PROFESSIONAL PYTHON®

CW00822469

PROFESSIONAL

Python®

PROFESSIONAL

Python®

Luke Sneeringer

A Wiley Brand

Professional Python®

Published by
John Wiley & Sons, Inc.
10475 Crosspoint Boulevard
Indianapolis, IN 46256
www.wiley.com

Copyright © 2016 by John Wiley & Sons, Inc., Indianapolis, Indiana

Published simultaneously in Canada

ISBN: 978-1-119-07085-6
ISBN: 978-1-119-07083-2 (ebk)
ISBN: 978-1-119-07078-8 (ebk)

Manufactured in the United States of America

10 9 8 7 6 5 4 3 2 1

To Meagan. My loving wife, and forever my best friend. You make "happily ever after" a reality.

ABOUT THE AUTHOR

LUKE SNEERINGER has designed, architected, built, and contributed to numerous Python applications for companies including FeedMagnet, May Designs, and Ansible, and is a frequent speaker at Python conferences. He lives in Austin, Texas, with his wife, Meagan, and a non-trivial contingent of cats and fish.

ABOUT THE TECHNICAL EDITORS

ALAN GAULD is a certified Enterprise Architect for The Open Group Architecture Framework (TOGAF), working in the telecommunications and customer service industries. He has been programming since 1974 and using Python since 1998. He is the author of two books on Python. When not working, he enjoys hiking, photography, travel, and music.

ELIAS BACHAALANY is a computer programmer, software reverse engineer, and a technical writer. Elias has also co-authored the books *Practical Reverse Engineering* (Wiley, 2014) and *The Antivirus Hacker's Handbook* (Wiley, 2015). During his employment period at Hex-Rays S.A, he amped up IDA Pro's scripting facilities and contributed to the IDAPython project.

CREDITS

PROJECT EDITOR
Kevin Shafer

TECHNICAL EDITOR
Alan Gauld; Elias Bachaalany

PRODUCTION EDITOR
Joel Jones

COPY EDITOR
Kimberly A. Cofer

MANAGER OF CONTENT DEVELOPMENT & ASSEMBLY
Mary Beth Wakefield

PRODUCTION MANAGER
Kathleen Wisor

MARKETING DIRECTOR
David Mayhew

MARKETING MANAGER
Carrie Sherrill

PROFESSIONAL TECHNOLOGY & STRATEGY DIRECTOR
Barry Pruett

BUSINESS MANAGER
Amy Knies

ASSOCIATE PUBLISHER
Jim Minatel

PROJECT COORDINATOR, COVER
Brent Savage

PROOFREADER
Kathryn Duggan

INDEXER
Jack Lewis

COVER DESIGNER
Wiley

COVER IMAGE
©Getty Images/Yagi Studio

ACKNOWLEDGMENTS

THIS BOOK WOULD NOT be a reality without the indispensible help of its editor, Kevin Shafer, and technical reviewers, Alan Gould and Elias Bachaalany. Their efforts made this book immeasurably better (and substantially reduced errata contained therein). The entire team at Wiley did an outstanding job of taking my rather unattractive starting manuscripts and making something beautiful.

A special thanks goes to Jason Ford, my dear friend and the brilliant entrepreneur who gives me an endless supply of entertaining work. He gave me my first opportunity to write Python professionally, and continues to be a daily source of interesting problems, fascinating debate, and endless excitement (oh, and a paycheck).

I am grateful also to many friends both inside and outside the Python community, who have worked or played with me over the past many years. While these are sadly too many to list, conscience would not forgive a failure to note a subset by name: Mickie Betz, Frank Burns, David Cassidy, Jon Chappell, Diana Clarke, George Dupere, John Ferguson, Alex Gaynor, Jasmin Goedtel, Chris Harbison, Boyd Hemphill, Rob Johnson, Daniel Lindsley, Jeff McHale, Doug Napleone, Elli Pope, Tom Smith, and Caleb Sneeringer.

Thanks to my parents, Jim and Cheryl Sneeringer, who taught me more things than I could ever enumerate. Among these was how to code, but greatest in importance was how to live.

Finally, the acknowledgements could hardly be considered complete without a paragraph citing the support, dedication, and love of my wife, Meagan. She convinced me that this book was worth writing, and graciously supported me during every step of the process. I could not be more blessed or more thankful to have her in my life every day.

—SOLI DEO GLORIA

CONTENTS

PART IV: EVERYTHING ELSE

INTRODUCTION

THIS BOOK INTRODUCES THE READER to more advanced Python programming by providing an intermediate course in the Python language.

Recently, Python has become more and more frequently the developer's language of choice. It is used all over the world, for myriad purposes. As adoption continues to increase, more and more developers are spending their days writing Python.

Python has grown so steadily *precisely because* it is a very powerful language, and even many seasoned Python developers have only scratched the surface of what the language is capable of doing.

WHO THIS BOOK IS FOR

This book is for developers who have already worked in Python, are already familiar with the language, and desire to learn more about it. This book assumes that readers have already done most basic tasks involved with developing in Python (such as having used the Python interactive terminal).

If you are a reader who seeks a general survey of intermediate to advanced Python language features, you should read this book from start to finish.

Alternatively, you may be a reader who has used some more-advanced language features in passing, or potentially needs to maintain code that uses such features. Consider using this book as a reference guide or index to flesh out your understanding when you are grappling with a particular implementation.

WHAT THIS BOOK COVERS

This book covers all recent versions of Python (including both Python 2 and Python 3). At the time of this writing, the most recent version available is Python 3.4, and Python 3.5 is in beta. This book primarily covers Python 2.6, 2.7, 3.3, and 3.4. Most code is provided in a manner that will run on both Python 2 and Python 3, with Python 2 code specifically noted as such.

Additionally, this book includes a chapter with a deep dive into distinctions between Python 2 and Python 3, which provides advice on writing code to run on multiple versions of Python, as well as porting over to Python 3.

This book primarily focuses on two areas. The first is features of the language itself. For example, this book includes several chapters about various aspects of how Python's class and object model works. The second area is modules provided as part of the standard library. For example, this book includes a chapter each on modules such as `asyncio`, `unittest`, and `argparse`.

HOW THIS BOOK IS STRUCTURED

This book is essentially divided into four parts.

The first three chapters in the book are fundamentally about *functions* in Python. This part includes a chapter each on decorators and context managers, which are reusable ways to modify or wrap functions to add functionality. It also includes a chapter on generators, which are a way to design functions that yield values one at a time, rather than creating an entire list of values in advance and returning them in one block.

The second part comprises the next four chapters, and they are all related somehow to Python *classes* and the language's object model. There is a chapter on magic methods. Then, there is a chapter each on metaclasses and class factories, which are two approaches to constructing classes in powerful ways. Finally, a chapter on abstract base classes explains the abc module and how to make classes declare patterns that they implement.

The third part comprises two chapters about strings and data. There is a chapter on how to navigate using Unicode strings (as opposed to byte strings) in Python, which also covers in detail how strings differ between Python 2 and Python 3. There is also a chapter on regular expressions, which covers the Python re module as well as how to write regular expressions.

Finally, the fourth part covers everything that does not neatly fit into one of the first three parts. This part begins with an in-depth look at the distinctions between Python 2 and Python 3, and how to write code that is interoperable with both. There is a chapter on unit testing, focusing on the unittest module. A chapter on command-line interface (CLI) tools teaches you about both optparse and argparse, which are Python's modules for writing command-line tools. There is a chapter on asyncio, which is a new asynchronous programming library that was added to the standard library in Python 3.4. Finally, the book closes with a chapter on style.

WHAT YOU NEED TO USE THIS BOOK

You will, first and foremost, need a machine running Python.

Although it does not make a difference in most chapters, this book is slightly Linux-focused in its approach (this will be most relevant in the chapter on CLI tools). Examples were run in a Linux environment, and output may vary slightly on Windows.

CONVENTIONS

To help you get the most from the text and keep track of what's happening, we've used a number of conventions throughout the book.

> **WARNING** *Boxes like this one hold important, not-to-be forgotten information that is directly relevant to the surrounding text.*

> **NOTE** *Notes, tips, hints, tricks, and asides to the current discussion are offset and placed in italics like this.*

As for styles in the text:

- ➤ We *highlight* new terms and important words when we introduce them.
- ➤ We show keyboard strokes like this: Ctrl+A.
- ➤ We show filenames, URLs, and code within the text like so: `persistence.properties`.
- ➤ We present code as follows:

```
We use a monofont type for most code examples.
```

ERRATA

We make every effort to ensure that there are no errors in the text or in the code. However, no one is perfect, and mistakes do occur. If you find an error in one of our books (like a spelling mistake or faulty piece of code), we would be very grateful for your feedback. By sending in errata, you may save another reader hours of frustration and, at the same time, you will be helping us to provide even higher quality information.

To find the errata page for this book, go to `http://www.wrox.com` and locate the title using the Search box or one of the title lists. Then, on the book details page, click the Book Errata link. On this page, you can view all errata that has been submitted for this book and posted by Wrox editors. A complete book list (including links to each book's errata) is also available at `www.wrox.com/misc-pages/booklist.shtml`.

If you don't spot "your" error on the Book Errata page, go to `www.wrox.com/contact/techsupport.shtml` and complete the form there to send us the error you have found. We'll check the information and, if appropriate, post a message to the book's errata page and fix the problem in subsequent editions of the book.

P2P.WROX.COM

For author and peer discussion, join the P2P forums at `p2p.wrox.com`. The forums are a web-based system for you to post messages relating to Wrox books and related technologies, and to interact with other readers and technology users. The forums offer a subscription feature to e-mail you topics of interest of your choosing when new posts are made to the forums. Some Wrox authors, editors, other industry experts, and your fellow readers are present on these forums.

At `http://p2p.wrox.com`, you will find a number of different forums that will help you not only as you read most Wrox books, but also as you develop your own applications. To join the forums, just follow these steps:

1. Go to `p2p.wrox.com` and click the Register link.
2. Read the terms of use and click Agree.
3. Complete the required information to join, as well as any optional information you wish to provide, and click Submit.
4. You will receive an e-mail with information describing how to verify your account and complete the joining process.

> **NOTE** *You can read messages in the forums without joining P2P. However, in order to post your own messages, you must join.*

Once you join, you can post new messages and respond to messages other users post. You can read messages at any time on the web. If you would like to have new messages from a particular forum e-mailed to you, click the Subscribe to this Forum icon by the forum name in the forum listing.

For more information about how to use the Wrox P2P, be sure to read the P2P FAQs for answers to questions about how the forum software works, as well as many common questions specific to P2P and Wrox books. To read the FAQs, click the FAQ link on any P2P page.

PART I
Functions

Decorators

A decorator is a tool for wrapping code around functions or classes. Decorators then explicitly apply that wrapper to functions or classes to cause them to "opt in" to the decorator's functionality. Decorators are extremely useful for addressing common prerequisite cases before a function runs (for example, ensuring authentication), or ensuring cleanup after a function runs (for example, output sanitization or exception handling). They are also useful for taking action on the decorated function or class itself. For example, a decorator might register a function with a signaling system or a URI registry in web applications.

This chapter provides an overview of what decorators are and how they interact with Python functions and classes. It enumerates certain decorators that appear in the Python standard library. Finally, it offers instruction in writing decorators and attaching them to functions and classes.

UNDERSTANDING DECORATORS

At its core, a *decorator* is a callable that *accepts* a callable and *returns* a callable. A decorator is simply a function (or other callable, such as an object with a __call__ method) that accepts the decorated function as its positional argument. The decorator takes some action using that argument, and then either returns the original argument or some other callable (presumably that interacts with it in some way).

Because functions are first-class objects in Python, they can be passed to another function just as any other object can be. A decorator is just a function that expects another function, and does something with it.

This sounds more confusing than it actually is. Consider the following very simple decorator. It does nothing except append a line to the decorated callable's docstring.

```
def decorated_by(func):
    func.__doc__ += '\nDecorated by decorated_by.'
    return func
```

Now, consider the following trivial function:

```
def add(x, y):
    """Return the sum of x and y."""
    return x + y
```

The function's docstring is the string specified in the first line. It is what you will see if you run `help` on that function in the Python shell. Here is the decorator applied to the `add` function:

```
def add(x, y):
    """Return the sum of x and y."""
    return x + y
add = decorated_by(add)
```

Here is what you get if you run `help`:

```
Help on function add in module __main__:

add(x, y)
    Return the sum of x and y.
    Decorated by decorated_by.
(END)
```

What has happened here is that the decorator made the modification to the function's `__doc__` attribute, and then returned the original function object.

DECORATOR SYNTAX

Most times that developers use decorators to decorate a function, they are only interested in the final, decorated function. Keeping a reference to the undecorated function is ultimately superfluous.

Because of this (and also for purposes of clarity), it is undesirable to define a function, assign it to a particular name, and then immediately reassign the decorated function to the same name.

Therefore, Python 2.5 introduced a special syntax for decorators. Decorators are applied by prepending an @ character to the name of the decorator and adding the line (without the implied decorator's method signature) immediately *above* the decorated function's declaration.

Following is the preferred way to apply a `decorated_by` decorator to the `add` method:

```
@decorated_by
def add(x, y):
    """Return the sum of x and y."""
    return x + y
```

Note again that no method signature is being provided to `@decorated_by`. The decorator is assumed to take a single, positional argument, which is the method being decorated. (You will see a method signature in some cases, but with other provided arguments. This is discussed later in this chapter.)

This syntax allows the decorator to be applied where the function is declared, which makes it easier to read the code and immediately realize that the decorator is in play. Readability counts.

Order of Decorator Application

When is a decorator applied? When the `@` syntax is being used, decorators are applied immediately *after* the decorated callable is created. Therefore, the two examples shown of how to apply `decorated_by` to `add` are exactly equivalent. First, the `add` function is created, and then, immediately after that, it is wrapped with `decorated_by`.

One important thing to note about this is that it is possible to use multiple decorators on a single callable (just as it is possible to wrap function calls multiple times).

However, note that if you use multiple decorators using the `@` syntax, they are applied in order, *from bottom to top*. This may be counterintuitive at first, but it makes sense given what the Python interpreter is actually doing.

Consider the following function with two decorators applied:

```
@also_decorated_by
@decorated_by
def add(x, y):
    """Return the sum of x and y."""
    return x + y
```

The first thing that occurs is that the `add` function is created by the interpreter. Then, the `decorated_by` decorator is applied. This decorator returns a callable (as all decorators do), which is then sent to `also_decorated_by`, which does the same; the latter result is assigned to `add`.

Remember that the application of `decorated_by` is syntactically equivalent to the following:

```
add = decorated_by(add)
```

The previous two-decorator example is syntactically equivalent to the following:

```
add = also_decorated_by(decorated_by(add))
```

In both cases, the `also_decorated_by` decorator comes first as a human reads the code. However, the decorators are applied bottom to top for the same reason that the functions are resolved from innermost to outermost. The same principles are at work.

In the case of a traditional function call, the interpreter must first resolve the inner function call in order to have the appropriate object or value to send to the outer call.

```
add = also_decorated_by(decorated_by(add))    # First, get a return value for
                                              # `decorated_by(add)`.
add = also_decorated_by(decorated_by(add))    # Send that return value to
                                              # `also_decorated_by`.
```

With a decorator, first the `add` function is created normally.

```
@also_decorated_by
@decorated_by
def add(x, y):
    """Return the sum of x and y."""
    return x + y
```

Then, the `@decorated_by` decorator is called, being sent the `add` function as its decorated method.

```
@also_decorated_by
@decorated_by
def add(x, y):
    """Return the sum of x and y."""
    return x + y
```

The `@decorated_by` function returns its own callable (in this case, a modified version of `add`). *That* value is what is then sent to `@also_decorated_by` in the final step.

```
@also_decorated_by
@decorated_by
def add(x, y):
    """Return the sum of x and y."""
    return x + y
```

When applying decorators, it is important for you to remember that they are applied bottom to top. Many times, order does matter.

WHERE DECORATORS ARE USED

The standard library includes many modules that incorporate decorators, and many common tools and frameworks make use of them for common functionality.

For example, if you want to make a method on a class not require an instance of the class, you use the `@classmethod` or `@staticmethod` decorator, which is part of the standard library. The `mock` module (which is used for unit testing, and which was added to the standard library in Python 3.3) allows the use of `@mock.patch` or `@mock.patch.object` as a decorator.

Common tools also use decorators. Django (which is a common web framework for Python) uses `@login_required` as a decorator to allow developers to specify that a user must be logged in to view a particular page, and uses `@permission_required` for applying more specific permissions. Flask (another common web framework) uses `@app.route` to serve as a registry between specific URIs and the functions that run when the browser hits those URIs.

Celery (a common Python task runner) uses a complex `@task` decorator to identify a function as an asynchronous task. This decorator actually returns an instance of a `Task` class, which illustrates how decorators can be used to make a very convenient API.

WHY YOU SHOULD WRITE DECORATORS

Decorators provide an excellent way to say, "I want this specific, reusable piece of functionality in these specific places." When written well, they are modular and explicit.

The modularity of decorators (you can apply or remove them from functions or classes easily) makes them ideal for avoiding the repetition of boilerplate setup and teardown code. Similarly, because decorators interact with the decorated function itself, they excel at registering functions elsewhere.

Also, decorators are explicit. They are applied, in-place, to all callables where they are needed. This is valuable for readability, and therefore for debugging. It is obvious exactly what is being applied and where.

WHEN YOU SHOULD WRITE DECORATORS

Several very good use cases exist for writing decorators in Python applications and modules.

Additional Functionality

Probably the most common reason to write a decorator is if you want to add additional functionality before or after the decorated method is executed. This could include use cases such as checking authentication or logging the result of a function to a consistent location.

Data Sanitization or Addition

A decorator could also sanitize the values of arguments being passed to the decorated function, to ensure consistency of argument type, or that a value conforms to a specific pattern. For example, a decorator could ensure that the values sent to a function conform to a specific type, or meet some other validation standard. (You will see an example of this shortly, a decorator called `@requires_ints`.)

A decorator can also transform or sanitize data that is *returned from* a function. A valuable use case for this is if you want to have functions that return native Python objects (such as lists or dictionaries), but ultimately receive a serialized format (such as JSON or YAML) on the other end.

Some decorators actually provide additional data to a function, usually in the form of additional arguments. The `@mock.patch` decorator is an example of this, because it (among other things) provides the mock object that it creates as an additional positional argument to the function.

Function Registration

Many times, it is useful to register a function elsewhere—for example, registering a task in a task runner, or a function with a signal handler. Any system in which some external input or routing mechanism decides what function runs is a candidate for function registration.

WRITING DECORATORS

Decorators are simply functions that (usually) accept the decorated callable as their only argument, and that return a callable (such as in the previous trivial example).

It is important to note that the decorator code itself runs when the decorator is *applied* to the decorated function, rather than when the decorated function is called. Understanding this is critical, and will become very clear over the course of the next several examples.

An Initial Example: A Function Registry

Consider the following simple registry of functions:

```
registry = []
def register(decorated):
    registry.append(decorated)
    return decorated
```

The `register` method is a simple decorator. It appends the positional argument, decorated to the registry variable, and then returns the decorated method unchanged. Any method that receives the `register` decorator will have itself appended to `registry`.

```
@register
def foo():
    return 3

@register
def bar():
    return 5
```

If you have access to the registry, you can easily iterate over it and execute the functions inside.

```
answers = []
for func in registry:
    answers.append(func())
```

The `answers` list at this point would now contain `[3, 5]`. This is because the functions are executed in order, and their return values are appended to `answers`.

Several less-trivial uses for function registries exist, such as adding "hooks" into code so that custom functionality can be run before or after critical events. Here is a `Registry` class that can handle just such a case:

```
class Registry(object):
    def __init__(self):
        self._functions = []

    def register(self, decorated):
        self._functions.append(decorated)
        return decorated

    def run_all(self, *args, **kwargs):
        return_values = []
        for func in self._functions:
            return_values.append(func(*args, **kwargs))
        return return_values
```

One thing worth noting about this class is that the `register` method—the decorator—still works the same way as before. It is perfectly fine to have a bound method as a decorator. It receives `self` as the first argument (just as any other bound method), and expects one additional positional argument, which is the decorated method.

By making several different registry instances, you can have entirely separate registries. It is even possible to take the same function and register it with more than one registry, as shown here:

```
a = Registry()
b = Registry()

@a.register
def foo(x=3):
    return x
```

```
@b.register
def bar(x=5):
    return x

@a.register
@b.register
def baz(x=7):
    return x
```

Running the code from either registry's `run_all` method gives the following results:

```
a.run_all()    # [3, 7]
b.run_all()    # [5, 7]
```

Notice that the `run_all` method is able to take arguments, which it then passes to the underlying functions when they are run.

```
a.run_all(x=4)    # [4, 4]
```

Execution-Time Wrapping Code

These decorators are very simple because the decorated function is passed through unmodified. However, sometimes you want additional functionality to run when the decorated method is *executed*. You do this by returning a different callable that adds the appropriate functionality and (usually) calls the decorated method in the course of its execution.

A Simple Type Check

Here is a simple decorator that ensures that every argument the function receives is an integer, and complains otherwise:

```
def requires_ints(decorated):
    def inner(*args, **kwargs):
        # Get any values that may have been sent as keyword arguments.
        kwarg_values = [i for i in kwargs.values()]

        # Iterate over every value sent to the decorated method, and
        # ensure that each one is an integer; raise TypeError if not.
        for arg in list(args) + kwarg_values:
            if not isinstance(arg, int):
                raise TypeError('%s only accepts integers as arguments.' %
                                decorated.__name__)

        # Run the decorated method, and return the result.
        return decorated(*args, **kwargs)
    return inner
```

What is happening here?

The decorator itself is `requires_ints`. It accepts one argument, `decorated`, which is the decorated callable. The only thing that this decorator does is return a new callable, the local function `inner`. This function replaces the decorated method.

You can see this in action by declaring a function and decorating it with `requires_ints`:

```
@requires_ints
def foo(x, y):
    """Return the sum of x and y."""
    return x + y
```

Notice what you get if you run `help(foo)`:

```
Help on function inner in module __main__:

inner(*args, **kwargs)
(END)
```

The `inner` function has been assigned to the name `foo` *instead of* the original, defined function. If you run `foo(3, 5)`, the `inner` function runs with those arguments. The inner function performs the type check, and then it runs the decorated method simply because the inner function calls it using return decorated(*args, **kwargs), returning 8. Absent this call, the decorated method would have been ignored.

Preserving the help

It often is not particularly desirable to have a decorator steamroll your function's docstring or hijack the output of `help`. Because decorators are tools for adding generic and reusable functionality, they are necessarily going to be more vague. And, generally, if someone using a function is trying to run `help` on it, he or she wants information about the guts of the function, not the shell.

The solution to this problem is actually … a decorator. Python implements a decorator called `@functools.wraps` that copies the important introspection elements of one function onto another function.

Here is the same `@requires_ints` decorator, but it adds in the use of `@functools.wraps`:

```
import functools


def requires_ints(decorated):
    @functools.wraps(decorated)
    def inner(*args, **kwargs):
        # Get any values that may have been sent as keyword arguments.
        kwarg_values = [i for i in kwargs.values()]

        # Iterate over every value sent to the decorated method, and
        # ensure that each one is an integer; raise TypeError if not.
        for arg in args + kwarg_values:
            if not isinstance(i, int):
                raise TypeError('%s only accepts integers as arguments.' %
                                decorated.__name__)

        # Run the decorated method, and return the result.
        return decorated(*args, **kwargs)
    return inner
```

The decorator itself is almost entirely unchanged, except for the addition of the second line, which applies the `@functools.wraps` decorator to the `inner` function. You must also import `functools` now (which is in the standard library). You will also notice some additional syntax. This decorator actually takes an argument (more on that later).

Now you apply the decorator to the same function, as shown here:

```
@requires_ints
def foo(x, y):
    """Return the sum of x and y."""
    return x + y
```

Here is what happens when you run `help(foo)` now:

```
Help on function foo in module __main__:

foo(x, y)
    Return the sum of x and y.
(END)
```

You see that the docstring for `foo`, as well as its method signature, is what is read out when you look at `help`. Underneath the hood, however, the `@requires_ints` decorator is still applied, and the `inner` function is still what runs.

Depending on which version of Python you are running, you will get a slightly different result from running `help` on `foo`, specifically regarding the function signature. The previous paste represents the output from Python 3.4. However, in Python 2, the function signature provided will still be that of `inner` (so, `*args` and `**kwargs` rather than x and y).

User Verification

A common use case for this pattern (that is, performing some kind of sanity check before running the decorated method) is user verification. Consider a method that is expected to take a user as its first argument.

The user should be an instance of this `User` and `AnonymousUser` class, as shown here:

```
class User(object):
    """A representation of a user in our application."""

    def __init__(self, username, email):
        self.username = username
        self.email = email


class AnonymousUser(User):
    """An anonymous user; a stand-in for an actual user that nonetheless
    is not an actual user.
    """
    def __init__(self):
        self.username = None
        self.email = None

    def __nonzero__(self):
        return False
```

A decorator is a powerful tool here for isolating the boilerplate code of user verification. A `@requires_user` decorator can easily verify that you got a `User` object and that it is not an anonymous user.

```python
import functools


def requires_user(func):
    @functools.wraps(func)
    def inner(user, *args, **kwargs):
        """Verify that the user is truthy; if so, run the decorated method,
        and if not, raise ValueError.
        """
        # Ensure that user is truthy, and of the correct type.
        # The "truthy" check will fail on anonymous users, since the
        # AnonymousUser subclass has a `__nonzero__` method that
        # returns False.
        if user and isinstance(user, User):
            return func(user, *args, **kwargs)
        else:
            raise ValueError('A valid user is required to run this.')
    return inner
```

This decorator applies a common, boilerplate need—the verification that a user is logged in to the application. When you implement this as a decorator, it is reusable and more easily maintainable, and its application to functions is clear and explicit.

Note that this decorator will only correctly wrap a function or static method, and will fail if wrapping a bound method to a class. This is because the decorator ignores the expectation to send `self` as the first argument to a bound method.

Output Formatting

In addition to sanitizing *input to* a function, another use for decorators can be sanitizing *output from* a function.

When you're working in Python, it is normally desirable to use native Python objects when possible. Often, however, you want a serialized output format (for example, JSON). It is cumbersome to manually convert to JSON at the end of every relevant function, and (and it's not a good idea, either). Ideally, you should be using the Python structures right up until serialization is necessary, and there may be other boilerplate that happens just before serialization (such as or the like).

Decorators provide an excellent, portable solution to this problem. Consider the following decorator that takes Python output and serializes the result to JSON:

```python
import functools
import json


def json_output(decorated):
    """Run the decorated function, serialize the result of that function
    to JSON, and return the JSON string.
    """
    @functools.wraps(decorated)
    def inner(*args, **kwargs):
        result = decorated(*args, **kwargs)
        return json.dumps(result)
    return inner
```

Apply the `@json_output` decorator to a trivial function, as shown here:

```
@json_output
def do_nothing():
    return {'status': 'done'}
```

Run the function in the Python shell, and you get the following:

```
>>> do_nothing()
'{"status": "done"}'
```

Notice that you got back a *string* that contains valid JSON. You did *not* get back a dictionary.

The beauty of this decorator is in its simplicity. Apply it to a function, and suddenly a function that did return a Python dictionary, list, or other object now returns its JSON-serialized version.

You might ask, "Why is this valuable?" After all, you are adding a one-line decorator that essentially removes a single line of code—a call to `json.dumps`. However, consider the value of having this decorator as the application's needs expand.

For example, what if certain exceptions should be trapped and output specifically formatted JSON, rather than having the exception bubble up and traceback? Because you have a decorator, that functionality is very easy to add.

```
import functools
import json


class JSONOutputError(Exception):
    def __init__(self, message):
        self._message = message

    def __str__(self):
        return self._message


def json_output(decorated):
    """Run the decorated function, serialize the result of that function
    to JSON, and return the JSON string.
    """
    @functools.wraps(decorated)
    def inner(*args, **kwargs):
        try:
            result = decorated(*args, **kwargs)
        except JSONOutputError as ex:
            result = {
                'status': 'error',
                'message': str(ex),
            }
        return json.dumps(result)
    return inner
```

By augmenting the `@json_output` decorator with this error handling, you have added it to *any function where the decorator was already applied*. This is part of what makes decorators so valuable. They are very useful tools for code portability and reusability.

Now, if a function decorated with `@json_output` raises a `JSONOutputError`, you will get this special error handling. Here is a function that does:

```
@json_output
def error():
    raise JSONOutputError('This function is erratic.')
```

Running the `error` function in the Python interpreter gives you the following:

```
>>> error()
'{"status": "error", "message": "This function is erratic."}'
```

Note that only the `JSONOutputError` exception class (and any subclasses) receives this special handling. Any other exception is passed through normally, and generates a traceback. Consider this function:

```
@json_output
def other_error():
    raise ValueError('The grass is always greener...')
```

When you run it, you will get the traceback you expect, as shown here:

```
>>> other_error()
Traceback (most recent call last):
  File "<stdin>", line 1, in <module>
  File "<stdin>", line 8, in inner
  File "<stdin>", line 3, in other_error
ValueError: The grass is always greener...
```

This reusability and maintainability is part of what makes decorators valuable. Because a decorator is being used for a reusable, generally applicable concept throughout the application (in this case, JSON serialization), the decorator becomes the place for housing that functionality as needs arise that are applicable whenever that concept is used.

Essentially, decorators are tools to avoid repeating yourself, and part of their value is in providing hooks for future maintenance.

This can be accomplished without the use of decorators. Consider the example of requiring a logged-in user. It is not difficult to write a function that does this and simply place it near the top of functions that require that functionality. The decorator is primarily syntactic sugar. The syntactic sugar has value, though. Code is read more often than it is written, after all, and it is easy to locate decorators at a glance.

Logging

One final example of execution-time wrapping of code is a general-use logging function. Consider the following decorator that causes the function call, timings, and result to be logged:

```
import functools
import logging
import time


def logged(method):
    """Cause the decorated method to be run and its results logged, along
```

```
        with some other diagnostic information.
        """
        @functools.wraps(method)
        def inner(*args, **kwargs):
            # Record our start time.
            start = time.time()

            # Run the decorated method.
            return_value = method(*args, **kwargs)

            # Record our completion time, and calculate the delta.
            end = time.time()
            delta = end - start

            # Log the method call and the result.
            logger = logging.getLogger('decorator.logged')
            logger.warn('Called method %s at %.02f; execution time %.02f '
                        'seconds; result %r.' %
                        (method.__name__, start, delta, return_value))

            # Return the method's original return value.
            return return_value
        return inner
```

When applied to a function, this decorator runs that function normally, but uses the Python `logging` module to log out information about the function call after it completes. Now, suddenly, you have (extremely rudimentary) logging of any function where this decorator is applied.

```
>>> import time
>>> @logged
... def sleep_and_return(return_value):
...         time.sleep(2)
...         return return_value
...
>>>
>>> sleep_and_return(42)
Called method sleep_and_return at 1424462194.70;
    execution time 2.00 seconds; result 42.
42
```

Unlike the previous examples, this decorator does not alter the function call in an obvious way. No cases exist where you apply this decorator and get a different result from the decorated function than you did from the undecorated function. The previous examples raised exceptions or modified the result if this or that check did not pass. This decorator is more invisible. It does some under-the-hood work, but in no situation should it change the actual result.

Variable Arguments

It is worth noting that the `@json_output` and `@logged` decorators both provide `inner` functions that simply take, and pass on with minimal investigation, variable arguments and keyword arguments.

This is an important pattern. One way that it is particularly important is that many decorators may be used to decorate plain functions as well as methods of classes. Remember that in Python, methods declared in classes receive an additional positional argument, conventionally known as `self`. This *does not change* when decorators are in use. (This is why the `requires_user` decorator shown earlier does not work on bound methods within classes.)

For example, if `@json_result` is used to decorate a method of a class, the `inner` function is called and it receives the instance of the class as the first argument. In fact, this is fine. In this case, that argument is simply `args[0]`, and it is passed to the decorated method unmolested.

Decorator Arguments

One thing that has been consistent about all the decorators enumerated thus far is that the decorators themselves appear not to take any arguments. As discussed, there is an implied argument—the method that is being decorated.

However, sometimes it is useful to have the decorator *itself* take some information that it needs to decorate the method appropriately. The difference between an argument passed to the decorator and an argument passed to the function at call time is precisely that. An argument to the decorator is processed once, when the function is declared and decorated. By contrast, arguments to the function are processed when that function is called.

You have already seen an example of an argument sent to a decorator with the repeated use of `@functools.wraps`. It takes an argument—the method being wrapped, whose help and docstring and the like should be preserved.

However, decorators have implied call signatures. They take one positional argument—the method being decorated. So, how does this work?

The answer is that it is complicated. Recall the basic decorators that have execution-time wrapping of code. They declare an inner method in local scope that they then return. This is the callable returned by the decorator. It is what is assigned to the function name. Decorators that take arguments add one more wrapping layer to this dance. This is because the decorator that takes the argument *is not actually the decorator*. Rather, it is a function that *returns the decorator*, which is a function that takes one argument (the decorated method), which then decorates the function and returns a callable.

That sounds confusing. Consider the following example where a `@json_output` decorator is augmented to ask about indentation and key sorting:

```
import functools
import json


class JSONOutputError(Exception):
    def __init__(self, message):
        self._message = message

    def __str__(self):
        return self._message


def json_output(indent=None, sort_keys=False):
    """Run the decorated function, serialize the result of that function
    to JSON, and return the JSON string.
```

```
    """
    def actual_decorator(decorated):
        @functools.wraps(decorated)
        def inner(*args, **kwargs):
            try:
                result = decorated(*args, **kwargs)
            except JSONOutputError as ex:
                result = {
                    'status': 'error',
                    'message': str(ex),
                }
            return json.dumps(result, indent=indent, sort_keys=sort_keys)
        return inner
    return actual_decorator
```

So, what has happened here, and why does this work?

This is a function, `json_output`, which accepts two arguments (`indent` and `sort_keys`). It returns another function, called `actual_decorator`, which is (as its name suggests) intended to be used as a decorator. That is a classic decorator—a callable that accepts a single callable (`decorated`) as an argument and returns a callable (`inner`).

Note that the `inner` function has changed slightly to accommodate the `indent` and `sort_keys` arguments. These arguments mirror similar arguments accepted by `json.dumps`, so the call to `json.dumps` accepts the values provided to `indent` and `sort_keys` in the decorator's signature and provides them to `json.dumps` in the antepenultimate line.

The `inner` function is what ultimately makes use of the `indent` and `sort_keys` arguments. This is fine, because Python's block scoping rules allow for this. It also is not a problem that this might be called with different values for `inner` and `sort_keys`, because `inner` is a local function (a different copy is returned each time the decorator is used).

Applying the `json_output` function looks like this:

```
@json_output(indent=4)
def do_nothing():
    return {'status': 'done'}
```

And if you run the `do_nothing` function now, you get a JSON block back with indentation and newlines added, as shown here:

```
>>> do_nothing()
'{\n    "status": "done"\n}'
```

How Does This Work?

But wait. If `json_output` is not a decorator, but a function that returns a decorator, why does it look like it is being applied as a decorator? What is the Python interpreter doing here that makes this work?

More explanation is in order. The key here is in the order of operations. Specifically, the function call (`json_output(indent=4)`) precedes the decorator application syntax (`@`). Thus, the *result of* the function call is used to apply the decorator.

The first thing that is happening is that the interpreter is seeing the function call for `json_output` and resolving that call (note that the boldface does *not* include the @):

```
@json_output(indent=4)
def do_nothing():
    return {'status': 'done'}
```

All the `json_output` function does is define another function, `actual_decorator`, and return it. As the result of that function, it is then provided to @, as shown here:

```
@actual_decorator
def do_nothing():
    return {'status': 'done'}
```

Now, `actual_decorator` is being run. It declares another local function, `inner`, and returns it. As previously discussed, that function is then assigned to the name `do_nothing`, the name of the decorated method. When `do_nothing` is called, the `inner` function is called, runs the decorated method, and JSON dumps the result with the appropriate indentation.

The Call Signature Matters

It is critical to realize that when you introduced your new, altered `json_output` function, you actually introduced a backward-incompatible change.

Why? Because now there is this extra function call that is expected. If you want the old `json_output` behavior, and do not need values for any of the arguments available, you still must call the method.

In other words, you must do the following:

```
@json_output()
def do_nothing():
    return {'status': 'done'}
```

Note the parentheses. They matter, because they indicate that the function is being called (even with no arguments), and then the result is applied to the @.

The previous code is *not*—repeat, *not*—equivalent to the following:

```
@json_output
def do_nothing():
    return {'status': 'done'}
```

This presents two problems. It is inherently confusing, because if you are accustomed to seeing decorators applied without a signature, a requirement to supply an empty signature is counterintuitive. Secondly, if the old decorator already exists in your application, you must go back and edit all of its existing calls. You should avoid backward-incompatible changes if possible.

In a perfect world, this decorator would work for three different types of applications:

➤   `@json_output`

➤   `@json_output()`

➤   `@json_output(indent=4)`

As it turns out, this is possible, by having a decorator that modifies its behavior based on the arguments that it receives. Remember, a decorator is just a function and has all the flexibility of any other function to do what it needs to do to respond to the inputs it gets.

Consider this more flexible iteration of `json_output`:

```python
import functools
import json


class JSONOutputError(Exception):
    def __init__(self, message):
        self._message = message

    def __str__(self):
        return self._message


def json_output(decorated_=None, indent=None, sort_keys=False):
    """Run the decorated function, serialize the result of that function
    to JSON, and return the JSON string.
    """
    # Did we get both a decorated method and keyword arguments?
    # That should not happen.
    if decorated_ and (indent or sort_keys):
        raise RuntimeError('Unexpected arguments.')

    # Define the actual decorator function.
    def actual_decorator(func):
        @functools.wraps(func)
        def inner(*args, **kwargs):
            try:
                result = func(*args, **kwargs)
            except JSONOutputError as ex:
                result = {
                    'status': 'error',
                    'message': str(ex),
                }
            return json.dumps(result, indent=indent, sort_keys=sort_keys)
        return inner

    # Return either the actual decorator, or the result of applying
    # the actual decorator, depending on what arguments we got.
    if decorated_:
        return actual_decorator(decorated_)
    else:
        return actual_decorator
```

This function is endeavoring to be intelligent about whether or not it is currently being used as a decorator.

First, it makes sure it is not being called in an unexpected way. You never expect to receive both a method to be decorated *and* the keyword arguments, because a decorator is always called with the decorated method as the only argument.

Second, it defines the `actual_decorator` function, which (as its name suggests) is the actual decorator to be either returned or applied. It defines the `inner` function that is the ultimate function to be returned from the decorator.

Finally, it returns the appropriate result based on how it was called:

➤ If `decorated_` is set, it was called as a plain decorator, without a method signature, and its responsibility is to apply the ultimate decorator and return the `inner` function. Here again, observe how decorators that take arguments are actually working. First, `actual_decorator(decorated_)` is called and resolved, then *its result* (which must be a callable, because this is a decorator) is called with `inner` provided as its only argument.

➤ If `decorated_` is not set, then this was called with keyword arguments instead, and the function must return an actual decorator, which receives the decorated method and returns `inner`. Therefore, the function returns `actual_decorator` outright. This is then applied by the Python interpreter as the actual decorator (which ultimately returns `inner`).

Why is this technique valuable? It enables you to maintain your decorator's functionality as previously used. This means that you do not have to update each case where the decorator has been applied. But you still get the additional flexibility of being able to add arguments in the cases where you need them.

DECORATING CLASSES

Remember that a decorator is, fundamentally, a callable that accepts a callable and returns a callable. This means that decorators can be used to decorate *classes* as well as functions (classes are callable, after all).

Decorating classes can have a variety of uses. They can be particularly valuable because, like function decorators, class decorators can interact with the attributes of the decorated class. A class decorator can add or augment attributes, or it can alter the API of a class to provide a distinction between how a class is *declared* versus how its instances are *used*.

You might ask, "Isn't the appropriate way to add or augment attributes of a class through sub classing?" Usually, the answer is "yes." However, in some situations an alternative approach may be appropriate. Consider, for example, a generally applicable feature that may apply to many classes in your application that live in distinct places in your class hierarchies.

By way of example, consider a feature of a class such that each instance knows when it was instantiated, and instances are sorted by their creation times. This has general applicability across many different classes, and requires the addition of three attributes—the instantiation timestamp, and the `__gt__` and `__lt__` methods.

You have multiple ways to go about adding this. Here is how you can do it with a class decorator:

```
import functools
import time
```

```
def sortable_by_creation_time(cls):
    """Given a class, augment the class to have its instances be sortable
    by the timestamp at which they were instantiated.
    """
    # Augment the class' original `__init__` method to also store a
    # `_created` attribute on the instance, which corresponds to when it
    # was instantiated.
    original_init = cls.__init__

    @functools.wraps(original_init)
    def new_init(self, *args, **kwargs):
        original_init(self, *args, **kwargs)
        self._created = time.time()
    cls.__init__ = new_init

    # Add `__lt__` and `__gt__` methods that return True or False based on
    # the created values in question.
    cls.__lt__ = lambda self, other: self._created < other._created
    cls.__gt__ = lambda self, other: self._created > other._created

    # Done; return the class object.
    return cls
```

The first thing that is happening in this decorator is that you are saving a copy of the class's original
__init__ method. You do not need to worry about whether the class has one. Because object has
an __init__ method, that attribute's presence is guaranteed. Next, you create a new method that
will be assigned to __init__, and this method first calls the original and then does
one piece of extra work, saving the instantiation timestamp to self._created.

It is worth noting that this is a very similar pattern to the execution-time wrapping code from previous examples—making a function that wraps another function, whose primary responsibility is to
run the wrapped function, but also adds a small piece of other functionality.

It is worth noting that if a class decorated with @sortable_by_creation_time defined its own
__lt__ and __gt__ methods, then this decorator would override them.

The _created value by itself does little good if the class does not recognize that it is to be used
for sorting. Therefore, the decorator also adds __lt__ and __gt__ magic methods. These cause the
< and > operators to return True or False based on the result of those methods. This also affects
the behavior of sorted and other similar functions.

This is all that is necessary to make an arbitrary class's instances sortable by their instantiation
time. This decorator can be applied to any class, including many classes with unrelated ancestry.

Here is an example of a simple class with instances sortable by when they are created:

```
>>> @sortable_by_creation_time
... class Sortable(object):
...     def __init__(self, identifier):
...         self.identifier = identifier
...     def __repr__(self):
...         return self.identifier
...
>>> first = Sortable('first')
>>> second = Sortable('second')
```

```
>>> third = Sortable('third')
>>>
>>> sortables = [second, first, third]
>>> sorted(sortables)
[first, second, third]
```

Bear in mind that simply because a decorator can be used to solve a problem, that does not mean that it is necessarily the appropriate solution.

For instance, when it comes to this example, the same thing could be accomplished by using a "mixin," or a small class that simply defines the appropriate __init__, __lt__, and __gt__ methods. A simple approach using a mixin would look like this:

```
import time


class SortableByCreationTime(object):
    def __init__(self):
        self._created = time.time()

    def __lt__(self, other):
        return self._created < other._created

    def __gt__(self, other):
        return self._created > other._created
```

Applying the mixin to a class can be done using Python's multiple inheritance:

```
class MyClass(MySuperclass, SortableByCreationTime):
    pass
```

This approach has different advantages and drawbacks. On the one hand, it will not mercilessly plow over __lt__ and __gt__ methods defined by the class or its superclasses (and it may not be obvious when the code is read later that the decorator was clobbering two methods).

On the other hand, it would be very easy to get into a situation where the __init__ method provided by SortableByCreationTime does not run. If MyClass *or* MySuperclass or any class in MySuperclass's ancestry defines an __init__ method, it will win out. Reversing the class order does not solve this problem; it simply reverses it.

By contrast, the decorator handles the __init__ case very well, simply by augmenting the effect of the decorated class's __init__ method and otherwise leaving it intact.

So, which approach is the correct approach? It depends.

TYPE SWITCHING

Thus far, the discussion in this chapter has only considered cases in which a decorator is expected to decorate a function and provide a function, or when a decorator is expected to decorate a class and provide a class.

There is no reason why this relationship must hold, however. The only requirement for a decorator is that it is a callable that accepts a callable and returns the callable. There is no requirement that it return *the same kind of* callable.

One more advanced use case for decorators is actually when they do not do this. In particular, it can be valuable for a decorator to decorate a function, but return a class. This can be a very useful tool for situations where the amount of boilerplate code grows, or for allowing developers to use a simple function for simple cases, but subclass a class in an application's API for more advanced cases.

An example of this in the wild is a decorator used in a popular task runner in the Python ecosystem: celery. The celery package provides a `@celery.task` decorator that is expected to decorate a function. What the decorator actually does is return a subclass of celery's internal `Task` *class*, with the decorated function being used within the subclass's `run` method.

Consider the following trivial example of a similar approach:

```python
class Task(object):
    """A trivial task class. Task classes have a `run` method, which runs
    the task.
    """
    def run(self, *args, **kwargs):
        raise NotImplementedError('Subclasses must implement `run`.')

    def identify(self):
        return 'I am a task.'

def task(decorated):
    """Return a class that runs the given function if its run method is
    called.
    """
    class TaskSubclass(Task):
        def run(self, *args, **kwargs):
            return decorated(*args, **kwargs)
    return TaskSubclass
```

What is happening here? The decorator creates a subclass of `Task` and returns the class. The class is callable calling a class creates an instance of that class and runs its __init__ method

The value of doing this is that it provides a hook for lots of augmentation. The base `Task` class can define much, much more than just the `run` method. For example, a `start` method might run the task asynchronously. The base class might also provide methods to save information about the task's status. Using a decorator that swaps out a function for a class here enables the developer to only consider the actual body of his or her task, and the decorator does the rest of the work.

You can see this in action by taking an instance of the class and running its `identify` method, as shown here:

```python
>>> @task
>>> def foo():
>>>     return 2 + 2
>>>
>>> f = foo()
>>> f.run()
4
>>> f.identify()
'I am a task.'
```

A Pitfall

This *exact* approach carries with it some problems. In particular, once a task function is decorated with the @task_class decorator, it becomes a class.

Consider the following simple task function decorated in this way:

```
@task
def foo():
    return 2 + 2
```

Now, attempt to run it directly in the interpreter:

```
>>> foo()
<__main__.TaskSubclass object at 0x10c3612d0>
```

That is a bad thing. This decorator alters the function in such a way that if the developer runs it, it does not do what anyone expects. It is usually not acceptable to expect the function to be declared as foo and then run using the convoluted foo().run() (which is what would be necessary in this case).

Fixing this requires putting a little more thought into how both the decorator and the Task class are constructed. Consider the following amended version:

```
class Task(object):
    """A trivial task class. Task classes have a `run` method, which runs
    the task.
    """
    def __call__(self, *args, **kwargs):
        return self.run(*args, **kwargs)

    def run(self, *args, **kwargs):
        raise NotImplementedError('Subclasses must implement `run`.')

    def identify(self):
        return 'I am a task.'


def task(decorated):
    """Return a class that runs the given function if its run method is
    called.
    """
    class TaskSubclass(Task):
        def run(self, *args, **kwargs):
            return decorated(*args, **kwargs)
    return TaskSubclass()
```

A couple of key differences exist here. The first is the addition of the __call__ method to the base Task class. The second difference (which complements the first) is that the @task_class decorator now returns *an instance of* the TaskSubclass, rather than the class itself.

This is acceptable because the only requirement for the decorator is that it return a callable, and the addition of the __call__ method to Task means that its instances are now callable.

Why is this pattern valuable? Again, the `Task` class is trivial, but it is easy to see how more functionality could be added here that is useful for managing and running tasks.

However, this approach maintains the spirit of the original function if it is invoked directly. Consider the decorated function again:

```
@task
def foo():
    return 2 + 2
```

And now, what do you get if you run it in the interpreter?

```
>>> foo()
4
```

This is what you expect, which makes this a far superior class and decorator design. Under the hood, the decorator has returned a `TaskSubclass` *instance*. When that instance is called in the interpreter, its __call__ method is invoked, which calls `run`, which calls the original function.

You can see that you still got your instance back, though, by using the `identify` method.

```
>>> foo.identify()
'I am a task.'
```

Now you have an instance that, when called directly, calls exactly like the original function. However, it can include other methods and attributes to provide for other functionality.

This is powerful. It allows a developer to write a function that is easily and explicitly grafted into a class that provides for alternate ways for that function to be invoked or other related functionality. This is a helpful paradigm.

SUMMARY

Decorators are very valuable tools that you can use to write maintainable, readable Python code. A decorator's value is in the fact that it is explicit, as well as the fact that decorators are reusable. They provide an excellent way to use boilerplate code, write it once, and apply it in many different situations.

This useful paradigm is possible because Python's data model provides functions and classes as first-class objects, capable of being passed around and augmented like any other object in the language.

On the other hand, there are also drawbacks to this model. In particular, the decorator syntax, while clean and easy to read, can obscure the fact that a function is being wrapped within another function, which can lead to challenges in debugging. Poorly written decorators may create errors by being careless about the nature of the callables they wrap (for example, by ignoring the distinction between bound methods and unbound functions).

Additionally, bear in mind that, like any function, the interpreter must actually run the code inside the decorator, which has a performance impact. Decorators are not immune to this; be mindful of what you are asking your decorators to do, in the same way that you would be for any other code you write.

Consider using decorators as a way to take leading or trailing functionality and wrap it around unrelated functions. Similarly, decorators are useful tools for function registries, signaling, certain cases of class augmentation, as well as many other things.

Chapter 2 "Context Managers," discusses context managers, which are another way to take bits of functionality that require reuse across an application, and compartmentalize them in an effective and portable way.

Context Managers

Context managers are the first cousins of decorators. Like their kindred, they are tools for wrapping code around other code. However, whereas decorators wrap *defined* blocks of code (such as functions or classes), context managers wrap *arbitrary*, *free-form* blocks of code.

In almost every other respect, the purposes of context managers and decorators are equivalent (and, it is often the case that APIs are written to allow you to use either, as discussed later in this chapter).

This chapter introduces and explains the concept of context managers, showing how and when to use them, and enumerating the different ways of handling exceptions that may occur within context blocks.

WHAT IS A CONTEXT MANAGER?

A *context manager* is an object that wraps an arbitrary block of code. Context managers ensure that setup is consistently performed when the context manager is entered, and that teardown is consistently performed when the context manager is exited.

It is important to note early that *the exit is guaranteed*. If a context manager is entered, it will, by definition, be exited. This holds true even if the internal code raises an exception. In fact, the context manager's exit code is given an opportunity to handle such exceptions if it sees fit to do so (although it is not obligated to do so).

Therefore, context managers perform a very similar function to the `try`, `except`, and `finally` keywords. They are often a useful mechanism to encapsulate boilerplate `try-except-finally` constructs that you may otherwise repeat.

This is probably the most common use of context managers—they are a way to ensure cleanup.

CONTEXT MANAGER SYNTAX

Consider a common use case where a context manager would be useful—opening a file. You open a file in Python with the built-in `open` function. When you open a file, it is your responsibility to close it again, as shown here:

```
try:
    my_file = open('/path/to/filename', 'r')
    contents = my_file.read()
finally:
    my_file.close()
```

You use a `finally` clause to ensure that, no matter what happens, `my_file` will, in fact, be closed. If an error occurs when reading the file, or something else goes wrong, the `finally` clause will still run, and `my_file` will be closed.

The *with* Statement

So, how you do the same thing—open a file and ensure that it is properly closed—with a context manager? Context managers were introduced in Python 2.5, which adds a new keyword to the language: `with`. You use the `with` statement to enter a context manager.

As it happens, Python's built-in `open` function can also be used as a context manager. This code is identical to what you saw previously:

```
with open('/path/to/filename', 'r') as my_file:
    contents = my_file.read()
```

Essentially, what is happening here is that the `with` statement evaluates the expression that comes after it (in this case, the `open` call). That expression is expected to return an object with two special methods: `__enter__` and `__exit__` (more on those shortly). The `__enter__` method returns a result that is assigned to the variable after the `as` keyword.

It is important to note that the result of the expression after `with` is *not* being assigned to said variable. In fact, it is not assigned to anything at all. It is what is returned from `__enter__` that is assigned.

Simplicity is a huge reason for doing it this way. More importantly, however, remember that the exception-handling and cleanup code can sometimes be very complex, and applying it in many different places is cumbersome. As with decorators, a key reason to use context managers is to avoid repetitive code.

The *enter* and *exit* Methods

Remember that the `with` statement's expression is responsible for returning an object that follows a particular protocol. Specifically, the object must define an `__enter__` and an `__exit__` method, and the latter method must take particular arguments.

The `__enter__` method takes no arguments except for the traditional `self` argument. It is run immediately when the object is returned, and its return value is assigned to the variable used after `as`, if any (the `as` clause is technically optional). Generally, the `__enter__` method is responsible for performing some kind of setup.

The __exit__ method, on the other hand, takes three positional arguments (not including the traditional self): an exception type, an exception instance, and a traceback. These three arguments are all set to None if there is no exception, but are populated if an exception occurs within the block.

Consider the following simple class whose instances act as context managers:

```python
class ContextManager(object):
    def __init__(self):
        self.entered = False

    def __enter__(self):
        self.entered = True
        return self

    def __exit__(self, exc_type, exc_instance, traceback):
        self.entered = False
```

This context manager does very little. It simply returns itself and sets its entered variable to True upon entrance, and then False upon exit.

You can observe this by looking at this context manager in the Python shell. If you create a new ContextManager instance, you find that its entered value is False as expected:

```python
>>> cm = ContextManager()
>>> cm.entered
False
```

If you use this same ContextManager instance as a context manager, observe that its entered attribute becomes True, then False again on exit.

```python
>>> with cm:
...     cm.entered
...
True
>>> cm.entered
False
```

If you do not need the ContextManager instance for anything else, you can instantiate it in the with statement. This works because its __enter__ method just returns itself.

```python
>>> with ContextManager() as cm:
...     cm.entered
...
True
```

Exception Handling

A context manager must define an __exit__ method, which may optionally handle exceptions that are raised in the wrapped code, or handle anything else needed to tear down the context manager state.

As mentioned previously, the __exit__ method must define three positional arguments: the type of the exception (called exc_type in this chapter), the instance of the exception (called exc_instance here), and the traceback option (called traceback here). If no exception occurred within the context manager code, all three of these values will be None.

If the __exit__ method receives an exception, it has the responsibility to handle that exception. Fundamentally, it has three options:

➤ It can propagate the exception (causing it to be re-raised after __exit__ finishes).

➤ It can suppress the exception.

➤ It can raise a different exception.

You can propagate exceptions by having an __exit__ method that returns `False`, or suppress exceptions by having an __exit__ method that returns `True`. Alternatively, if __exit__ raises a different exception, it is used in place of the exceptions it was sent.

Each of these options is covered in more detail in examples throughout this chapter.

WHEN YOU SHOULD WRITE CONTEXT MANAGERS

Several common reasons exist to write context managers. Generally, these involve ensuring that a certain resource is both initialized and de-initialized in an expected manner, or trying to avoid repetition.

Resource Cleanliness

One of the key reasons to write context managers is for situations in which you are opening and closing a resource (such as a file or a database connection). It is often important to ensure that the handle in question is closed properly, to avoid ending up with a situation where many zombie processes can build up over time.

Context managers excel here. By opening a resource in the __enter__ method and returning it, the __exit__ method is guaranteed to be run, and can close the resource before allowing the exception to bubble.

Consider the following context manager that opens a PostgreSQL database connection:

```python
import psycopg2


class DBConnection(object):
    def __init__(self, dbname=None, user=None,
                       password=None, host='localhost'):
        self.host = host
        self.dbname = dbname
        self.user = user
        self.password = password

    def __enter__(self):
        self.connection = psycopg2.connect(
            dbname=self.dbname,
            host=self.host,
            user=self.user,
            password=self.password,
        )
        return self.connection.cursor()
```

```
        def __exit__(self, exc_type, exc_instance, traceback):
            self.connection.close()
```

Within the context manager, it is possible to run queries against the database and retrieve results.

```
    >>> with DBConnection(user='luke', dbname='foo') as db:
    ...     db.execute('SELECT 1 + 1')
    ...     db.fetchall()
    ...
    [(2,)]
```

However, as soon as the context manager exists, the database cursor that you assigned to db becomes closed, and further queries cannot be made against it.

```
    >>> with DBConnection(user='luke', dbname='foo') as db:
    ...     db.execute('SELECT 1 + 1')
    ...     db.fetchall()
    ...
    [(2,)]
    >>> db.execute('SELECT 1 + 1')
    Traceback (most recent call last):
      File "<stdin>", line 1, in <module>
    psycopg2.InterfaceError: cursor already closed
```

What has happened here? This context manager creates a psycopg2 connection object and returns a cursor, which the developer can use to interact with the database. What is important here, though, is that the connection is guaranteed to be closed when the context manager exits.

This is important because, as mentioned, lingering database connections not only consume memory, but they also open files or ports on both the application machine and the database machine. Additionally, some databases also have maximum connection allowances.

Note also that, unlike the previous example, this context manager does *not* simply return itself at the end of the __enter__ method. Instead, it returns a database cursor. This is fine, and a useful paradigm. However, it is still the context manager's __exit__ method that runs.

Most frameworks that work with databases handle opening and closing your database connections for you, but this principle remains: if you are opening a resource and must ensure that it is being properly closed, a context manager is an excellent tool.

Avoiding Repetition

When it comes to avoiding repetition, the most common place where this is useful is in exception handling. Context managers can both propagate and suppress exceptions, which makes them ideal for taking repetitive except clauses and defining them in one place.

Propagating Exceptions

An __exit__ method that just propagates the exception up the chain can do so by returning False. It need not interact with the exception instance at all. Consider the following context manager:

```
    class BubbleExceptions(object):
        def __enter__(self):
            return self
```

```
def __exit__(self, exc_type, exc_instance, traceback):
    if exc_instance:
        print('Bubbling up exception: %s.' % exc_instance)
    return False
```

Running a normal block of code (that does not raise an exception) with this context manager will do nothing particularly interesting.

```
>>> with BubbleExceptions():
...     5 + 5
...
10
```

On the other hand, this block of code does actually raise an exception:

```
>>> with BubbleExceptions():
...     5 / 0
...
Bubbling up exception: integer division or modulo by zero.
Traceback (most recent call last):
  File "<stdin>", line 2, in <module>
ZeroDivisionError: integer division or modulo by zero
```

A couple important things are worth noting here. The first printed line (which begins with `Bubbling up exception: integer...`) was generated by the `__exit__` method itself. It corresponds to the `print` statement on the second line of `__exit__`. This means that `__exit__` did run, and complete. Because it returned `False`, the exception that was sent to `__exit__` in the first place is simply re-raised.

Suppressing Exceptions

As mentioned previously, another option that the `__exit__` method has is to suppress the exception that it receives. The following context manager suppresses any and every exception that might be sent to its `__exit__` method (you should never actually do this, however):

```
class SuppressExceptions(object):
    def __enter__(self):
        return self

    def __exit__(self, exc_type, exc_instance, traceback):
        if exc_instance:
            print('Suppressing exception: %s.' % exc_instance)
        return True
```

The bulk of this code is similar to the `BubbleExceptions` class from earlier, with the primary difference being that now the `__exit__` method returns `True` instead of `False`.

The example of showing normal, uninteresting code that does not raise any exception at all remains unchanged:

```
>>> with SuppressExceptions():
...     5 + 5
...
10
```

However, if you do something that raises an exception, you see a different result:

```
>>> with SuppressExceptions():
...     5 / 0
...
Suppressing exception: integer division or modulo by zero.
```

The first and most obvious thing to note is that the traceback is gone. The exception was handled (suppressed) by the __exit__ method, so program execution continues with no exception raised.

The second thing to note is that no value was ever returned. Whereas the expression 5 + 5, when entered into the interpreter, gave a value of 10, the exception-raising 5 / 0 simply never shows a value. The exception was raised in the process of computing a value, which triggered the running of __exit__. A value is never actually returned. It is also worth noting that if any code was present after 5 / 0, it would never run.

As you would expect, however, exception handlers that are defined *within* the context block are handled before the context block completes. Exceptions handled within a context block are considered to be dealt with and are not sent to __exit__.

Consider the following example:

```
with SuppressExceptions():
    try:
        5 / 0
    except ZeroDivisionError:
        print('Exception caught within context block.')
```

If you run this, the "Exception caught within context block." message will print, and no exception will be sent to __exit__.

Although propagating exceptions is fairly straightforward, suppressing exceptions is always something that you should do carefully. Suppressing too many exceptions leads to code that is extremely difficult to debug. Simply suppressing all exceptions is fundamentally equivalent to a try block that looks like this:

```
try:
    [do something]
except:
    pass
```

Suffice it to say that this is very rarely wise.

__exit__ methods *can*, however, conditionally suppress or handle exceptions, because they are provided the type and instance of the exception, as well as a full traceback. In fact, the exception handling is extremely customizable.

Handling Certain Exception Classes

A simple exception-handling __exit__ function may simply check to see if the exception is an instance of a particular exception class, perform whatever exception handling is necessary, and return True (or return False) if it gets any other exception class.

```
class HandleValueError(object):
    def __enter__(self):
        return self
```

```
def __exit__(self, exc_type, exc_instance, traceback):
    # Return True if there is no exception.
    if not exc_type:
        return True

    # If this is a ValueError, note that it is being handled and
    # return True.
    if issubclass(exc_type, ValueError):
        print('Handling ValueError: %s' % exc_instance)
        return True

    # Propagate anything else.
    return False
```

If you use this context manager and raise `ValueError` inside the block, you see that it prints and then suppresses the exception.

```
>>> with HandleValueError():
...     raise ValueError('Wrong value.')
...
Handling ValueError: Wrong value.
```

Similarly, if you use this context manager but raise a different class of exception (such as `TypeError`, instead), it will bubble and you will still get your traceback.

```
>>> with HandleValueError():
...     raise TypeError('Wrong type.')
...
Traceback (most recent call last):
  File "<stdin>", line 2, in <module>
TypeError: Wrong type.
```

By itself, this does not have a whole lot of value. After all, this is really just a substitute for a much more straightforward `try` clause.

```
try:
    [do something]
except ValueError as exc_instance:
    print('Handling ValueError: %s' % exc_instance)
```

One way that the context manager can be valuable is when the work that must be done in the `except` clause is both non-trivial and must be repeated in multiple places throughout the application. The context manager encapsulates not only the `except` clause, but also its body.

Excluding Subclasses

There is also a little more flexibility in how the class or instance check is done. For example, suppose that you want to catch a given class of exception, but *explicitly not* its subclasses. You cannot do that in a traditional `except` block (nor should you be able to), but a context manager is able to address such an edge case, as shown here:

```
class ValueErrorSubclass(ValueError):
    pass
```

```
class HandleValueError(object):
    def __enter__(self):
        return self

    def __exit__(self, exc_type, exc_instance, traceback):
        # Return True if there is no exception.
        if not exc_type:
            return True

        # If this is a ValueError (but not a ValueError subclass),
        # note that it is being handled and return True.
        if exc_type == ValueError:
            print('Handling ValueError: %s' % exc_instance)
            return True

        # Propagate anything else.
        return False
```

Note that the `HandleValueError` context manager has changed slightly now. It checks its type using == rather than the more traditional `issubclass` check that the previous example used. This means that although it will handle `ValueError` as before, it will not handle a `ValueError` subclass such as the `ValueErrorSubclass` defined previously:

```
>>> with HandleValueError():
...     raise ValueErrorSubclass('foo bar baz')
...
Traceback (most recent call last):
  File "<stdin>", line 2, in <module>
__main__.ValueErrorSubclass: foo bar baz
```

Attribute-Based Exception Handling

Similarly, a context manager might decide whether to handle an exception based on not the *type* of the exception (which is what an `except` clause must do), but rather based on an *attribute* of the exception.

Consider the following function designed to run shell commands conveniently, and use an exception class that is designed to be raised in response to shell errors:

```
import subprocess


class ShellException(Exception):
    def __init__(self, code, stdout='', stderr=''):
        self.code = code
        self.stdout = stdout
        self.stderr = stderr

    def __str__(self):
        return 'exit code %d - %s' % (self.code, self.stderr)


def run_command(command):
    # Run the command and wait for it to complete.
    proc = subprocess.Popen(command.split(' '), stdout=subprocess.PIPE,
                                                stderr=subprocess.PIPE)
```

```
    proc.wait()

    # Get the stdout and stderr from the shell.
    stdout, stderr = proc.communicate()

    # Sanity check: If the shell returned a non-zero exit status, raise an
    # exception.
    if proc.returncode > 0:
        raise ShellException(proc.returncode, stdout, stderr)

    # Return stdout.
    return stdout
```

Such a function (and exception class) is very easy to use. The following is an attempt to rm a bogus file:

```
    run_command('rm bogusfile')
```

Running this will generate the ShellException traceback as expected.

```
    Traceback (most recent call last):
      File "<stdin>", line 1, in <module>
      File "<stdin>", line 11, in run_command
    __main__.ShellException: exit code 1 - rm: bogusfile: No such file or directory
```

What happens when it comes time to *handle* these exceptions? Handling any generic ShellException is easy, but imagine a situation where you receive a ShellException but only want to handle a particular exit code. A context manager is one possible way to approach this.

For example, say that you want to remove a file, but you are okay with a situation where the file was already removed. (For the purpose of this example, ignore that os.remove exists.) In this case, you would be fine with a return code of 0, which indicates successful removal of the file, as well as a return code of 1, which indicates that the file was already absent. On the other hand, an exit code of 64 is still problematic, because this would indicate a usage error of some kind. This should still be raised.

Here is a context manager that would allow some ShellException instances based on their code:

```
    class AcceptableErrorCodes(object):
        def __init__(self, *error_codes):
            self.error_codes = error_codes

        def __enter__(self):
            return self

        def __exit__(self, exc_type, exc_instance, traceback):
            # Sanity check: If this is not an exceptional situation, then just
            # be done.
            if not exc_type:
                return True

            # Sanity check: If this is anything other than a ShellException,
            # then we do not actually know what to do with it.
            if not issubclass(exc_type, ShellException):
                return False
```

```
# Return True if and only if the ShellException has a code that
# matches one of the codes on our error_codes list.
return exc_instance.code in self.error_codes
```

This example code actually introduces a new pattern. The context manager is given the error codes that it should allow when the context manager is initiated. In this case, `AcceptableErrorCodes` takes any number of integers as arguments, and those are used to determine which error codes are actually acceptable.

If you want to attempt to remove a non-existent file when using the `AcceptableErrorCodes` context manager, it will work without incident.

```
>>> with AcceptableErrorCodes(1):
...     run_command('rm bogusfile')
...
```

What this context manager will *not* do, however, is just blindly swallow up every `ShellException` it gets. Consider the following case where you actually use `rm` incorrectly:

```
>>> with AcceptableErrorCodes(1):
...     # -m is not a switch available to rm (at least in Mac OS X).
...     run_command('rm -m bogusfile')
...
Traceback (most recent call last):
  File "<stdin>", line 3, in <module>
  File "<stdin>", line 11, in run_command
__main__.ShellException: exit code 64 - rm: illegal option -- m
usage: rm [-f | -i] [-dPRrvW] file ...
       unlink file
```

So, why did this cause a traceback? Because the exit code was 64 (on Mac OS X; this may vary based on the exact operating system you are using), and you told the context manager that the only acceptable erratic exit code was 1. Therefore, __exit__ returned `False`, and the exception was bubbled as usual.

A SIMPLER SYNTAX

Many of the context managers explored thus far are actually very simple. Although they are fully constructed classes, their only real purpose is to provide straightforward, linear __enter__ and __exit__ functionality.

This structure is extremely powerful. It allows for the creation of very complex and context managers that can do a great deal of customizable logic. However, many context managers are very simple, and creating a class and manually defining __enter__ and __exit__ may seem like overkill.

A simpler approach is designed around handling the simple cases. The Python standard library provides a decorator that will decorate a simple function and make it into a context manager class.

This decorator is `@contextlib.contextmanager`, and functions it decorates are expected to `yield` a single value somewhere during the function. (The `yield` statement is discussed in more detail in Chapter 3, "Generators.")

Consider what the `AcceptableErrorCodes` class might look like as a single, more straightforward function:

```
import contextlib


@contextlib.contextmanager
def acceptable_error_codes(*codes):
    try:
        yield
    except ShellException as exc_instance:
        # If this error code is not in the list of acceptable error
        # codes, re-raise the exception.
        if exc_instance.code not in codes:
            raise

        # This was an acceptable error; no need to do anything.
        pass
```

This function ultimately does the exact same thing that your class did. (It is worth noting that the `pass` line is for instructional purposes—it is obviously not necessary.)

```
>>> with acceptable_error_codes(1):
...     run_command('rm bogusfile')
```

Similarly, error codes are still checked, and only the appropriate ones are intercepted.

```
>>> with acceptable_error_codes(1):
...     run_command('rm -m bogusfile')
...
Traceback (most recent call last):
  File "<stdin>", line 2, in <module>
  File "<stdin>", line 11, in run_command
__main__.ShellException: exit code 64 - rm: illegal option -- M
usage: rm [-f | -i] [-dPRrvW] file ...
       unlink file
```

This simpler syntax (just declaring a function with a single `yield` and using the `@contextlib.contextmanager` decorator) is more than sufficient to create most simple context managers, and is easier to read later. Create a context manager class yourself when you need the power that this provides, and use the decorator with a function otherwise.

SUMMARY

Context managers provide an excellent way to ensure that resources are handled appropriately, as well as to take exception-handling code that would be repeated in multiple different places throughout an application and giving that code a single home.

Along with decorators, context managers are tools for employing the simple principle of *not repeating yourself* unless you absolutely must. Where decorators encase named functions and classes, context managers are ideal for encasing arbitrary blocks of code.

Chapter 3 discusses generators, which produce values one by one when iterated, as each value is needed, rather than having to compute an entire set of values in advance.

Generators

Generators allow sequences of values to be handled while computing each value of the sequence only as it is needed, rather than as a traditional list (which must compute all of its values ahead of time).

Using generators where appropriate can result in substantial memory savings, because large collections of data do not need to be stored in memory in their entirety. Similarly, generators are uniquely able to handle representation of some sequences that cannot be accurately represented by lists.

This chapter explains what a generator is, and the syntax for using generators in Python. It also covers some of the common generators that are provided in the Python standard library.

UNDERSTANDING WHAT A GENERATOR IS

A *generator* is a function that, instead of executing and returning a single value, sends back one or more values in a sequence. A generator function executes until it is told to *yield* a value, and then it continues execution until told to do so again. This continues until the function is complete, or until iteration over that generator terminates.

There is no explicit requirement that a generator terminate at all; generators may represent infinite sequences. There is nothing inherently wrong with this. In cases where this occurs, it is simply the responsibility of the code iterating over the generator to break out of the sequence when appropriate (such as with a `break` statement).

UNDERSTANDING GENERATOR SYNTAX

A generator function is recognizable by the presence of one or more `yield` statements inside the function, usually instead of a `return` statement. In Python 2, a `yield` statement and a `return` statement cannot coexist in the same function. However, in Python 3, it is possible to have both `yield` and `return` (discussed in more detail later).

Like the `return` statement, the `yield` statement commands the function to send back a value to the caller. Unlike the `return` statement, however, the `yield` statement does not actually terminate the function's execution. Rather, execution is temporarily halted until the generator is resumed by the calling code, at which point it picks up where it left off.

Consider the following very simple generator:

```
def fibonacci():
    yield 1
    yield 1
    yield 2
    yield 3
    yield 5
    yield 8
```

This generator represents the beginning of the Fibonacci sequence (that is, the sequence in which each integer is the sum of the previous two). You can iterate generators, as you can see by using a simple for...in loop in the Python interactive terminal.

```
>>> for i in fibonacci():
...     print(i)
...
1
1
2
3
5
8
```

Obviously, this particular generator is probably better represented as a plain Python list. However, consider a generator which, instead of returning six Fibonacci numbers, returns an infinite series of them, as shown here:

```
def fibonacci():
    numbers = []
    while True:
        if len(numbers) < 2:
            numbers.append(1)
        else:
            numbers.append(sum(numbers))
            numbers.pop(0)
        yield numbers[-1]
```

This generator will yield an infinite sequence of Fibonacci numbers. Using the simple for...in from the interactive terminal shown previously would simply print numbers, which very quickly become humorously long (that is, to the screen into perpetuity).

> **NOTE** *For the curious, I tried running this for a few minutes in a Python 3.4 terminal to see how long it would take to overflow the maximum integer size. However, after about five minutes, I got bored and said, "*KeyboardInterrupt *to the rescue!" The computations themselves would probably get to* sys.max- size *reasonably quickly, but the terminal I/O is much slower.*

Unlike the previous `fibonacci` function, this one is not better represented as a simple Python list. In fact, not only would it be unwise to try to represent this as a simple Python list, it would be impossible. Python lists cannot store infinite sequences of values.

The *next* Function

You can ask a generator for a value without using a for...in loop. Sometimes you may want to just get a single value, or a fixed number of values. Python provides the built-in `next` function, which can ask a generator (actually, any object with a __next__ method, called `next` in Python 2) for its next value.

The earlier `fibonacci` function yields an infinite sequence of Fibonacci numbers. Instead of iterating over the entire thing, you can ask for values one at a time.

First, you simply create your generator by calling the `fibonacci` function and saving its returned value. Because the function has `yield` statements rather than a `return` statement, the Python interpreter knows to just return the `generator` object.

```
>>> gen = fibonacci()
>>> gen
<generator object fibonacci at 0x101555dc8>
```

At this point, it is worth noting that none of the code within `fibonacci` has actually run. The only thing that the interpreter has done is recognize that a generator is present and return a `generator` object, which is ready to run the code once a value is requested.

You can use the built-in `next` function to request your first value, as shown here:

```
>>> next(gen)
1
```

Now (and only now) some of the actual code in the `fibonacci` function has been run. (To make the explanation as clear as possible, an explicit `continue` statement has been added at the end of the loop.)

```
def fibonacci():
    numbers = []
    while True:
        if len(numbers) < 2:   # True; numbers == []
            numbers.append(1)
        else:
            numbers.append(sum(numbers))
            numbers.pop(0)
        yield numbers[-1]
        continue
```

The function is entered, and it begins the first iteration of the `while` loop. Because the `numbers` list is empty at this point, the value 1 is appended to the list. Finally, you get to the `yield numbers[-1]` statement. At this point, the generator has been given a value to yield, so execution halts, and the value 1 is yielded. This is where the execution ends; the `continue` statement does not yet run.

Now, issue `next(gen)` again, as shown here:

```
>>> next(gen)
1
```

Execution picks up where it left off, which means the *first* thing to run is the `continue` statement.

```
def fibonacci():
    numbers = []
    while True:
        if len(numbers) < 2:
            numbers.append(1)
        else:
            numbers.append(sum(numbers))
            numbers.pop(0)
        yield numbers[-1]
        continue
```

This sends you back to the top of the `while` loop. Your `numbers` list only has one member (it is `[1]`), so `len(numbers)` is still less than 2, and that path is chosen at the `if` statement again. Your numbers list is now `[1, 1]`, and the final element of the list is yielded, stopping execution.

```
def fibonacci():
    numbers = []
    while True:
        if len(numbers) < 2:   # True; numbers == [1]
            numbers.append(1)
        else:
            numbers.append(sum(numbers))
            numbers.pop(0)
        yield numbers[-1]
        continue
```

Now, issue `next(gen)` yet again, as shown here:

```
>>> next(gen)
2
```

Again, execution picks up where it left off, meaning the next thing to run is the `continue` statement.

```
def fibonacci():
    numbers = []
    while True:
        if len(numbers) < 2:
            numbers.append(1)
        else:
            numbers.append(sum(numbers))
            numbers.pop(0)
        yield numbers[-1]
        continue
```

The `continue` statement sends the interpreter back to the stop of the `while` loop. However, now it takes the `else` pathway when it gets to the `if` statement, because `numbers` is now a list with two elements (`[1, 1]`). The sum of the two elements is then appended to the end of the list, and the first element is removed. Again, you get to the `yield` statement, and it yields the final element of the list, which is 2.

```
def fibonacci():
    numbers = []
    while True:
        if len(numbers) < 2:  # False; numbers == [1, 1]
            numbers.append(1)
        else:
            numbers.append(sum(numbers))
            numbers.pop(0)
        yield numbers[-1]
        continue
```

If you issue `next(gen)` again, the interpreter will follow the same path (because the length of the numbers list is still 2). Of course, now the `numbers` list itself has changed from `[1, 1]` to `[1, 2]`, so the result is different. The value 3 is appended to the list, the 1 is lopped off of the beginning, and 3 is yielded.

```
>>> next(gen)
3
```

If you continue to ask for more values, you see this pattern repeat. The same code runs, but against an updated `numbers` list, so the yielded values continue along the Fibonacci series.

```
>>> next(gen)
5
>>> next(gen)
8
>>> next(gen)
13
>>> next(gen)
21
```

Notice that a few things are not happening. You are not storing a huge list of Fibonacci numbers in memory. The only numbers that you must store are the most recent two, because they are required to find the next number in the series. The generator scraps anything that is out of date. This would matter if the generator were to continue on indefinitely, because if you needlessly held on to every previous value, eventually the list would fill up free memory.

Similarly, the generator only computes each value in the series when it is specifically requested. At this point in code execution, the generator has not bothered to determine that the *next* value that it will need to yield back (if asked) is 34, precisely because it may not be asked.

The *StopIteration* Exception

As with other functions, with generators, you may want to have more than one potential exit path. For example, the following "plain" function has multiple exit paths using multiple `return` statements:

```
def my_function(foo, add_extra_things=True):
    foo += '\nadded things'
    if not add_extra_things:
        return foo
    foo += '\n added extra things'
    return foo
```

This function normally returns at the end of the block. However, if the keyword argument add_extra_things is provided and set to False, the earlier return statement on the third line of the function will be hit instead, and function execution will be cut off there.

Plenty of reasons exist to do this, and generators must have a mechanism to serve a similar purpose.

Python 2

The correct approach for this depends somewhat on which version of Python you are using. In Python 2, generators are not allowed to have return statements. If you attempt to write a function with both a yield statement and a return statement, you get a syntax error, as shown here:

```
>>> def my_generator():
...     yield 1
...     return
...
  File "<stdin>", line 3
SyntaxError: 'return' with argument inside generator
```

Instead, Python provides a built-in exception called StopIteration, which serves a similar purpose. When a generator is being iterated over and StopIteration is raised, this signals that the generator's iteration is complete, and it exits. The exception is caught in this case, and there is no traceback. On the other hand, if next is being used, the StopIteration exception bubbles.

Consider the following simple generator:

```
>>> def my_generator():
...     yield 1
...     yield 2
...     raise StopIteration
...     yield 3
```

If you iterate over this, you will get the values 1 and 2, and then the generator will exit cleanly. The yield 3 statement never runs (similar to code that exists after a return statement).

```
>>> [i for i in my_generator()]
[1, 2]
```

If you manually run next on the generator, the first two next calls will yield values, and the third (and any subsequent) call will raise a StopIteration exception, as shown here:

```
>>> gen = my_generator()
>>> next(gen)
1
>>> next(gen)
2
>>> next(gen)
Traceback (most recent call last):
  File "<stdin>", line 1, in <module>
  File "<stdin>", line 4, in my_generator
StopIteration
```

Python 3

In Python 3, the situation is similar, but you have one additional syntactic option. Python 3 removes the restriction that `yield` and `return` cannot appear together in a function. In this case, using `return` effectively becomes an alias for `raise StopIteration`.

It is worth noting that if you return a value in your `return` statement, it *does not* become a final yielded value. Rather, the value is sent as the exception message. Consider the following statement:

```
return 42
```

This is equivalent to the following:

```
raise StopIteration(42)
```

And, very importantly, it is *not* equivalent to the following:

```
yield 42
return
```

In code that is intended to be cross-compatible with Python 2 and Python 3, it is probably preferable to use the `raise StopIteration` form explicitly. In code that only runs on Python 3, it likely does not matter much.

COMMUNICATION WITH GENERATORS

The generators explored thus far are unidirectional in their communication. They yield values to the calling code; nothing is ever sent to the generator.

However, the generator protocol also supports an additional `send` method that allows communication back to a generator. This works because the `yield` statement is actually an expression. In addition to yielding back its value, if a generator is resumed with `send` rather than `next`, the value provided to `send` can actually be assigned to the result of the `yield` expression.

Consider the following generator to return the perfect squares in order. This is trivial.

```
def squares():
    cursor = 1
    while True:
        yield cursor ** 2
        cursor += 1
```

However, you may want to tell the generator to move to a certain point, forward or backward. You could implement that capability with a small change to your generator code, as shown here:

```
def squares(cursor=1):
    while True:
        response = yield cursor ** 2
        if response:
            cursor = int(response)
        else:
            cursor += 1
```

Now you are *assigning the result of the yield expression* to the `response` variable (if and only if there is a result—you do not want to plow over your value with `None`).

This enables you to jump around within the squares generator, as shown here:

```
>>> sq = squares()
>>> next(sq)
1
>>> next(sq)
4
>>> sq.send(7)
49
>>> next(sq)
64
```

What has happened here? First, the interpreter entered the generator and was asked to yield two values (1 and 4). But, the next time, the generator was *sent* the value 7. The squares generator is coded such that if a value is sent back, the `cursor` variable is set to that value. So, instead of `cursor` being incremented to 3, it is set to 7.

The generator then continues as before. The interpreter goes back to the top of the `while` loop. Because `cursor` is now 7, the value yielded is 49 (7^2). This generator is written such that it simply continues from there, so when `next` is called against it again, `cursor` increments as before, to 8, and the next value to be yielded is 64 (8^2).

It is entirely up to the generator to determine how (and whether) sent values are handled. The generators previously explored in this chapter simply ignore them. A generator could, by contrast, use the sent `cursor` value as a one-off, and then return to its previous spot, as shown here:

```
def squares(cursor=1):
    response = None
    while True:
        if response:
            response = yield response ** 2
            continue
        response = yield cursor ** 2
        cursor += 1
```

This version of the squares generator does exactly that:

```
>>> sq = squares()
>>> next(sq)
1
>>> next(sq)
4
>>> sq.send(7)
49
>>> next(sq)
9
```

The difference here is entirely in the behavior of the generator. There is no magic for how `send` behaves. The purpose of `send` is to provide a mechanism for two-way communication with a generator. It is the responsibility of the generator to determine whether (and how) it handles values sent to it.

ITERABLES VERSUS ITERATORS

Generators in Python are a kind of *iterator.* An iterator in Python is any object that has a __next__ method (and, therefore, is able to respond to the next function).

This is distinct from an *iterable*, which is any object that defines an __iter__ method. An iterable object's __iter__ method is responsible for returning an iterator.

For an example of the subtle distinction here, consider the Python 3 range function (known as xrange in Python 2). It is commonly believed that range objects are, in fact, generators. However, they are not, as shown here:

```
>>> r = range(0, 5)
>>> r
range(0, 5)
>>> next(r)
Traceback (most recent call last):
  File "<stdin>", line 1, in <module>
TypeError: 'range' object is not an iterator
```

This is confusing to many, because an idiom such as for i in range(0, 5) is often one of the first things that you learn in Python. This works because the range function returns an iterable.

The *actual iterator* that the range object's __iter__ method returns, however, is a generator, and responds as expected to the next method.

```
>>> r = range(0, 5)
>>> iterator = iter(r)
>>> iterator
<range_iterator object at 0x10055ecc0>
>>> next(iterator)
0
>>> next(iterator)
1
```

Also, as you would expect, calling next after the generator has finished yielding values will raise StopIteration.

```
>>> next(iterator)
2
>>> next(iterator)
3
>>> next(iterator)
4
>>> next(iterator)
Traceback (most recent call last):
  File "<stdin>", line 1, in <module>
StopIteration
```

When thinking about generators, remember that generators are *iterators*, but they are not necessarily *iterables*. Similarly, not all iterables are iterators.

> **NOTE** *Similarly, not all iterators are actually instances of the* `generator` *class. The iterator in this example is an instance of* `range_iterator`, *which implements a similar pattern. However, as an implementation detail, it lacks a* `send` *method.*

GENERATORS IN THE STANDARD LIBRARY

The Python standard library includes several generators, which you may already use, possibly without even realizing that they are generators.

range

During the earlier discussion about the distinction between iterables and iterators, you learned about the `range` function, which returns an iterable `range` object.

> **NOTE** *As previously mentioned, this function is called* `xrange` *in Python 2.*

The `range` object's iterator is a generator. It returns sequential values, beginning with the `range` object's floor, and continuing through its ceiling. By default, its sequence is simply adding one to each value to get the next value to yield. But an optional third argument to the `range` function, `step`, enables you to specify a different increment, including a negative one.

dict.items and Family

The built-in dictionary class in Python includes three methods that allow for iterating over the dictionary, and all three are iterables whose iterators are generators: `keys`, `values`, and `items`.

> **NOTE** *These three methods are called* `iterkeys`, `itervalues`, *and* `iteritems` *in Python 2.*

The purpose of these methods is to allow for iteration over the keys, values, or two-tuples of keys and values (items) of a dictionary, as shown here:

```
>>> dictionary = {'foo': 'bar', 'baz': 'bacon'}
>>> iterator = iter(dictionary.items())
>>> next(iterator)
```

```
('foo', 'bar')
>>> next(iterator)
('baz', 'bacon')
```

One value of using a generator here is that it prevents the need to make an additional copy of the dictionary (or pieces of the dictionary) in another format. `dict.items` does not need to reformat the entire dictionary into a list of two-tuples. It simply returns back one two-tuple at a time, when it is requested.

You can see a side effect of this if you attempt to alter the dictionary during iteration, as shown here:

```
>>> dictionary = {'foo': 'bar', 'baz': 'bacon'}
>>> iterator = iter(dictionary.items())
>>> next(iterator)
('foo', 'bar')
>>> dictionary['spam'] = 'eggs'
>>> next(iterator)
Traceback (most recent call last):
  File "<stdin>", line 1, in <module>
RuntimeError: dictionary changed size during iteration
```

Because the `items` iterator is a generator that simply reads from the referenced dictionary, it does not know what it should do if the dictionary changes while it is working. In the face of ambiguity, it refuses the temptation to guess, and raises `RuntimeError` instead.

zip

Python includes a built-in function called `zip` that takes multiple iterable objects and iterates over them together, yielding the first element from each iterable (in a tuple), then the second, then the third, and so on, until the end of the shortest iterable is reached. Following is an example:

```
>>> z = zip(['a', 'b', 'c', 'd'], ['x', 'y', 'z'])
>>> next(z)
('a', 'x')
>>> next(z)
('b', 'y')
>>> next(z)
('c', 'z')
>>> next(z)
Traceback (most recent call last):
  File "<stdin>", line 1, in <module>
StopIteration
```

The reasons to use `zip` are similar to the reasons to use `dict.items` and family. Its purpose is to yield back members of its iterables in a different structure, one set at a time. This alleviates the need to copy over the entire thing in memory if such an operation is not necessary.

map

A cousin to the `zip` function is the built-in `map` function. The `map` function takes a function that accepts N arguments as well as N iterables, and computes the result of the function against the sequential members of each iterable, stopping when it reaches the end of the shortest one.

Similarly to `zip`, a generator is used for the iterator here, precisely because it is undesirable to compute every value in advance. After all, these values may or may not be needed. Instead, each value is computed when and only when it is requested.

```
>>> m = map(lambda x, y: max([x, y]), [4, 1, 7], [3, 4, 5])
>>> next(m)
4
>>> next(m)
4
>>> next(m)
7
>>> next(m)
Traceback (most recent call last):
  File "<stdin>", line 1, in <module>
StopIteration
```

As before, this is a trivial operation when dealing with small iterables. However, given a larger data structure, the use of a generator may entail serious savings in computation time or memory use, because the entire structure does not need to be computed and transformed at once.

File Objects

One of the most commonly used generators in Python is the open file object. Although you can interact in many ways with open files in Python, and it is common with smaller files to just call `read` to read the entire file into memory, the file object does support the generator pattern, which reads the file from disk one line at a time. This is very important when operating on larger files. It is not always reasonable to read the entirety of a file into memory.

For historical reasons, file objects have a special method called `readline` used for reading a line at a time. However, the generator protocol is also implemented, and calling `next` on a file does the same thing.

Consider the following simple file:

```
$ cat lines.txt
line 1
line 2
line 3
line 4
line 5
```

You read it in the Python shell by using the built-in `open` function. The resulting object is, among other things, a generator.

```
>>> f = open('lines.txt')
>>> next(f)
'line 1\n'
>>> next(f)
'line 2\n'
```

Note that the generator reads one line at a time and yields the entire line, including the trailing newline (\n) character.

If you attempt to call `next` after the end of the file is reached, `StopIteration` is raised as expected.

```
>>> next(f)
'line 5\n'
>>> next(f)
Traceback (most recent call last):
  File "<stdin>", line 1, in <module>
StopIteration
```

It is worth noting that `__next__` and `readline` are not exact aliases for one another here. Once end of file is reached, `__next__` raises `StopIteration` as it would for any other generator, whereas `readline` actually catches this exception and returns an empty string:

```
>>> next(f)
Traceback (most recent call last):
  File "<stdin>", line 1, in <module>
StopIteration
>>> f.readline()
''
```

WHEN TO WRITE GENERATORS

Essentially, you have two primary reasons to write generators. Both of them spring from the same fundamental concept, which is determining the value *only when it is needed*, rather than well ahead of time.

The basic principle at play here is this: *You do yourself no favors by having your code do a bunch of work or store a bunch of data in advance*. Often, you may not need large chunks of data. Even if you need all of it, you are still doing unnecessary storage if you do not need all of it *at once*.

The two use cases that branch out from this fundamental principle are the need to *access* data in pieces, and the need to *compute* data in pieces.

Accessing Data in Pieces

The first (and probably most common) reason to write generators is to cover cases where you must access data in chunks, but where it is undesirable to store copies of the entire thing.

This is essentially what happens in the file object generator explored previously, as well as the `dict.items` (and family) methods. When dealing with small files, it is entirely reasonable to read the entire file into memory and do whatever work needs to be done against that in-memory string.

On the other hand, what if a file is large? What if you need to restructure a dictionary that is large? Sometimes, making a copy to manipulate data is not a feasible operation. This is where accessing data in pieces is a valuable capability.

When iterating over a large file with the generator method, it does not matter how large the file is. Each line will be read and yielded, one at a time. When iterating over a dictionary with `dict.items`, it does not matter whatsoever how large the source dictionary is. The iterator will iterate over it one piece at a time, and yield only that two-tuple.

The same principle applies to generators that you write. A generator is a useful tool in any situation where you want to iterate over a substantial amount of data, and it is unnecessary to store or copy the entirety of that data in memory at once.

Computing Data in Pieces

The second common reason to write generators is to *compute* data only as it is needed. Consider the range function or the fibonacci function discussed earlier in this chapter. A program that must loop over each number between zero and a googleplex need not store a list of every number between those figures. It is sufficient to simply keep adding one until the maximum is reached.

Similarly, the fibonacci function does not need to compute every Fibonacci number (an impossible task, because there exists an infinite number of them—more on this shortly). It simply must determine *the single next* Fibonacci number and yield it back.

This can be important because sometimes the computation of each item in a sequence can be expensive. It is not useful to compute the entire series unnecessarily.

Sequences Can Be Infinite

One aspect that the earlier discussion about the fibonacci function explored briefly is the fact that some sequences are actually infinite. In such cases, it is not possible to represent the entire sequence in a list, but a generator is capable of representing this.

This is because a generator is not concerned with being aware of every value it must generate. It only needs to generate the next one. It does not matter that the Fibonacci sequence goes on forever. As long as your generator stores the most recent two numbers in the sequence, it is perfectly reasonable to compute the next one.

There is nothing wrong with this. It is the responsibility of the code calling the generator in such cases to deal with the fact that the sequence that the generator represents is an infinite one, and to break out of the sequence when appropriate.

WHEN ARE GENERATORS SINGLETONS?

One important (and often overlooked) fact about generators is that many generators are singletons. This is most often the case when an object is both iterable and an iterator. Because the iterable simply returns self, calling iter on such an object repeatedly will return *the same object*. This essentially means that the object supports only one active iterator.

A simple generator function is not a singleton. Calling the function multiple times returns distinct generators, as shown here:

```
>>> gen1 = fibonacci()
>>> next(gen1), next(gen1), next(gen1), next(gen1), next(gen1)
(1, 1, 2, 3, 5)
>>> gen2 = fibonacci()
>>> next(gen2)
1
>>> next(gen1)
8
```

The following iterable class serves a similar purpose, and returns itself in its __iter__ method:

```python
class Fibonacci(object):
    def __init__(self):
        self.numbers = []

    def __iter__(self):
        return self

    def __next__(self):
        if len(self.numbers) < 2:
            self.numbers.append(1)
        else:
            self.numbers.append(sum(self.numbers))
            self.numbers.pop(0)
        return self.numbers[-1]

    def send(self, value):
        pass

    # For Python 2 compatibility
    next = __next__
```

This is a `Fibonacci` *class*, which implements the generator protocol. However, note that it is also iterable, and responds to iter... with itself. This means that each `Fibonacci` *object* has only one iterator: itself.

```python
>>> f = Fibonacci()
>>> i1 = iter(f)
>>> next(i1), next(i1), next(i1), next(i1), next(i1)
(1, 1, 2, 3, 5)
>>> i2 = iter(f)
>>> next(i2)
8
```

There is nothing inherently wrong with this. It is worth noting, however, because some generators may be implemented as singletons, whereas others are not. Be aware of what the relationship is between the iterable and the iterators, and whether or not an iterable allows multiple iterators. Some do; others do not.

GENERATORS WITHIN GENERATORS

It is often desirable for functions to call other functions. This is a key way that developers structure code for reusability. Similarly, it is often desirable for generators to call other generators. Python 3.3 introduces the new `yield from` statement to provide a straightforward way for a generator to call out to other generators.

Consider the following two trivial, finite generators:

```python
def gen1():
    yield 'foo'
    yield 'bar'
```

```
def gen2():
    yield 'spam'
    yield 'eggs'
```

Prior to Python 3.3, the common way to combine these subgenerators into one would be to iterate over them explicitly in the wrapping generator, as shown here:

```
def full_gen():
    for word in gen1():
        yield word
    for word in gen2():
        yield word
```

It is also possible to do this with the `itertools.chain` method:

```
def full_gen():
    for word in itertools.chain(gen1(), gen2()):
        yield word
```

The Python 3.3 `yield from` syntax provides a cleaner way to do the same thing, and looks much more in line with a function call within another function.

```
def full_gen():
    yield from gen1()
    yield from gen2()
```

Use of this syntax is referred to as *generator delegation*. And, in fact, the previous two implementations of `full_gen` are not actually equivalent. This is because the former implementation discards any value sent to the generator using `send`.

The `yield from` syntax, on the other hand, preserves this, because the generator is simply delegating to another generator. This means that any values sent to the wrapping generator will *also* be sent to the current delegate generator, avoiding the need for the developer to handle this.

SUMMARY

Generators are valuable tools in Python that are used to perform computations or iterate over large amounts of data while only storing and computing what you actually need at the time. This can mean substantial cost savings in terms of both memory and performance.

Consider using generators when dealing with substantial amounts of data or computational work, when not all the work needs to be done in advance. Also consider generators as a way to represent infinite or branching sequences.

In Chapter 4, "Magic Methods," you begin your study of classes in Python, starting with an introduction to magic methods.

PART II
Classes

Magic Methods

Python classes may optionally define a long list of methods that, when defined, are called when the instances of the class are used in certain situations. For example, a class may define under what situations its instances should be considered equivalent by defining a method called __eq__. If the __eq__ method is defined, it is invoked if the class meets an equality test using the == operator.

The purpose of these so-called "magic methods" is to overload Python operators or built-in methods. They are defined using the __ syntax to avoid a case where a programmer accidentally defines a method with the same name without explicitly opting in to the functionality. Magic methods provide consistency between the contracts that built-in classes (including primitives such as integers and strings) provide, as well as the contracts that custom classes provide. If you want to test for equivalence in Python, you should always be able to use == to do so, regardless of whether you are testing two integers, two instances of a class that you wrote for your specific application, or even two instances of unrelated classes.

This chapter explores magic methods, how they work, and what magic methods are available.

MAGIC METHOD SYNTAX

In Python, magic methods follow a consistent pattern—the name of the method is wrapped on both sides by two underscores. For example, when an instance of a class is instantiated, the method that runs is __init__ (not init).

This convention exists to provide a certain level of future-proofing. You can name methods as you please, and not have to worry that your method name will later be used by Python to assign some special (and unintended) significance, provided that you do not name your methods such that they both begin and end with two underscores.

When verbally referring to such methods (for example, in talks at conferences), many people choose to use the coined term "dunder" to describe them. So, __init__ ends up being pronounced as *dunder-init*.

Each magic method serves a specific purpose; it is a hook that is run when particular syntax appears. For example, the __init__ method is run when a new instance of a class is created. Consider the following simple class:

```
class MyClass(object):
    def __init__(self):
        print('The __init__ method is running.')
```

Of course, this class does nothing, except for print to standard out upon instantiation. That is enough to establish that the __init__ method runs in this situation, though.

```
>>> mc = MyClass()
The __init__ method is running.
>>>
```

What is important to realize here is that you are not actually calling the __init__ method directly. Rather, the Python interpreter simply knows to call __init__ upon object instantiation.

Each of the magic methods works this way. There is a particular spelling and method signature that is taken (sometimes the method signature is variable), and the method is actually invoked in a particular situation.

The __eq__ method (mentioned earlier) takes both the obligatory self argument and a second positional argument, which is the object being compared against.

```
class MyClass(object):
    def __eq__(self, other):
        # All instances of MyClass are equivalent to one another, and they
        # are not equivalent to instances of other classes.
        return type(self) == type(other)
```

Notice that this __eq__ method takes a second argument, other. Because the __eq__ method runs when Python is asked to make an equivalence check with the == operator, other will be set to the object on the other side of ==.

This example __eq__ method simply decides equality based solely on whether it is another instance of MyClass. Therefore, you get the following results:

```
>>> MyClass() == MyClass()
True
>>> MyClass() == 42
False
```

Two different instances of MyClass are equivalent because isinstance(other, type(self)) evaluates to True. On the other hand, 42 is an int, and, therefore, not an instance of MyClass. Thus, __eq__ (and, therefore, the == operator) returns False.

AVAILABLE METHODS

The Python interpreter understands a rich set of magic methods that serve many different purposes, from comparison checks and sorting, to hooks for various language features. This book has already explored some of these in Chapter 2, "Context Managers," and Chapter 3, "Generators."

Creation and Destruction

These methods are run when instances of the class are created or destroyed.

__init__

The __init__ method of an object runs immediately after the instance is created. It must take one positional argument (self) and then can take any number of required or optional positional arguments, and any number of keyword arguments.

This method signature is flexible because the arguments passed to the class instantiation call are what are sent to __init__.

Consider the following class with an __init__ method that takes an optional keyword argument:

```python
import random


class Dice(object):
    """A class representing a dice with an arbitrary number
    of sides.
    """
    def __init__(self, sides=6):
        self._sides = sides

    def roll(self):
        return random.randint(1, self._sides)
```

To instantiate a standard, six-sided die, you need only call the class with no arguments: `die = Dice()`. This creates the Dice instance (more on that later), and then calls the new instance's __init__ method, passing no arguments except self. Because the sides argument is not provided, the default of 6 is used.

To instead create a d20, however, you simply pass the sides argument to the call to Dice, which forwards it to the __init__ function.

```python
>>> die = Dice(sides=20)
>>> die._sides
20
>>> die.roll()
20
>>> die.roll()
18
```

It is worth noting that the purpose of the __init__ method is not to actually create the new object (that is performed by __new__). Rather, the purpose is to provide initial data to the object after it has been created.

What this means in practice is that the __init__ method does not (and should not) actually return anything. All __init__ methods in Python return None, and returning anything else will raise TypeError.

The __init__ method is probably the single most common magic method that custom classes define. Most classes are instantiated with extra variables that customize their implementation in some way, and the __init__ method is the appropriate place for this behavior.

__new__

The __new__ method actually precedes the __init__ method in the dance of creating an instance of a class. Whereas the __init__ method is responsible for customizing an instance once it has been created, the __new__ method is responsible for actually creating and returning that instance.

The __new__ method is always static. It does not need to be explicitly decorated as such. The first and most important argument is the class of which an instance is being created (by convention, called cls).

In most cases, the remaining arguments to __new__ should mirror the arguments to __init__. The arguments sent to the call to the class will be sent first to __new__ (because it is called first), and then to __init__.

Realistically, most classes do not actually need to define __new__ at all. The built-in implementation is adequate. When classes do need to define __new__, they will almost always want to reference the superclass implementation first, as shown here, before doing whatever work is necessary on the instance:

```
class MyClass(object):
    def __new__(cls, [...]):
        instance = super(MyClass, cls).__new__(cls, [...])
        [do work on instance]
        return instance
```

Normally, you will want the __new__ method to return an instance of the class being instantiated. However, occasionally this may not be true. Note, however, that the __init__ half of the dance will only be performed if you return an instance of the class whose __new__ method is being run. If you return something else, the instance's __init__ method will not be invoked.

You do this primarily because, in situations where an instance of a different class is returned, the __init__ method was likely run by whatever means created that instance within the __new__ method, and running it twice would be problematic.

__del__

Whereas the __new__ and __init__ methods are invoked when an object is being created, the __del__ method is invoked when an object is being destroyed.

It is relatively rare for developers to destroy their objects in Python directly. (You should do so with the del keyword if you need to.) Python's memory management is good enough that it is generally acceptable simply to allow the garbage collector to do so.

That said, the `__del__` method is run regardless of how an object comes to be destroyed, whether it is through a direct deletion, or through memory reclamation by the garbage collector. You can see this behavior at work by making the following class that deletes noisily:

```
class Xon(object):
    def __del__(self):
        print('AUUUUUUGGGGGGHH!')
```

If you make `Xon` objects but do not assign them to variables, they will be marked as collectable by the garbage collector, which will collect them in short order as other program statements run.

```
>>> Xon()
<__main__.Xon object at 0x1022b8890>
>>> 'foo'
AUUUUUUGGGGGGHH!
'foo'
>>>
```

What happened here? First, an `Xon` object was created (but not assigned to a variable, so there is no real reason for the Python interpreter to keep it around). Next, the interpreter was sent an immutable string, which it must assign to memory (and then immediately release, because it was not assigned to a variable either, but that is not important).

In the particular interpreters I was using (CPython 3.4.0 and CPython 2.7.6), that memory operation causes the garbage collector to take a pass through its table. It finds the `Xon` object and deletes it. This triggers the `Xon` object's `__del__` method, which then loudly screams as it is unceremoniously sent to the great bit bucket beyond.

You see similar (but more immediate) behavior if you delete an `Xon` object directly, as shown here:

```
>>> x = Xon()
>>> del x
AUUUUUUGGGGGGHH!
```

In both cases, the principle is the same. No matter whether the deletion is directly invoked in code or automatically triggered by the garbage collector, the `__del__` method is invoked identically.

It is worth noting that `__del__` methods are generally unable to raise exceptions in any meaningful way. Because deletions are usually triggered in the background by the garbage collector, there is no good way for exceptions to bubble. Therefore, raising any kind of exception in a `__del__` method just prints some nastiness to standard error, and it is generally considered inappropriate to raise exceptions there.

Type Conversion

Several magic methods are available in Python to take a complex object and make it into a more primitive, or more widely used type. For example, types such as `int`, `str`, and `bool` are used everywhere in Python, and it is useful for complex objects to know what their representations are in these formats.

__str__, __unicode__, and __bytes__

By far, the most commonly used type conversion magic method is `__str__`. This method takes one positional argument (`self`), is invoked when an object is passed to the `str` constructor, and is expected to return a string.

```
>>> class MyObject(object):
...     def __str__(self):
...         return 'My Awesome Object!'
...
>>> str(MyObject())
'My Awesome Object!'
```

Because strings are so ubiquitous, it is very often useful for classes to define a __str__ method.

There is a bit more to this situation, however. In Python 2, strings are ASCII strings, whereas in Python 3, strings are Unicode strings. This actually causes a great deal of pain, and this book devotes an entire chapter to the subject (Chapter 8, "Strings and Bytestrings").

Suffice it to say here, however, that Python 2 does have Unicode strings, and Python 3 introduces a type called bytes (or *bytestrings*, as they are sometimes called), which are roughly analogous to the old Python 2 ASCII strings.

These string brethren have their own magic methods. Python 2 honors a __unicode__ method that is invoked when an object is passed to the unicode constructor. Similarly, Python 3 honors a __bytes__ method that is invoked when an object is passed to the bytes constructor. In both cases, the method is expected to return the proper type.

The __str__ method is invoked in certain other situations, too (essentially, situations where str is called under the hood). For example, encountering %s in a format string will run the corresponding argument through str, as shown here:

```
>>> 'This is %s' % MyObject()
'This is My Awesome Object!'
```

In this case, however, the formatting method is a bit smarter. For example, if %s is encountered when formatting a unicode object in Python 2, it will attempt to use __unicode__ first. Consider the following code, running in Python 2.7:

```
>>> class Which(object):
...     def __str__(self):
...         return 'string'
...     def __unicode__(self):
...         return u'unicode'
...
>>> u'The %s was used.' % Which()
u'The unicode conversion was performed.'
>>> 'The %s was used.' % Which()
'The string conversion was performed.'
```

__bool__

Another common need is for an object to define whether it should be considered True or False, either if expressly converted to a Boolean, or in a situation where a Boolean representation is required (such as if the object is the subject of an if statement).

This is handled in Python 3 with the __bool__ magic method, which in Python 2 is instead called __nonzero__. In both cases, the method takes one positional argument (self) and returns either True or False.

It is often unnecessary to define an explicit __bool__ method. If no __bool__ method is defined but a __len__ method (explained further shortly) is defined, the latter will be used, and these often overlap.

__int__, __float__, and __complex__

Occasionally, it is valuable for complex objects to be able to convert to primitive numbers. If an object defines an __int__ method, which should return an int, it will be invoked if the object is passed to the int constructor.

Similarly, objects that define __float__ and __complex__ will have those methods invoked if they are passed to float and complex, respectively.

> **NOTE** *Python 2 has a separate* long *type, and, therefore, a* __long__ *method. This works exactly as you expect.*

Comparisons

Objects are being compared when they are checked for equivalence (with == or !=), or for relative value to one another (such as with <, <=, >, and >=).

Each of these operators maps to a magic method in Python.

Binary Equality

The following methods support testing equality using == and !=.

__eq__

As already explored, the __eq__ method is called when two objects are compared with the == operator. The method must take two positional arguments (by convention, self and other), which are the two objects being compared.

Under most circumstances, the object on the left side has its __eq__ method checked first. It is used if it is defined (and returns something other than NotImplemented). Otherwise, the __eq__ method of the object on the right side is used instead (with the argument order reversed).

Consider the following class that is noisy when given equivalence tests (and then returns False unless it is the exact same object):

```
class MyClass(object):
    def __eq__(self, other):
        print('The following are being tested for equivalence:\n'
              '%r\n%r' % (self, other))
        return self is other
```

You can see the order in action based on which side of the operator your objects are on.

```
>>> c1 = MyClass()
>>> c2 = MyClass()
>>> c1 == c2
The following are being tested for equivalence:
<__main__.MyClass object at 0x1066de590>
<__main__.MyClass object at 0x1066de390>
False
>>> c2 == c1
The following are being tested for equivalence:
<__main__.MyClass object at 0x1066de390>
<__main__.MyClass object at 0x1066de590>
False
>>> c1 == c1
The following are being tested for equivalence:
<__main__.MyClass object at 0x1066de590>
<__main__.MyClass object at 0x1066de590>
True
```

Notice how the order in which the objects are dumped to standard out is reversed. This is because the order in which they were sent to __eq__ was reversed. This also means that there is no inherent requirement that your equivalence check be commutative. However, unless you have a really good reason, you should ensure that equivalence is consistently commutative.

You can observe another facet of this behavior by comparing a MyClass object against something of a different type. Consider the following type with a plain __eq__ method that does nothing but return False:

```
class Unequal(object):
    def __eq__(self, other):
        return False
```

And, when you run equivalence tests against instances of these classes, you see different behavior based on the order in which they are called. When an instance of MyClass is on the left, its __eq__ method is called. When an instance of Unequal is on the left, its quieter brethren is called instead.

```
>>> MyClass() == Unequal()
The following are being tested for equivalence:
<__main__.MyClass object at 0x1066de5d0>
<__main__.Unequal object at 0x1066de450>
False
>>> Unequal() == MyClass()
False
```

There is one exception to this rule on order of objects sent to __eq__: direct subclasses. If one of the two objects being compared is an instance of a direct subclass of the other, this will override the ordering rules, and the __eq__ method of the subclass will be used.

```
class MySubclass(MyClass):
    def __eq__(self, other):
        print('MySubclass\' __eq__ method is testing:\n'
                '%r\n%r' % (self, other))
        return False
```

Now, the same method with the same argument order will be invoked, regardless of the order in which arguments are provided to the operator.

```
>>> MyClass() == MySubclass()
MySubclass' __eq__ method is testing:
<__main__.MySubclass object at 0x1066de690>
<__main__.MyClass object at 0x1066de450>
False
>>> MySubclass() == MyClass()
MySubclass' __eq__ method is testing:
<__main__.MySubclass object at 0x1066de5d0>
<__main__.MyClass object at 0x1066de450>
False
```

__ne__

The __ne__ method is the converse of the __eq__ method. It works the same way, except that it is invoked when the != operator is used.

Normally, it is not necessary to define an __ne__ method, provided that you always want the result to be the opposite of the returned value of __eq__. If no __ne__ method is defined, the Python interpreter will run the __eq__ method and flip the result.

It is possible to explicitly provide an __ne__ method for situations where you do not want this behavior.

Relative Comparisons

These methods also handle comparison, but using comparison operators that test relative value (such as >).

__lt__, __le__, __gt__, __ge__

The __lt__, __le__, __gt__, and __ge__ methods map to the <, <=, >, and >= operators, respectively. Like the equivalence methods, each of these methods should take two arguments (by convention, self and other), and return True if the relative comparison should be considered to hold, and False otherwise.

Usually, it is unnecessary to define all four of these methods. The Python interpreter will rightly consider __lt__ to be the inverse of __ge__, and __gt__ to be the inverse of __le__. Similarly, the Python interpreter will consider the __le__ method to be the disjunction of __lt__ and __eq__, and the __ge__ method to be the disjunction of __gt__ and __eq__.

This means that, in practice, it is usually only necessary to define __eq__ and __lt__ (or __gt__), and all six of the comparison operators will work in the way that you expect.

Another important (but easily overlooked) aspect of defining these methods is that they are what the built-in sorted function uses for sorting objects. Therefore, if you have a list of objects with these methods defined, passing that list to sorted automatically returns a sorted list, from least to greatest, based on the result of the comparison methods.

__cmp__

The __cmp__ method is an older (and less preferred) way of defining relative comparisons for objects. It is checked if (and only if) the comparison methods described previously are not defined.

This method takes two positional arguments (by convention, `self` and `other`), and should return a negative integer if `self` is less than `other`, or a positive integer if `self` is greater than `other`. If `self` and `other` are equivalent, the method should return `0`.

The `__cmp__` method is deprecated in Python 2, and not available in Python 3.

Operator Overloading

These methods provide a mechanism to override the standard Python operators.

Binary Operators

A set of magic methods is also available for overloading the various binary operators available in Python, such as `+`, `-`, and so on. Python actually supplies three magic methods for each operator, each of which takes two positional arguments (by convention, `self` and `other`).

The first of these is a *vanilla method*, in which an expression `x + y` maps to `x.__add__(y)`, and the method simply returns the result.

The second is a *reverse method*. The reverse methods are called (with the operands swapped) if (and only if) the first operand does not supply the traditional method (or returns `NotImplemented`) and the operands are of different types. These methods are spelled the same way, but the method name is preceded by an `r`. Therefore, the expression `x + y`, where `x` does not define an `__add__` method, would call `y.__radd__(x)`.

The third and final magic method is the *in-place method*. In-place methods are called when the operators that modify the former variable in place (such as `+=`, `-=`, and so on) are used. These are spelled the same way, but the method name is preceded by an `i`. Therefore, the expression `x += y` would call `x.__iadd__(y)`.

Normally, the in-place methods simply modify `self` in place and return it. However, this is not a strict requirement. It is also worth noting that it is only necessary to define an in-place method if the behavior of the straightforward method does not cleanly map. The straightforward method is called and its return value assigned to the left operand in the event that the in-place method is not defined.

Table 4-1 shows the full set of operator overloading magic methods.

TABLE 4-1 Operator Overloading Magic Methods

OPERATOR	METHOD	REVERSE	IN-PLACE
+	`__add__`	`__radd__`	`__iadd__`
-	`__sub__`	`__rsub__`	`__isub__`
*	`__mul__`	`__rmul__`	`__imul__`
/	`__truediv__`	`__rtruediv__`	`__itruediv__`
//	`__floordiv__`	`__rfloordiv__`	`__ifloordiv__`
%	`__mod__`	`__rmod__`	`__imod__`

OPERATOR	METHOD	REVERSE	IN-PLACE
**	__pow__	__rpow__	__ipow__
&	__and__	__rand__	__iand__
|	__or__	__ror__	__ior__
^	__xor__	__rxor__	__ixor__
<<	__lshift__	__rlshift__	__ilshift__
>>	__rshift__	__rrshift__	__irshift__

These methods allow for overloading of all of the binary operators that are available in Python. Custom classes can (and should) define them when it is sensible to do so.

Division

One binary operator, division (/), requires slightly more discussion. First, you need a bit of background. Originally, in Python, the division operator between two integers would always return an int, not a float. Essentially, what happens is that the division is performed and the floor of the result is taken. Therefore, 5 / 2 would return 2, and -5 / 2 would return -3. If you wanted a float result, at least one of the operands had to be a float. Therefore, 5.0 / 2 would return 2.5.

Python 3 changes this behavior, because many developers found it to be counterintuitive. In Python 3, division between two integers returns a float, and does so even if the result is a whole number. Thus, 5 / 2 is 2.5, and 4 / 2 is 2.0 (not 2). This is one of the backward-incompatible changes that Python 3 introduced to the language.

Because Python 3 introduced backward-incompatible changes, subsequent releases of the Python 2 series used a mechanism already in place to "opt in" to the new behavior: a special module called __future__, from which future behavior can be imported. In Python 2.6 and 2.7, developers can opt-in to the Python 3 behavior by issuing from __future__ import division.

This is important to discuss here because it alters which magic method is used. The __truediv__ (and siblings) method in Table 5-1 is the Python 3 method. Python 2 originally provided __div__, and calls __div__ for the / operator unless division is imported from __future__, in which case it conforms to the Python 3 behavior and calls __truediv__.

In most cases, code that runs on Python 2 probably needs to be agnostic as to which division scheme is in effect. This means defining both the __div__ and __truediv__ methods. In most cases, it is probably completely acceptable to just map them to each other, as shown here:

```python
class MyClass(object):
    def __truediv__(self, other):
        [...]

    __div__ = __truediv__
```

It is probably wise to make __truediv__ be the "proper" method, and __div__ the alias. The broader principle here is that any code that may even eventually run on Python 3 should be written to target Python 3 and accommodate Python 2, as opposed to the other way around.

Unary Operators

Python also provides three unary operators: +, -, and ~. Notice that two of the symbols here are reused between unary and binary operators. This is fine. The interpreter is able to determine which is in use based on whether the expression is unary or binary.

The unary operator methods simply take a single positional argument (self), perform the operation, and return the result. The methods are called __pos__ (which maps to +), __neg__ (which maps to -), and __invert__ (which maps to ~).

Unary operators are straightforward. The expression ~x, for example, calls x.__invert__(). Consider the following string-like class that is able to return the string backward:

```python
class ReversibleString(object):
    def __init__(self, s):
        self.s = s

    def __invert__(self):
        return self.s[::-1]

    def __str__(self):
        return self.s
```

And, in the Python interpreter, you would see the following:

```python
>>> rs = ReversibleString('The quick brown fox jumped over the lazy dogs.')
>>> ~rs
'.sgod yzal eht revo depmuj xof nworb kciuq ehT'
```

So, what is happening here? The ReversibleString object is created and assigned to rs. The second statement, ~rs, is a simple unary expression. The result is not being assigned to a variable, which means that it is simply being discarded. The rs variable is not being modified in place. The interpreter, however, shows you the result, which is a str object that represents your string, backward.

Note that the return value is a str, not a ReversibleString. There is no obligation that these methods return a value of the same type as the operand, and your __invert__ method does not do so.

There is no reason why it cannot return a ReversibleString, however, and often returning an object of the same type is desirable.

```python
class ReversibleString(object):
    def __init__(self, s):
        self.s = s

    def __invert__(self):
        return type(self)(self.s[::-1])

    def __repr__(self):
        return 'ReversibleString: %s' % self.s

    def __str__(self):
        return self.s
```

This iteration of `ReversibleString` returns a new `ReversibleString` instance from its `__invert__` method. A custom `repr` has been added for demonstration purposes, because having the interpreter provide a memory address in the output is not useful.

> **NOTE** *You may note the use of* `type(self)()`, *rather than simply calling* `ReversibleString()` *directly. This ensures that if* `ReversibleString` *is subclassed, the subclass would be correctly used there.*

The Python interpreter now shows slightly different output:

```
>>> rs = ReversibleString('The quick brown fox jumped over the lazy dogs.')
>>> ~rs
ReversibleString: .sgod yzal eht revo depmuj xof nworb kciuq ehT
```

Instead of getting a `str` object back, you now have a `ReversibleString`. This means that your inverted output is now invertible.

```
>>> ~~rs
ReversibleString: The quick brown fox jumped over the lazy dogs.
```

This is straightforward. The `rs` object is having its `__invert__` method called. Then, the result of that expression is having *its* `__invert__` method called. This is, therefore, equivalent to `rs.__invert__().__invert__()`.

Overloading Common Methods

Python includes many built-in methods (the most common example being `len`) that are widely used and almost as much of the contract that an object observes as are the operators. Therefore, Python supplies magic methods that are invoked when an object is passed to those methods.

__len__

The most common method to be overloaded in this way is almost certainly `len`, which is the Pythonic way to determine the "length" of an item. The length of a string is the number of characters in the string, the length of a list is the number of elements within the list, and so on.

Objects can describe their length by defining a `__len__` method. This method takes one positional argument (`self`) and should return an integer.

Consider the following class to represent a span of time:

```python
class Timespan(object):
    def __init__(self, hours=0, minutes=0, seconds=0):
        self.hours = hours
        self.minutes = minutes
        self.seconds = seconds

    def __len__(self):
        return (self.hours * 3600) + (self.minutes * 60) + self.seconds
```

This class essentially takes a number of hours, minutes, and seconds; it then calculates the seconds that this represents and uses that as the length.

```
>>> ts = Timespan(hours=2, minutes=30, seconds=1)
>>> len(ts)
9001
```

It is worth noting that the `__len__` method, if defined, also is used to determine whether an object is considered `True` or `False` if typecast to a `bool` or is used in an `if` statement, *unless* the object also defines a `__bool__` method (or, in Python 2, `__nonzero__`).

This will actually do exactly what you expect the bulk of the time, so it often is not necessary to define a separate `__bool__`.

```
>>> bool(Timespan(hours=1, minutes=0, seconds=0))
True
>>> bool(Timespan(hours=0, minutes=0, seconds=0))
False
```

In Python 3.4, an additional method, `__length_hint__`, has been added. Its purpose is to provide an *estimate* of an object's length, which is allowed to be somewhat greater than or less than an object's actual length, and can be used as a performance optimization. It takes one positional argument (`self`), and must return an integer greater than `0`.

__repr__

One of the most important built-in methods in Python is also potentially one of the most overlooked: `repr`. Any object can define a `__repr__` method, which takes one positional argument (`self`).

Why is `repr` so important? An object's `repr` is how it will represent itself when output on the Python interactive terminal.

It is not generally useful to return an object in the terminal and have it render as `<__main__.O object at 0x102cdf950>`. In the vast majority of cases, an object's class and address in memory are not what you want to know.

Defining `__repr__` allows you to give objects a more useful representation. Consider the following `Timespan` class with a useful `__repr__` method:

```
class Timespan(object):
    def __init__(self, hours=0, minutes=0, seconds=0):
        self.hours = hours
        self.minutes = minutes
        self.seconds = seconds

    def __repr__(self):
        return 'Timespan(hours=%d, minutes=%d, seconds=%d)' % \
                (self.hours, self.minutes, self.seconds)
```

What happens when you work with `Timespan` objects on the terminal now?

```
>>> Timespan()
Timespan(hours=0, minutes=0, seconds=0)
>>> Timespan(hours=2, minutes=30)
Timespan(hours=2, minutes=30, seconds=0)
```

This is much more useful than a memory address!

Notice that in addition to communicating all the key attributes of a `Timespan`, the `repr` prints as a valid expression that instantiates a `Timespan`. This is incredibly valuable when it is possible. It intuitively communicates that you are working with an object generally, and a `Timespan` object specifically. Just printing out the timing information might leave open the interpretation that you are looking at a `str` or a `timedelta`, for example. Also, the Python interpreter could parse it if it's copied and pasted. That is a good thing.

What this really points to is a more general distinction that is important: `repr` and `str` have different purposes. Exactly how you delineate them is a matter of subtle differences of opinion, depending on what you read. But an all-encompassing understanding should be that an object's `repr` is intended for programmers (and machines, possibly), whereas an object's `str` is geared toward more public consumption. You would not want the `Timespan`'s `str` to look like a class instantiation call. Most likely, it would be something intended for humans instead.

It is often very useful for an object's `repr` to return a valid Python expression to reconstruct the object. Many Python built-ins do this. The `repr` of an empty list is `[]`, which is the expression to make an empty list.

When this is impossible or impractical, a good rule of thumb is to return something that looks like it is obviously an object, and is noisy about what its key properties are. As an example, an alternative `repr` for a `Timestamp` object might be `<Timestamp: X hours, Y minutes, Z seconds>`. The Python interpreter will not be able to parse that (unlike the `repr` used previously), but it is clear exactly what it is, and nobody will errantly expect it to be able to be parsed, either.

__hash__

Another often overlooked built-in function is the `hash` function. The purpose of the `hash` function is to uniquely identify objects, and to do so using a numeric representation.

When an object is passed to hash, its `__hash__` method is invoked (if defined). The `__hash__` method takes one positional argument (`self`), and should return an integer. It is acceptable for this integer to be negative.

The object class provides a `__hash__` function, which normally simply returns the `id` of the object. An object's `id` is implementation-specific, but in CPython, it is its memory address.

However, if an object defines an `__eq__` method, the `__hash__` method is implicitly set to `None`. This is done because of an ambiguity in the purpose of hashing generally. Depending on how they are being used, it may be desirable for every object to have a unique hash, or for equivalent objects to have matching hashes. And, "in the face of ambiguity, avoid the temptation to guess."

Therefore, if a class should understand equivalence and be hashable, it must explicitly define its own `__hash__` method.

Hashes are used in several places in the Python ecosystem. The two most common uses for them are for dictionary keys and in `set` objects. Only hashable objects can be used as dictionary keys. Similarly, only hashable objects can exist in Python `set` objects. In both cases, the hash is used to determine equivalence for testing set membership and dictionary key lookup.

__format__

Another common Python built-in function is the `format` function, which is capable of formatting various kinds of objects according to Python's format specification.

Any object can provide a `__format__` method, which is invoked if an object is passed to `format`. This method takes two positional arguments, the first being `self`, and the second being the format specification string.

In Python 3, the `str.format` method has replaced the `%` operator as the preferred way to handle templating within strings. If you pass an object with a `__format__` method as an argument to `str.format`, this method will be called.

```
>>> from datetime import datetime
>>>
>>>
>>> class MyDate(datetime):
...     def __format__(self, spec_str):
...         if not spec_str:
...             spec_str = '%Y-%m-%d %H:%M:%S'
...         return self.strftime(spec_str)
...
>>>
>>> md = MyDate(2012, 4, 21, 11)
>>>
>>> '{0}'.format(md)
'2012-04-21 11:00:00'
```

Because the string used `{0}` with no additional formatting information, there was no format specification, and the default is used. However, note what happens when you provide one:

```
>>> '{0:%Y-%m-%d}'.format(md)
'2012-04-21'
```

The `__format__` method is only called in this way when using the `format` method. It is *not* called if `%`-substitution is used within a string.

__instancecheck__ and __subclasscheck__

Although most type checking in Python is done using so-called *duck typing* (if `obj.look()`-s like a `Duck` and `obj.quack()`-s like a `Duck`, it's probably a `Duck`), it is also possible to test whether an object is an instance of a particular class using the built-in `isinstance` method. Similarly, a class can test whether it inherits from another class using `issubclass`.

It is rarely necessary to customize this behavior. The `isinstance` method returns `True` if the object is an instance of the provided class *or any subclass thereof* (which is almost always what you want). Similarly, `issubclass` (despite its name) returns `True` if the same class is provided for both arguments (which is also almost always what you want).

Occasionally, though, it is desirable to allow classes to fake their identities. Python 2.6 introduces this possibility by providing the `__instancecheck__` and `__subclasscheck__` methods. Each of these methods takes two arguments, the first being `self`, and the second being the object being tested against this class (so, the *first* argument to `isinstance`). This allows classes to determine what objects may masquerade as their instances or subclasses.

__abs__ and __round__

Python provides built-in `abs` and `round` functions, which return the absolute value of a number and a rounded value, respectively.

Although it is not usually necessary for custom classes to define this behavior, they can do so by defining `__abs__` and `__round__`, respectively. Both take one positional argument (`self`), and should return a numeric value.

Collections

Many objects are *collections* of various kinds of other objects. Most complex classes functionally come down to a collection of attributes (sorted in a meaningful way), as well as actions that the object can take.

Python has several ways of understanding "membership" of one object within another. For lists and dictionaries, for example, it is possible to test whether an object is a member of the collection by the expression `needle in haystack` (where `needle` is the variable being searched for, and `haystack` is the collection).

Dictionaries are made up of keys, and can perform lookup based on the key by evaluating `haystack[key]`. Similarly, most objects have attributes that are set during initialization or by other methods, which are accessed using dot notation (`haystack.attr_name`).

Python has magic methods that interact with all of these.

__contains__

The `__contains__` method is invoked when an expression such as `needle in haystack` is evaluated. This method takes two positional arguments (`self`, and then the `needle`), and should return `True` if the `needle` is considered to be present, and `False` if it is absent.

There is no strict requirement that this conform to object presence within another object, although that is the most common use case. Consider the following class that represents a range of dates:

```
class DateRange(object):
    def __init__(self, start, end):
        self.start = start
        self.end = end

    def __contains__(self, needle):
        return self.start <= needle <= self.end
```

In this case, the `__contains__` method determines whether the date is between the boundaries of the range.

```
>>> dr = DateRange(date(2015, 1, 1), date(2015, 12, 31))
>>> date(2015, 4, 21) in dr
True
>>> date(2012, 4, 21) in dr
False
```

__getitem__, __setitem__, and __delitem__

The __getitem__ method and its siblings are used for key lookups on collections (such as dictionaries), or index or slice lookups on sequences (such as lists). In both cases, the fundamental expression being evaluated is haystack[key].

The __getitem__ method takes two arguments: self and key. It should return the appropriate value if present, or raise an appropriate exception if absent. What exception is appropriate varies somewhat based on the situation, but is usually one of IndexError, KeyError, or TypeError.

The __setitem__ method is used in the same situation, except that it is invoked when a value is being *set* to the collection, rather than being looked up. It takes three positional arguments rather than two: self, key, and value.

It is *not* a requirement that every object that supports item lookup necessarily support item changes. In other words, it is entirely acceptable to define __getitem__ and not define __setitem__ if this is the behavior that you want.

Finally, the __delitem__ method is invoked in the unusual situation where key is deleted with the del keyword (for example, del haystack[key]).

__getattr__ and __setattr__

The other major way that Python classes serve as collections is by being collections of attributes and objects. When a date object contains year, month, and day, those are attributes (which are set to integers in that case).

The __getattr__ method is invoked when attempting to get an attribute from an object, either with dot notation (such as obj.attr_name), or using the getattr method (such as getattr(obj, 'attr_name')).

However, unlike other magic methods, it is important to realize that __getattr__ is only invoked *if the attribute is not found on the object in the usual places*. In other words, the Python interpreter will *first* do a standard attribute lookup, return that if there is a match, and if there is not a match (in other words, AttributeError would be raised), then and only then is the __getattr__ method called.

In other respects, it works similarly to __getitem__ (discussed previously). It accepts two positional arguments (self and key), and is expected to return an appropriate value, or raise AttributeError.

Similarly, the __setattr__ method is the writing equivalent of __getattr__. It is invoked when attempting to write to an object, whether by dot notation or using the setattr method. Unlike __getattr__, it is always invoked (the method would be meaningless otherwise), and, therefore, should call the superclass method in situations where the traditional implementation is desired.

__getattribute__

The reason why __getattr__ is only invoked if the attribute is not found is because this is ordinarily the desired behavior (otherwise, it would be *very* easy to fall into infinite recursion traps). However, the __getattribute__ method, unlike its more common counterpart, is called unconditionally.

The logical order here is that __getattribute__ is called first, and is ordinarily responsible for doing the traditional attribute lookup. If a class defines its own __getattribute__, it becomes responsible for calling the superclass implementation if it needs to do so. If (and only if) __getattribute__ raises AttributeError, __getattr__ is called.

OTHER MAGIC METHODS

A few other magic methods exist in addition to the ones described so far. In particular, Python implements an iterator protocol, which uses the __iter__ and __next__ methods. These are not discussed in detail here because they are discussed at length in Chapter 3, "Generators."

Similarly, Python implements a rich language feature known as context managers, which make use of the __enter__ and __exit__ magic methods. These are also not discussed in detail here because they are discussed at length in Chapter 2, "Context Managers."

SUMMARY

The magic methods available to classes provide the Python language with a consistent data model that can be used across custom classes. This greatly enhances the readability of the language, in addition to providing hooks for classes of disparate types to interact with each other in predictable ways.

There is no reason to require that every custom class implement all of these methods, or even any of them. When writing a class, consider what functionality you need. However, if the functionality needed maps cleanly to an already defined method here, it is preferable to implement these rather than provide your own custom spelling.

In Chapter 5, you will learn about metaclasses.

Metaclasses

Classes in Python are also objects.

This is a key concept. In Python, almost everything is an object, including both functions and classes. This means that functions and classes can be provided as arguments, exist as members of class instances, and do anything that any other object is capable of doing.

What else does it mean to say that classes are objects? Chapter 4, "Magic Methods," discussed how object instantiation works. The __new__ and __init__ methods of the class are called, in that order, to create the new object. Classes are not an exception to this process. Classes themselves, being objects, are instances of another class, which is responsible for creating them.

The classes responsible for generating other classes are called *metaclasses*. "Meta-" is a Greek prefix that simply means "post-" or "after." For example, a portion of Aristotle's work is called "The Physics," and the subsequent portion is called "The Metaphysics," which simply means "the stuff that comes after the physics." However, the meaning assigned to this prefix has since evolved to refer to a level of self-reference—an instantiation of a concept in order to work on that concept. If you have ever been unfortunate enough to be forced to sit through a meeting to plan other meetings, that particular atrocity could rightly be called a meta-meeting.

This chapter covers metaclasses. First, it delves into the philosophy behind Python's object model, and how metaclasses, classes, and objects connect to one another. Then, it explores examples of specific ways metaclasses can be used.

CLASSES AND OBJECTS

The relationship between a class and an instance of that class is straightforward and two-fold. First, a class defines the properties and available actions of its instances. Second, a class serves as a factory that creates said instances.

With this in mind, the only additional understanding necessary to grasp metaclasses is the realization that this relationship can be hierarchical. When you instantiate a class that you write, your class serves as the definition of the instance's properties and actions, and performs the generation of the instance. When you defined the class, you were simply using a special, substitute syntax that stands in for the instantiation of a different class, called `type`.

Using *type* Directly

This can best be illustrated by simply creating a class using `type` directly, rather than using the Python `class` keyword. This is syntactically quite ugly, but it offers a clear view into what is going on under the hood.

Therefore, consider the following simple set of classes:

```python
class Animal(object):
    """A class representing an arbitrary animal."""

    def __init__(self, name):
        self.name = name

    def eat(self):
        pass

    def go_to_vet(self):
        pass


class Cat(Animal):
    def meow(self):
        pass

    def purr(self):
        pass
```

The `Animal` class obviously represents an animal, and defines certain things that the animal is capable of doing, such as eating and being taken to the vet. The `Cat` subclass additionally knows how to meow and purr, functions not available to other animals. (The method bodies are stubbed, and left to the reader's intuition.)

What happens here is that when the Python interpreter gets to the top statement in the code, `class Animal(object)`, it invokes the `type` constructor under the hood. As alluded to earlier, `type` is a built-in class in Python, which is the default class for other class objects. It is the default class that creates other classes—or, the default metaclass.

However, nothing stops you from simply doing this directly. The `type` constructor takes three positional arguments: `name`, `bases`, and `attrs`. The `name` argument (a string) is simply the name of the class. The `bases` argument is a tuple of the superclasses for that class. Python supports multiple inheritance, which is why this is a tuple. If you are only inheriting from a single class, just send a tuple with a single element. Finally, the `attrs` argument is a dictionary of all the attributes on the class.

Creating a Class

The following code is (roughly) equivalent to the previous `class Animal` block:

```
def init(self, name):
    self.name = name

def eat(self):
    pass

def go_to_vet(self):
    pass


Animal = type('Animal', (object,), {
    '__doc__': 'A class representing an arbitrary animal.',
    '__init__': init,
    'eat': eat,
    'go_to_vet': go_to_vet,
})
```

This is, obviously, *not* the preferred way to instantiate a new class. Also, note that it is only roughly equivalent. It has a couple of differences, most notably that this code leaves functions called init, eat, and go_to_vet, unattached to the class, in that namespace. This is worth noting, but not particularly important for the purposes of this discussion.

Focus on the call to `type`. The first argument is just the string `'Animal'`. There is some repetition here. You are sending this string to assign the name of the class, but you are also assigning the result of the type call to the variable `Animal`. The `class` keyword handled this for you. Because this is a direct call to `type`, you must manually assign the result to a variable, as you would for a new instance of any other class.

The second argument is a tuple with a single item: `(object,)`. This means that the `Animal` class inherits from `object`, as it did in the initial class. You need the trailing comma to disambiguate to the Python interpreter that you want a tuple here. Parentheses have other uses in Python, and so a trailing comma is required for tuples with only a single element.

The third argument is a dictionary that defines the attributes of the class, equivalent to the indented portion of the `class` block. You previously defined functions that map to the functions in your original class, and pass them into the `attrs` dictionary. The dictionary *keys* are used to determine the name of the attribute within the class. One thing to note here is the docstring. The Python interpreter automatically takes the docstring in a class call and assigns it to the attribute __doc__. Because you are instantiating `type` directly, you must do that manually.

Creating a Subclass

You can create the `Cat` class similarly, as shown here:

```
def meow(self):
    return None

def purr(self):
    return None
```

```
Cat = type('Cat', (Animal,), {
    'meow': meow,
    'purr': purr,
})
```

This is mostly more of the same. The big change here is that you are now subclassing `Animal` rather than `object`. What you are passing here is the `Animal` class itself. Also, note that it is still a tuple with a single element. You are not passing `(Animal, object)`. The fact that `object` is `Animal`'s superclass is baked into the `Animal` class already. Sending in a tuple with more than one element is only necessary for multiple inheritance situations.

The *type* Chain

Consider the following instance of the `Cat` class:

```
louisoix = Cat(name='Louisoix')
```

Notice the three things that are on deck. `louisoix` is an object, and an instance of `Cat`. The `Cat` class is also an object (because classes are objects), and is an instance of `type`. Finally, `type` is the top of the chain.

You can also observe this in another way. Passing a single object to `type` returns its class, as shown here:

```
>>> type(5)
<type 'int'>
```

So, observe the following chain:

```
>>> type(louisoix)
<class '__main__.Cat'>

>>> type(Cat)
<class 'type'>
>>> type(type)
<class 'type'>
```

The `type` class is the base case here. It is the top of the chain, and, therefore, `type(type)` returns itself.

> **NOTE** *In a Python 2 terminal, note that the output will show* `<type 'type'>` *instead of* `<class 'type'>`. *This is fine. It is still the same type; it simply represents itself differently on the terminal.*

The Role of *type*

`type` is the primary metaclass in Python. Ordinary classes that are created with the `class` keyword, by default, have `type` as their metaclass.

Colloquially, you can refer to `type` as the metaclass for both the class (`Cat`) and its instances (`louisoix`).

Additionally, `type` is also the superclass from which other metaclasses inherit. This is analogous to `object` being the class from which other classes inherit. Just as `object` is the top of the class hierarchy, `type` is the top of the metaclass hierarchy.

WRITING METACLASSES

Writing a metaclass is syntactically very straightforward. You simply declare a class (using the `class` keyword) that inherits from `type`. The beauty of this object model shines through here. Classes are just objects, and metaclasses are just classes. The behaviors that metaclasses take on are inherited from `type`. Any class that subclasses `type` is, therefore, capable of functioning as a metaclass.

Before going into examples, note as an aside that you should never attempt to declare or use a metaclass that does not directly subclass `type`. This will cause havoc with Python's multiple inheritance. Python's inheritance model requires any class to have exactly one metaclass. Inheriting from two classes with different metaclasses is acceptable if (and only if) one of the metaclasses is a direct subclass of the other (in which case, the subclass is used). Attempting to implement a metaclass that does not subclass `type` will break multiple inheritance with any classes that use that metaclass, along with any classes that use `type` (that is, virtually all of them). You do not want to do this.

The __*new*__ Method

The most important method that custom metaclasses must define is the `__new__` method. This method actually handles the creation of the class, and must return the new class.

The `__new__` method is a class method (that does not need to be explicitly decorated as such). The arguments sent to `__new__` in custom metaclasses must mirror the arguments sent to `type`'s `__new__` method, which takes four positional arguments.

The first argument is the metaclass itself, prepended to arguments in a manner similar to that of bound methods. By convention, this argument is called `cls`.

Beyond this, `__new__` expects three positional arguments:

➤ First, the desired name of the class as a string (`name`)

➤ Second, a tuple of the class's superclasses (`bases`)

➤ Third, a dictionary of attributes that the class should contain (`attrs`)

Most custom implementations of `__new__` in metaclasses should ensure that they call the superclass implementation, and perform whatever work is needed in the code around that.

__*new*__ Versus __*init*__

Recall at this point the distinction between the `__new__` method and the `__init__` method. In a class or a metaclass, the `__new__` method is responsible for creating and returning the object.

Conversely, the __init__ method is responsible for customizing the object after it has been created, and returns nothing.

In ordinary classes, you generally do not define a custom __new__ method at all. By contract, defining a custom __init__ method is extremely common. This is because the implementation of __new__ provided by object is essentially always sufficient, but it is also necessary. Overriding it (even in direct subclasses of object) would require calling the superclass method and being careful to return the result (the new instance). By contrast, overriding __init__ is easy and relatively risk-free. An object's implementation of __init__ is a no-op, and the method does not return anything at all.

When you're writing custom metaclasses, this behavior changes. Custom metaclasses generally should override the __new__ method, and generally do not implement an __init__ method at all. When doing this, keep in mind that you almost always *must* call the superclass implementation. type's implementation of __new__ will actually provide you with the object you need to do work on and return.

A Trivial Metaclass

Before diving into a metaclass that customizes behavior, consider a custom metaclass that does nothing but check all the boxes that have been covered thus far.

```
class Meta(type):
    """A custom metaclass that adds no actual functionality."""

    def __new__(cls, name, bases, attrs):
        return super(Meta, cls).__new__(cls, name, bases, attrs)
```

This discussion has not yet explored how to assign a metaclass within class creation using the class keyword (more on that shortly). But you can create a class that uses the Meta metaclass by calling Meta directly, similar to the direct invocation of type earlier.

```
>>> C = Meta('C', (object,), {})
```

This creates a class, C, which is an instance of Meta rather than an instance of type. Observe the following:

```
>>> type(C)
<class '__main__.Meta'>
```

This is distinct from what you observe from a "normal" class, as shown here:

```
>>> class N(object):
...     pass
...
>>> type(N)
<class 'type'>
```

Metaclass Inheritance

It is worth noting that metaclasses are inherited. Therefore, subclasses of C will be instances of Meta, rather than being direct instances of type as shown in the following code and illustrated in Figure 5-1.

```
>>> class D(C):
...     pass
...
>>> type(D)
<class '__main__.Meta'>
```

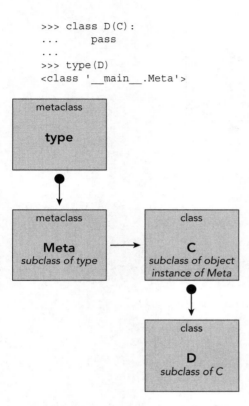

FIGURE 5-1: Metaclass inheritance

In this case, D is an instance of Meta not because it has an explicit metaclass declared, or because you called Meta to create it, but rather because its superclass is an instance of Meta, and, therefore, it is also.

It is important to note here that classes may only have one metaclass. Under most circumstances, this is fine, even in scenarios where multiple inheritance is in play. If a class subclasses two or more distinct classes with distinct metaclasses, the Python interpreter will try to resolve this by checking the ancestry of the metaclasses. If they are direct ancestors, the subclass will be used.

Consider the following class that subclasses both C (an instance of Meta) and N (an instance of type)

```
>>> class Z(C, N):
...     pass
...
>>> type(Z)
<class '__main__.Meta'>
```

Figure 5-2 shows what is happening in this code.

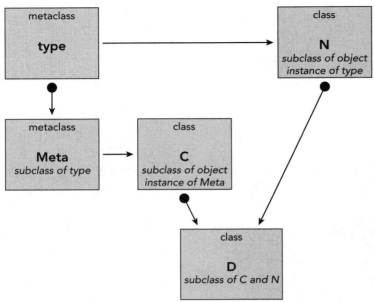

FIGURE 5-2: Metaclass inheritance with subclasses

What is going on here? The Python interpreter is told to create class Z, and that it should subclass both C and N. This would be the equivalent of type('Z', (C, N), {}).

First, the Python interpreter examines C, and realizes that it is an instance of Meta. Then it examines N, and realizes that it is an instance of type. This is a potential conflict. The two superclasses have different metaclasses. However, the Python interpreter also realizes that Meta is a direct subclass of type. Therefore, it knows it can safely use Meta, and does so.

What happens if you have two metaclasses where one is not a direct descendent of the other? Now there is a conflict, and the Python interpreter does not know how to solve it. And it will cowardly refuse to try, as shown here:

```
>>> class OtherMeta(type):
...     def __new__(cls, name, bases, attrs):
...         return super(OtherMeta, cls).__new__(cls, name, bases, attrs)
...
>>> OtherC = OtherMeta('OtherC', (object,), {})
>>>
>>> class Invalid(C, OtherC):
...     pass
...
Traceback (most recent call last):
  File "<stdin>", line 1, in <module>
  File "<stdin>", line 4, in __new__
TypeError: Error when calling the metaclass bases
```

```
metaclass conflict: the metaclass of a derived class must be a (non-
strict) subclass of the metaclasses of all its bases
```

This happens because Python can only have one metaclass for each class, and will not try to guess which metaclass to use in an ambiguous case.

USING METACLASSES

Before delving into more complex metaclasses, let's explore how to use them. Although it is, of course, possible to instantiate metaclasses directly (as shown with `type` and `Meta` earlier), it is not the desirable method.

The `class` construct in Python provides a mechanism to declare the metaclass if `type` is not the metaclass being used. However, the syntax to define which metaclass is different, depending on which version of Python you are using.

Python 3

In Python 3, metaclasses are declared alongside the superclasses (if any). The syntax resembles that of a keyword argument in a function declaration or a function call, and the "keyword argument" is `metaclass`.

Earlier, you created the `C` class by calling `Meta` directly. Here is the preferred way to do this in Python 3:

```
class C(metaclass=Meta):
    pass
```

This `class` keyword call does the exact same thing as creating the class by directly calling `Meta`. This, however, is the preferred style.

One thing to note here is that you did not explicitly specify `object` as the superclass. In most of the examples used in this book, you have explicitly specified `object` as the superclass. This is because this book intends examples to be run on either Python 2 or Python 3. In Python 2, specifying this matters, because subclassing `object` is what makes the class be a "new-style class," which is a construct introduced a long time ago (Python 2.2) that altered Python's method-resolution order, as well as some of the other guts of how Python classes work. The direct subclassing of `object` was used as a way to ensure backward-compatibility, forcing developers to "opt-in" to new-style classes, rather than to opt out of them.

In Python 3, which was a backward-incompatible release, all classes are new-style, and directly subclassing `object` is no longer necessary, and thus is not done here. That said, the previous code is exactly equivalent to the following:

```
class C(object, metaclass=Meta):
    pass
```

This style allows you to observe more explicitly the distinction between superclasses, which are declared here using a syntax akin to positional arguments in a function declaration, as opposed to the metaclass that is declared with the keyword argument syntax. They must be specified in this order, with `metaclass` last, just like function arguments.

When directly subclassing `object` in Python 3, either style (explicitly including it or omitting it) is acceptable.

Python 2

Python 2 has an entirely different syntax for metaclass declaration. The Python 2 syntax is *not* supported under Python 3, and the Python 3 syntax is *not* supported under Python 2. (Skip down a section to see how to declare a metaclass in a way that does the right thing on both.)

The Python 2 syntax for declaring a metaclass is to assign a `__metaclass__` attribute to the class. Consider the earlier creation of class `C` using a call to `Meta`. Following is the equivalent code in Python 2:

```
class C(object):
    __metaclass__ = Meta
```

In this case, the metaclass is being assigned in the class body. This is fine. The Python interpreter looks for this when the class keyword is invoked, and uses `Meta` rather than `type` to create the new class.

What About Code That Might Run on Either Version?

Because Python 3 introduced backward-incompatible changes to the Python language, Python developers have come up with strategies for running the same set of code under either the Python 3 interpreter or the Python 2 interpreter with similar results.

One of the most popular ways to do this involves using a tool called `six`, which was written by Benjamin Peterson and is available from PyPI.

`six` provides two ways to declare a metaclass: by creating a stand-in class and using it as a direct superclass, or by using a decorator to add the metaclass.

The first method (which is the stand-in class method) looks like this:

```
import six

class C(six.with_metaclass(Meta)):
    pass
```

What is happening here? `six.with_metaclass` creates a dummy class of sorts that subclasses `object`, and has `Meta` as its metaclass, but which does nothing else. By applying this class as the superclass to `C`, and based on how metaclasses interact with class inheritance (discussed previously), `C` is now an instance of `Meta`, regardless of which Python version is in use.

Depending on exactly what the metaclass in question does, sometimes this solution will not actually work. Because `six.with_metaclass` actually instantiates a class, some metaclasses may want to do work, and it is possible that said work would not be compatible with having an abstract superclass.

`six` provides one other way to assign a metaclass to a class, which is using a decorator: `@six.add_metaclass`. The syntax for that looks like this:

```
import six

@six.add_metaclass(Meta)
class C(object):
    pass
```

The result here becomes the same to the Python 2- or Python 3-specific implementations. Class `c` is created, using the `class` keyword, and the `Meta` metaclass, rather than using `type`. The decorator does this without instantiating an abstract class.

When Is Cross-Compatibility Important?

Because there are two incompatible syntaxes for Python 2 as opposed to Python 3, it's important to explore at this point when it is better to use the "pure" language approach, and when it is the right time to introduce `six`.

Without delving too deeply into the theory, a good rule of thumb here is that if you are running Python 2, assume that you may at some point want to migrate to Python 3, and try to write cross-compatible code. This will entail using `six` for any number of things (this among them), and so probably introducing `six` into your codebase is wise. By contrast, if you are already exclusively in a Python 3 environment, it is unlikely that you will ever want to shift backward, and just writing Python 3 code should be fine.

WHEN TO USE METACLASSES

One of the trickiest things when you're learning about metaclasses is understanding when it is really appropriate to actually use them. Realistically, most code fits pretty well into the traditional class and object structure, and does not really require the use of metaclasses.

Similarly, using metaclasses needlessly adds a layer of complexity and challenge to that code. Code is read more often than it is written, and, therefore, it is usually desirable to solve problems in the simplest possible way that meets the objectives.

That said, when in situations where metaclasses are appropriate, they are often a very clear solution that can make code much simpler to understand. Realizing when metaclasses can make code simpler rather than more complex is a valuable skill.

Declarative Class Declaration

The most common reason to use a custom metaclass is to create a delineation between class *declaration* and class *structure*, particularly when you're creating APIs for other developers to use.

An Existing Example

First, consider an example from the wild. Many Python developers are familiar with Django models, which is a popular web framework. Django models usually correspond to discrete database tables in a relational database.

A Django model declaration is quite straightforward. The following sample model might represent a book:

```
from django.db import models

class Book(models.Model):
    author = models.CharField(max_length=100)
```

```
title = models.CharField(max_length=250)
isbn = models.CharField(max_length=20)
publication_date = models.DateField()
pages = models.PositiveIntegerField()
```

Given what you know about normal classes in Python, what do you expect to happen here? Clearly, `models.CharField`, `models.DateField`, and the like are instantiations of objects. So, you expect that when you create a `Book` instance, you should get back those instances if you access those attributes.

Those familiar with Django know well that this is not what happens. If you try to get the `author` attribute of a `Book` instance, it will be a string. The same goes for `title` and `isbn`. The `publication_date` attribute will be a `datetime.date` object, and pages will be an `int`. If any of these are not yet provided to the model, they will be `None`.

How does this happen? What magic is going on under the hood to differentiate between how this class was *declared* (the code provided to generate it) and how it is *structured* when inspected? When the class is declared, its attributes are complex field objects. However, when you look at an instance of the class, those same attributes are set to values for a particular book.

The answer is, of course, that Django models use a special metaclass that ships with Django, which happens to be called `ModelBase`. This is largely invisible when you're using Django, because `django.db.models.Model` uses the `ModelBase` metaclass. Therefore, subclasses get it for free.

`ModelBase` does quite a lot of things. (Django is a mature framework, and its ORM has undergone a lot of iteration.) But a major thing it does is translate between how the model classes in Django are declared versus how their objects are structured. It is advantageous to Django to have a model declaration syntax that is extremely simple and straightforward. A model represents a table; the attributes on the model correspond to columns on the table.

Instances in the Django ecosystem represent rows within a table. When you are accessing a field on the instance, what you really want is the value for that row. So, a specific `Book` instance might be *The Hobbit*, and you would want `book.title` to be `'The Hobbit'` in this case.

Essentially, using a metaclass here is desirable because it allows both the declaration of your `Book` class and accessing data on your `Book` instances to be very clean, and to use a very intuitive API, even though those attributes do not match.

How This Works

Going into every detail of the implementation of `ModelBase` is beyond the scope of this book, but the implementation of this particular concept is actually extremely straightforward.

First, when the model class is being created, recall that the attributes of that class are passed to the metaclass's `__new__` method in a dictionary, usually called `attrs`. In this example model, this dictionary would include `author`, `title`, and so on, as keys in that dictionary. The values for those keys would be the `Field` objects (all of these classes are subclasses of `django.db.models.Field`).

The `ModelBase` metaclass has a `__new__` method that (among other things) iterates over the `attrs` dictionary looking for `Field` subclasses. Any fields that it finds are popped off of the `attrs` dictionary and placed in another location—a separate dictionary called `fields` (which actually lives in an object called _meta that is written to the class). This implementation detail is not particularly important except to know that the actual field classes live somewhere else, hidden away where internal Django code can get at them when needed. But the average person who just wants to write a Django model does not need to see it.

Then, when an instance is created, the attributes corresponding to the field are instantiated and set to None unless a default or a specific value for that row is provided, in which case that value takes precedence. Now, suddenly, when the attribute is accessed on that instance, the value for that row is returned instead of the Field subclass. Similarly, the value can be written in a straightforward manner, without plowing over the Field.

Essentially, what the metaclass does is take the class declaration, reorganize the structure of the attributes of the class, and then create the class with the new structure.

Why This Is a Good Use for Metaclasses

This paradigm is exceptionally useful when you're designing APIs. A primary goal of a good API is to be as simple as possible, and contain as little boilerplate code as possible. This means both that *declaring a class* should be simple and straightforward, and that *using the class* should be similarly simple and straightforward.

In the case of a Django model, those two goals are somewhat in conflict. The ModelBase metaclass resolves that conflict.

Using metaclasses is an excellent way to bridge this gap. They do this by essentially making the class declaration into a front, and then transforming the declaration of the class into the actual class structure in the __new__ method.

Class Verification

Another key use for metaclasses is for class verification. If a class must conform to a particular interface, a metaclass can be a very effective way to enforce this. Usually, it is preferable that this sort of problem be handled by a sensible default. Occasionally, however, this is not possible.

For example, consider a class that requires either one or another attribute to be set, but not both. This is difficult to handle with a sensible default if it is important that one attribute be *unset* (as opposed to set to None).

This concept can be handled using a metaclass. The following simple metaclass requires classes to contain either a foo attribute or a bar attribute:

```python
class FooOrBar(type):
    def __new__(cls, name, bases, attrs):
        if 'foo' in attrs and 'bar' in attrs:
            raise TypeError('Class %s cannot contain both `foo` and '
                            '`bar` attributes.' % name)
        if 'foo' not in attrs and 'bar' not in attrs:
            raise TypeError('Class %s must provide either a `foo` '
                            'attribute or a `bar` attribute.' % name)
        return super(FooOrBar, cls).__new__(cls, name, bases, attrs)
```

The following Python 3 class uses this metaclass and conforms to this interface:

```
>>> class Valid(metaclass=FooOrBar):
...        foo = 42
...
>>>
```

Everything here works fine. What happens if you try to set both attributes, or neither?

```
>>> class Invalid(metaclass=FooOrBar):
...        pass
...
Traceback (most recent call last):
  File "<stdin>", line 1, in <module>
  File "<stdin>", line 9, in __new__
TypeError: Class Invalid must provide either a `foo` attribute or a `bar`
    attribute.
>>>
>>> class Invalid(metaclass=FooOrBar):
...        foo = 42
...        bar = 42
...
Traceback (most recent call last):
  File "<stdin>", line 1, in <module>
  File "<stdin>", line 6, in __new__
TypeError: Class Invalid cannot contain both `foo` and `bar` attributes.
```

This particular implementation has a problem. It will not work well continuing down the subclass chain. The reason for this is because the metaclass examines the attrs dictionary directly, but this only contains attributes set for the class being declared. It does not know anything about attributes that are inherited from superclasses.

```
>>> class Valid(metaclass=FooOrBar):
...        foo = 42
...
>>> class AlsoValid(Valid):
...        pass
...
Traceback (most recent call last):
  File "<stdin>", line 1, in <module>
  File "<stdin>", line 8, in __new__
TypeError: Class AlsoValid must provide either a `foo` attribute or a `bar`
    attribute.
```

This is a problem. After all, your AlsoValid class is also valid. It contains a foo attribute. An alternate approach to the FooOrBar metaclass is necessary.

```
class FooOrBar(type):
    def __new__(cls, name, bases, attrs):
        answer = super(FooOrBar, cls).__new__(cls, name, bases, attrs)
        if hasattr(answer, 'foo') and hasattr(answer, 'bar'):
            raise TypeError('Class %s cannot contain both `foo` and '
                            '`bar` attributes.' % name)
        if not hasattr(answer, 'foo') and not hasattr(answer, 'bar'):
            raise TypeError('Class %s must provide either a `foo` '
                            'attribute or a `bar` attribute.' % name)
        return answer
```

What is the difference here? This time, you are checking for the attributes *on the instantiated class* before it is returned, rather than looking at the attrs dictionary.

The new class will get all the attributes from the superclass as part of the call to type's constructor on the first line of the __new__ method. Therefore, the hasattr calls work, regardless of whether the attribute is declared on this class or inherited from a superclass.

Could this be handled without a metaclass? Absolutely. Nothing prevents writing a simple method that receives the class as an argument and does this same check. In fact, this is an excellent use for a decorator. However, the class must be manually sent to the verification method. With a metaclass, this is just handled when the class is created. Sometimes, an explicit opt-in is preferable; other times, it is not. It simply depends on the use case.

Non-Inheriting Attributes

Metaclasses can also be used as a tool to cause certain attributes of a class to *not* automatically inherit. The most common scenario in which you might want to do this is in conjunction with other metaclass behavior. For example, suppose that a metaclass provides functionality for its classes, but some classes will be created as abstract classes, and you do not want said functionality to run in this case.

An obvious way to go about this would be to allow the class to set an abstract attribute, and only perform the special functionality of the metaclass if its abstract is either not set or set to False.

```
class Meta(type):
    def __new__(cls, name, bases, attrs):
        # Sanity check: If this is an abstract class, then we do not
        # want the metaclass functionality here.
        if attrs.get('abstract', False):
            return super(Meta, cls).__new__(cls, name, bases, attrs)

        # Perform actual metaclass functionality.
        [...]
```

There is one problem with this approach, however. The abstract attribute, like any other attribute, will be inherited by subclasses. That means that any subclass would have to explicitly declare itself not to be abstract, which seems strange.

```
class AbstractClass(metaclass=Meta):
    abstract = True

class RegularClass(AbstractClass):
    abstract = False
```

Intuitively, you want abstract to have to be declared on all abstract classes, but for that attribute not to be inherited. It turns out that this is very easy, because instead of just reading the attrs dictionary like your metaclass is doing, it can modify it, disposing of the abstract attribute once it is no longer necessary.

In this case, you can do this by just popping the `abstract` value off of the `attrs` dictionary, as shown here:

```
class Meta(type):
    def __new__(cls, name, bases, attrs):
        # Sanity check: If this is an abstract class, then we do not
        # want the metaclass functionality here.
        if attrs.pop('abstract', False):
            return super(Meta, cls).__new__(cls, name, bases, attrs)

        # Perform actual metaclass functionality.
        [...]
```

The difference here is subtle, but important. The `abstract` attribute is being *removed entirely* from the actual class being created. In this example, `AbstractClass` would not get the metaclass functionality, but the actual `abstract` attribute would be gone. Most importantly, this means that subclasses do not inherit the attribute, which is exactly the behavior you want.

THE QUESTION OF EXPLICIT OPT-IN

Both of the examples provided earlier as potential use cases for metaclasses can be solved without using metaclasses. In fact, essentially any major use case for metaclasses does not explicitly require their use.

A class decorator can easily handle requiring a class to conform to a particular interface, for example. It is a trivial matter to decorate each class, and the decorator is easily capable of ensuring that either `foo` or `bar` is set, but not both.

This raises an important question. What is the value of doing this with a metaclass? What value does a metaclass provide that a class decorator does not?

The answer to this sort of question is largely dependent on how the final classes are being used. The key difference between an approach that uses a metaclass as opposed to an approach that uses a class decorator is that the class decorator must be applied explicitly to each subclass. If the programmer implementing the subclasses forgets to apply it, the check does not happen.

By contrast, metaclasses are automatic and invisible to the programmer declaring the classes that use them. Few (if any) APIs ask a programmer to directly use a metaclass, but many of them ask a programmer to subclass a base class that the API package provides. By assigning a metaclass to that base class, all subclasses receive it, too. This causes that functionality of the metaclass to be applied without the end programmer having to think about it.

Put more simply, one of the first lines in the Zen of Python states, "Explicit is better than implicit." But, like most things in that document, this adage is true … until it is not. For example, being implicit is better if you are talking about extraneous information or boilerplate. Similarly, sometimes being more explicit just means more maintenance, which is not usually a win.

META-CODING

Metaclasses really start to stand out as the operation on the metaclass becomes greater. It would not be reasonable or as maintainable to mark every Django model with an explicit decorator.

Similarly, consider meta-coding situations. In this context, the term *meta-coding* refers to code that inspects other code in the application. For example, consider code that should log itself.

A metaclass that causes all method calls from instances of a class to be logged somehow is quite easy to implement. The following metaclass causes its classes to "log" their function calls (except substituting actual logging for just printing to `sys.stdout`):

```python
class Logged(type):
    """A metaclass that causes classes that it creates to log
    their function calls.
    """
    def __new__(cls, name, bases, attrs):
        for key, value in attrs.items():
            if callable(value):
                attrs[key] = cls.log_call(value)
        return super(Logged, cls).__new__(cls, name, bases, attrs)

    @staticmethod
    def log_call(fxn):
        """Given a function, wrap it with some logging code and
        return the wrapped function.
        """
        def inner(*args, **kwargs):
            print('The function %s was called with arguments %r and '
                'keyword arguments %r.' % (fxn.__name__, args, kwargs))
            try:
                response = fxn(*args, **kwargs)
                print('The function call to %s was successful.' %
                    fxn.__name__)
                return response
            except Exception as exc:
                print('The function call to %s raised an exception: %r' %
                    (fxn.__name__, exc))
                raise
        return inner
```

Let's first review what is happening here. `Logged` is being declared as a subclass of `type`, which means it is a metaclass. The `Logged` class has a `__new__` method, and what that method does is iterate over all the attributes in the `attrs` dictionary, check to see if they are callables (using the Python built-in function `callable`), and wrap them if they are.

The wrapping function itself is very straightforward, especially if you are already familiar with the concept of decorators. It declares a local function that performs some logic (in this case, calling `print`), and then calls the function that was passed as an argument to the `log_call` method. To learn more about this pattern, see Chapter 1, "Decorators," which makes extensive use of this paradigm.

What happens when a class uses this metaclass? Consider the following Python 3 class that has `Logged` as its metaclass:

```
class MyClass(metaclass=Logged):
    def foo(self):
        pass

    def bar(self):
        raise TypeError('oh noes!')
```

When you create an instance of `MyClass`, you discover that calling methods on it becomes ... er, loud.

```
>>> obj = MyClass()
>>> obj.foo()
The function foo was called with arguments (<__main__.MyClass object at
    0x1022a37f0>,) and keyword arguments {}.
The function call to foo was successful.
```

If you try to call `obj.bar()`, you get an exception.

```
>>> obj.bar()
The function bar was called with arguments (<__main__.MyClass object at
    0x1022a37f0>,) and keyword arguments {}.
The function call to bar raised an exception: TypeError('oh noes!',)
Traceback (most recent call last):
  File "<stdin>", line 1, in <module>
  File "<stdin>", line 19, in inner
  File "<stdin>", line 5, in bar
TypeError: oh noes!
```

Astute readers probably noticed something. When `MyClass` was instantiated, why was there no logging of the call to __init__? After all, __init__ is certainly callable. It seems like it should have been noisy along with `foo` and `bar`.

Recall, however, that your metaclass loops over attributes in the `attrs` dictionary, and you did not explicitly define __init__ in your `MyClass` class. Rather, it is inherited from `object`. This is the behavior you really want as well. Otherwise, subclassing would cause the `log_call` "decorator" to be applied repeatedly on the same callables, which would result in repeated `print` statements.

By explicitly defining __init__, however, you can observe the noisy behavior there.

```
>>> class MyClass(metaclass=Logged):
...     def __init__(self):
...         pass
...
>>>
>>> obj = MyClass()
The function __init__ was called with arguments (<__main__.MyClass object
    at 0x1022a3550>,) and keyword arguments {}.
The function call to __init__ was successful.
```

Also, note that, even though __init__ was not explicitly called in the Python shell, it is still the function that is logged, because the Python interpreter calls __init__ under the hood when a new instance is created.

It is worth noting, however, that this behavior only occurs at class creation time. If a method is added to the class after it is created (which usually should not be happening anyway), it will not be wrapped.

```
>>> MyClass.foo = lambda self: 42
>>> obj.foo()
42
```

In this case, your call to foo was not noisy, because MyClass had already been created, and so the metaclass had already done its job. Therefore, you just get a plain function call rather than a wrapped one.

SUMMARY

Metaclasses are extremely powerful tools in Python. The fact that classes are first-class objects allows for those classes to be manipulated outside of when they are declared. Metaclasses are a way to accomplish this.

The presence of metaclasses in the Python language overcomes many of the limitations of other object-oriented languages, in which classes are statically declared at coding time.

The ultimate result is that Python's object model ends up being the best of all worlds. It combines the simplicity of languages with a traditional class structure and the power of languages that follow other models, such as prototypal inheritance in JavaScript and LUA.

It is a common misconception that metaclasses are difficult to understand. However, some of the power in Python's object model is in its simplicity and consistency. Metaclasses are, in fact, a very straightforward implementation that adds a huge amount of power to the language.

Chapter 6, "Class Factories," covers another way to make classes, which is by constructing them on-the-fly.

Class Factories

As described in Chapter 5, "Metaclasses," Python classes are also objects. The fact that classes are first-class objects in Python also allows for the possibility to employ other powerful patterns. A *class factory* is one of these patterns. Essentially, this is a function that creates a class, and does so at runtime. This concept allows for the creation of a class whose attributes are determined, for example, as a result of user input.

This chapter covers class factories, first by reviewing generating classes on the fly, and showing how to do so within functions. Then, it covers a couple of common cases where class factories are valuable.

A REVIEW OF TYPE

Recall from the discussion in Chapter 5 that, like other objects in Python, classes are instantiated by a class. For example, say that you create a class, `Animal`, as shown here:

```
class Animal(object):
    """A class representing an arbitrary animal."""

    def __init__(self, name):
        self.name = name

    def eat(self):
        pass

    def go_to_vet(self):
        pass
```

The `Animal` class is responsible for creating `Animal` objects when its constructor is called. But, in the same way that `Animal` creates its objects, so, too, is `Animal` an object itself. *Its* class is `type`, a built-in class in Python that creates all other classes.

`type` is primary metaclass, and custom metaclasses (as you learned in Chapter 5) subclass `type`.

It is also possible to invoke `type` directly to create a class, in lieu of using the class keyword. `type` takes three positional arguments: `name`, `bases`, and `attrs`, which correspond to the name of the class, the superclass or superclasses for the class (specified as a tuple), and, finally, any attributes for the class, as a dictionary.

UNDERSTANDING A CLASS FACTORY FUNCTION

A *class factory function* is exactly what the name implies—a function that creates and returns a class.

Consider the previous `Animal` class. You can use code to create an equivalent class using `type` rather than using the `class` keyword, as shown here:

```
def init(self, name):
    self.name = name

def eat(self):
    pass

def go_to_vet(self):
    pass


Animal = type('Animal', (object,), {
    '__doc__': 'A class representing an arbitrary animal.',
    '__init__': init,
    'eat': eat,
    'go_to_vet': go_to_vet,
})
```

This is not ideal, for several reasons. One of these reasons is that it leaves functions in the namespace alongside `Animal`. It is usually not desirable to use `type` directly instead of the `class` keyword unless you really need to do so.

However, sometimes you do, in fact, need to do so. In this kind of case, you can minimize the clutter by wrapping this code in a function, which can then be passed around and used. This is a class factory. Consider the following function for the example `Animal` class:

```
def create_animal_class():
    """Return an Animal class, built by invoking the type
    constructor.
    """
    def init(self, name):
        self.name = name

    def eat(self):
        pass

    def go_to_vet(self):
        pass

    return type('Animal', (object,), {
        '__doc__': 'A class representing an arbitrary animal.',
```

```
        '__init__': init,
        'eat': eat,
        'go_to_vet': go_to_vet,
    })
```

What has changed here? The `init`, `eat`, and `go_to_vet` functions that were previously cluttering the namespace (as well as the creation of the `Animal` class itself) have been moved inside a `create_animal_class` function.

Now, you can get a custom-built `Animal` class by calling said function, as shown here:

```
Animal = create_animal_class()
```

It is important to note here that multiple calls to `create_animal_class` *will return distinct classes*. That is, while the classes returned would all have the same name and the same attributes, they will not actually be the same class. The similarity between those classes is based on the fact that each run of the function assigns the same dictionary keys and similar functions.

In other words, the similarity between the classes that would be returned is *contingent*. There is no reason why the function could not take one or more parameters and return wildly different classes based on those parameters. In fact, this is the entire purpose of class factory functions.

Consider the following distinct classes returned from distinct calls to `create_animal_class`:

```
>>> Animal1 = create_animal_class()
>>> Animal2 = create_animal_class()
>>> Animal1
<class '__main__.Animal'>
>>> Animal2
<class '__main__.Animal'>
>>> Animal1 == Animal2
False
```

Similarly, consider the following instances:

```
>>> animal1 = Animal1('louisoix')
>>> animal2 = Animal2('louisoix')
>>> isinstance(animal1, Animal1)
True
>>> isinstance(animal1, Animal2)
False
```

While these classes are both called `Animal` internally, they are *not* the same class. They are distinct results from two distinct function runs.

This example creates the `Animal` class by invoking `type`, but this is actually not necessary. It is far more straightforward to create the class using the `class` keyword. This works, even within the function, and then you can return the class at the end of the function:

```
def create_animal_class():
    """Return an Animal class, built using the class keyword
    and returned afterwards.
    """
    class Animal(object):
        """A class representing an arbitrary animal."""
        def __init__(self, name):
```

```
        self.name = name

    def eat(self):
        pass

    def go_to_vet(self):
        pass

return Animal
```

It is almost always preferable to create a class using the `class` keyword rather than by invoking `type` directly. However, it is not always feasible to do so.

DETERMINING WHEN YOU SHOULD WRITE CLASS FACTORIES

The primary reason to write a class factory function is when it is necessary to create a class based on execution-time knowledge, such as user input. The `class` keyword assumes that you know the attributes you wish to assign to the class (albeit not necessarily the instances) *at coding time.*

If you do not know the attributes to be assigned to the class at coding time, a class factory function can be a convenient alternative.

Runtime Attributes

Consider the following function that creates a class, but this time, the attributes of that class can vary based on parameters sent to the function:

```
def get_credential_class(use_proxy=False, tfa=False):
    """Return a class representing a credential for the given service,
    with an attribute repsenting the expected keys.
    """
    # If a proxy, such as Facebook Connect, is being used, we just
    # need the service name and the e-mail address.
    if use_proxy:
        keys = ['service_name', 'email_address']
    else:
        # For the purposes of this example, all other services use
        # username and password.
        keys = ['username', 'password']

        # If two-factor auth is in play, then we need an authenticator
        # token also.
        if tfa:
            keys.append('tfa_token')

    # Return a class with a proper __init__ method which expects
    # all expected keys.
    class Credential(object):
        expected_keys = set(keys)

        def __init__(self, **kwargs):
            # Sanity check: Do our keys match?
```

```
        if self.expected_keys != set(kwargs.keys()):
            raise ValueError('Keys do not match.')

        # Write the keys to the credential object.
        for k, v in kwargs.items():
            setattr(self, k, v)

    return Credential
```

This `get_credential_class` function is asking for information about the type of login that is occurring—either a traditional login (with username and password), or using an OpenID service. If it is a traditional login, it also may use two-factor authentication, which adds the need for an authentication token.

The function returns *a class* (not an instance) that represents the appropriate type of credential. For example, if the `use_proxy` variable is set to `True`, then the class will be returned with the `expected_keys` attribute set to `['service_name', 'email_address']`, representing the keys necessary to authenticate through the proxy. Alternate inputs to the function will return a class with a different `expected_keys` attribute.

Then, the `__init__` method on the class itself checks the keyword arguments that it gets against the keys identified in the `expected_keys` attribute. If they do not match, the constructor raises an error. If they do, it writes the values to the instance.

You were able to create this class within the function using the `class` keyword, rather than invoking `type`. Because the `class` block was *within* the `def` block, the class was created locally to the function.

Understanding Why You Should Do This

You may be asking why a class factory is even valuable in this case. After all, there are only three possibilities. These classes could just be hard-coded, rather than dynamically created on the fly. That said, it is easy to extrapolate a case from this example where a hard-coded class is no longer tenable.

After all, there are lots of websites with a non-trivial number of authentication paradigms. For example, some use custom usernames, while others use an e-mail address. For development services, you are likely to have an API key and potentially one or more secret tokens.

There is really no way to programmatically determine what credentials a website requires (at least not reliably), but consider a service that did try to represent credentials from lots of different, supported third-party sites. That service would likely store the required keys and types of values in a database.

Now, suddenly, you have a class *with attributes generated based on a database lookup*. This is important because database lookups happen at runtime, not at coding time. Now, suddenly, you have a functionally infinite number of possibilities for how the `expected_keys` attribute of the classes might need to be written, and it is no longer feasible to code them all up front.

Storing that kind of data in the database also means that, as the data changes, the code need not do so. A website may alter or augment what kind of credentials it supports, and this would require adding or removing rows from the database, but the `Credential` class would still be up to the task.

Attribute Dictionaries

Just because some attributes are only known at execution time does not always mean that a class factory is the correct approach. Often, attributes can be written to the class on the fly, or a class can simply store a dictionary with an arbitrary set of attributes.

If this is a sufficient solution, it is likely an easier and more straightforward one.

```
class MyClass(object):
    attrs = {}
```

The most common case where attribute dictionaries are most likely to fall short is in a situation where you are subclassing an existing class over which you do not have direct control, and you require the class's existing functionality to work against the modified attributes. You will see a subclassing example shortly.

Fleshing Out the Credential Class

Consider a credentials database with a single table, and that table has two columns: a service name (such as `Apple` or `Amazon`), and a credential key (such as `username`).

This mock database is obviously still far too simple to cover all use cases. In this example, support for alternative modes of login (such as OpenID) has been dropped. Also, the example does not have any concept for presenting credentials in a specific order (username before password, for example). All of this is fine; it is sufficient for a proof of concept.

Now, consider a class factory that reads from this database (which will simply be stored as a CSV flat file) and returns an appropriate class.

```
import csv


def get_credential_class(service):
    """Return a class representing a credential for the given service,
    with an attribute representing the expected keys.
    """
    # Open our "database".
    keys = []
    with open('creds.csv', 'r') as csvfile:
        for row in csv.reader(csvfile):
            # If this row does not correspond to the service we
            # are actually asking for (e.g., if it is a row for
            # Apple and we are asking for an Amazon credential class),
            # skip it.
            if row[0].lower() != service.lower():
                continue

            # Add the key to the list of expected keys.
            keys.append(row[1])

    # Return a class with a proper __init__ method which expects
    # all expected keys.
    class Credential(object):
        expected_keys = keys
```

```
        def __init__(self, **kwargs):
            # Sanity check: Do our keys match?
            if set(self.expected_keys) != set([i for i in kwargs.keys()]):
                raise ValueError('Keys do not match.')

            # Write the keys to the credential object.
            for k, v in kwargs.items():
                setattr(self, k, v)

    return Credential
```

The inputs for the `get_credential_class` function have now been entirely replaced. Instead of describing the type of credential, you simply specify whom the credential is for.

For example, a sample CSV "database" might look like this:

```
Amazon,username
Amazon,password
Apple,email_address
Apple,password
GitHub,username
GitHub,password
GitHub,auth_token
```

The value that `get_credential_class` takes is a string, and it corresponds to the first column in the CSV file. Therefore, calling `get_credential_class('GitHub')` will return a class with expected keys of `username`, `password`, and `auth_token`. The lines in the CSV file corresponding to `Apple` and `Amazon` will be skipped.

The Form Example

One place where you can see this concept at work is in the forms API of a popular web framework, Django. This framework includes an abstract class, `django.forms.Form`, which is used to create HTML forms.

Django forms have a custom metaclass that takes the attributes declared on the form and erects a distinction between form fields and form data. Creating a credential form in this API is very easy if you know what your fields are.

```
from django import forms


class CredentialForm(forms.Form):
    username = forms.CharField()
    password = forms.CharField(widget=forms.PasswordInput)
```

On the other hand, if you *do not* know what your fields are (as in the case of the previous example), this is a more complicated task. A class factory becomes the perfect approach.

```
import csv

from django import forms
```

```python
def get_credential_form_class(service):
    """Return a class representing a credential for the given service,
    with attributes representing the expected keys.
    """
    # Open our "database".
    keys = []
    with open('creds.csv', 'r') as csvfile:
        for row in csv.reader(csvfile):
            # If this row does not correspond to the service we
            # are actually asking for (e.g. if it is a row for
            # Apple and we are asking for an Amazon credential class),
            # skip it.
            if row[0].lower() != service.lower():
                continue

            # Add the key to the list of expected keys.
            keys.append(row[1])

    # Put together the appropriate credential fields.
    attrs = {}
    for key in keys:
        field_kw = {}
        if 'password' in key:
            field_kw['widget'] = forms.PasswordInput
        attrs[key] = forms.CharField(**field_kw)

    # Return a form class with the appropriate credential fields.
    metaclass = type(forms.Form)
    return metaclass('CredentialForm', (forms.Form,), attrs)
```

In this case, you have substituted your custom `Credential` class for a Django form subclass. It is no longer the case that you are just setting an `expected_keys` attribute. Rather, you are setting one attribute for each expected key. The previous code puts these together in a dictionary (doing a blatant hand-wave for passwords and `PasswordInput`), and then creates a new form subclass and returns it.

It is worth calling out explicitly that Django's `Form` class uses a custom metaclass, which subclasses `type`. Therefore, it is important that you call *its* constructor, rather than `type` directly. You do this on the last two lines by asking `forms.Form` for its metaclass, and then using that constructor directly.

It is also worth noting that this is a case where it really is necessary to use the metaclass constructor, rather than creating the class using the `class` keyword. You are not able to create the class using the `class` keyword here because, even within a function, you would have to create the class and then write the attributes to the class, and the metaclass behavior will not be applied to the attributes assigned to the class after it is built. (Chapter 5 covers this in more detail.)

Dodging Class Attribute Consistency

Another reason to write class factory functions deals with how attributes differ between classes and instances.

Class Attributes Versus Instance Attributes

The following two code blocks do *not* produce equivalent classes or instances:

```
##########################
###   CLASS ATTRIBUTE   ###
##########################

class C(object):
    foo = 'bar'


##########################
### INSTANCE ATTRIBUTE ###
##########################

class I(object):
    def __init__(self):
        self.foo = 'bar'
```

The first and most obvious thing that is different about these classes is where the foo attribute can be accessed. It is not particularly surprising that C.foo is a string, and I.foo raises AttributeError.

```
>>> C.foo
'bar'
>>> I.foo
Traceback (most recent call last):
  File "<stdin>", line 1, in <module>
AttributeError: type object 'I' has no attribute 'foo'
```

After all, foo was instantiated as an attribute on C, but not on I. Since I is being accessed directly, rather than by way of an instance, the __init__ function has not even run yet. Even if an instance of I had been created, the *instance* would have the foo attribute while the *class* would not.

```
>>> i = I()
>>> i.foo
'bar'
>>> I.foo
Traceback (most recent call last):
  File "<stdin>", line 1, in <module>
AttributeError: type object 'I' has no attribute 'foo'
```

There is, however, a lesser-noticed difference between C and I, which involves what happens if the foo attribute is modified against one of their instances.

Consider the following two instantiated C instances:

```
>>> c1 = C()
>>> c2 = C()
```

Now, say you modify the foo attribute on one of them, as shown here:

```
>>> c1.foo = 'baz'
```

You see that the c2 instance still uses the attribute of the class, while c1 has its own.

```
>>> c1.foo
'baz'
>>> c2.foo
'bar'
```

The lookup happening here is not quite the same. c1 has written an *instance attribute*, called foo, with the value of 'baz'. However, c2 has no such instance attribute. However, because the class, c, *does*, the lookup uses the class attribute.

Consider what happens if you modify the class attribute, as shown here:

```
>>> C.foo = 'bacon'
>>> c1.foo
'baz'
>>> c2.foo
'bacon'
```

Here, c1.foo was unaffected, because c1 has an instance attribute called foo. However, the value of c2.foo has changed, because it has no such attribute on the instance. Therefore, when the attribute of the class changes, you observe the change on the instance.

You can view this within Python's internal data model by examining the __dict__ attribute of both instances.

```
>>> c1.__dict__
{'foo': 'baz'}
>>> c2.__dict__
{}
```

Under normal circumstances, the special __dict__ attribute is what stores all the attributes (and their values) for an object. There are exceptions to this rule. A class may define a custom __getattr__ or __getattribute__ method (as discussed in Chapter 4, "Magic Methods"), or may define a special attribute __slots__, which also introduces alternative attribute behavior. (This is rarely needed except in particular situations where memory use is paramount, and is not discussed in this book.) Notice that c1 has a foo key in its __dict__, and c2 does not.

The Class Method Limitation

This situation gets really interesting when classes define class methods. Remember that class methods are methods that do not expect or require an instance of the class to execute, but do require the class itself. They are usually declared by decorating a method with the @classmethod decorator, and their first argument is traditionally called cls rather than self.

Consider the following c class with a class method that accesses and returns foo from the class:

```
class C(object):
    foo = 'bar'

    @classmethod
    def classfoo(cls):
        return cls.foo
```

In the context of the classfoo method, the foo attribute is being accessed *explicitly on the class*, rather than on the instance. Re-run the example using the new class definition, and then consider the following:

```
>>> c1.foo
'baz'
>>> c1.classfoo()
'bacon'
>>> c2.classfoo()
'bacon'
```

There is, in fact, no actual way to access the instance attribute from the class method. That is the entire point of class methods, after all. They do not require an instance.

Tying This in with Class Factories

One of the biggest reasons to need class factories is when you are subclassing existing classes that rely on class attributes that must be adjusted.

Essentially, in code that you do not control, if an existing class sets a class attribute that must be customized, class factories are an attractive approach to generating appropriate subclasses with the overridden attributes.

Consider a situation where a class has an attribute that must be overridden at runtime (or where there are too many options for subclassing in static code to be reasonable). In this case, a class factory can be a very useful approach. Following is a continuation of the use of C as an instructive example:

```
def create_C_subclass(new_foo):
    class SubC(C):
        foo = new_foo
    return SubC
```

What matters here is that it is not necessary to know what the value of foo should be until the class is created, which is *when the function runs*. Like most other use of class factories, then, this is about knowing the attribute value at runtime.

Running your classfoo class method on C subclasses created this way gives you what you expect.

```
>>> S = create_C_subclass('spam')
>>> S.classfoo()
'spam'
>>> E = create_C_subclass('eggs')
>>> E.classfoo()
'eggs'
```

It is worth noting that, in many cases, it is much easier to simply create a subclass that accepts this value as part of its __init__ method. However, there are some cases where this is an insufficient solution. If the parent class relies on class methods, for example, then writing a new value to an instance will not cause the class methods to receive the new value, and this model of subclass creation becomes a valuable solution.

Answering the Singleton Question

One thing that can make class factory functions somewhat awkward to use is that, as their name suggests, their responsibility is to return *classes*, rather than instances of those classes.

This means that if you want an instance, you must call *the result of* the class factory function to get one. The correct code to instantiate a subclass generated with `create_C_subclass`, for example, would be `create_C_subclass('eggs')()`.

There is nothing inherently wrong with this, but it is not always what you really want. Sometimes classes created through class factories are functionally *singletons*. A singleton is a class pattern where only one instance is permitted.

In the case of classes generated in functions, it is possible that the purpose of the function is simply to act like a class constructor. This is problematic if the end developer must constantly think about instantiating the class that comes back.

This is not a requirement, though. If there is not a need to deal with reusing the class elsewhere, or if the class factory is able to handle the reuse itself, it is completely reasonable and useful to simply have the class factory return *an instance of the class it creates,* rather than the class itself.

To continue the simple example of `C`, consider this factory:

```
def CPrime(new_foo='bar'):
    # If `foo` is set to 'bar', then we do not need a
    # custom subclass at all.
    if new_foo = 'bar':
        return C()

    # Create a custom subclass and return an instance.
    class SubC(C):
        foo = new_foo
    return SubC()
```

Now, calling `CPrime` will return *an instance of* the appropriate `C` subclass with the `foo` attribute modified as needed.

One issue with this is that many (probably most) classes do expect arguments to be sent to their `__init__` methods, which this function is not able to handle. The pattern for this is simple enough, though. Consider an example of a credential form, with the method retooled to return an instance.

```
import csv

from django import forms


def get_credential_form(service, *args, **kwargs):
    """Return a form instance representing a credential for the
    given service.
    """
    # Open our "database".
    keys = []
    with open('creds.csv', 'r') as csvfile:
        for row in csv.reader(csvfile):
            # If this row does not correspond to the service we
            # are actually asking for (e.g. if it is a row for
            # Apple and we are asking for an Amazon credential class),
            # skip it.
            if row[0].lower() != service.lower():
```

```
            continue

            # Add the key to the list of expected keys.
            keys.append(row[1])

    # Put together the appropriate credential fields.
    attrs = {}
    for key in keys:
        field_kw = {}
        if 'password' in key:
            field_kw['widget'] = forms.PasswordInput
        attrs[key] = forms.CharField(**field_kw)

    # Return a form class with the appropriate credential fields.
    metaclass = type(forms.Form)
    cls = metaclass('CredentialForm', (forms.Form,), attrs)
    return cls(*args, **kwargs)
```

This does not actually entail very many changes from the previous class factory. There are really only two changes:

➤ First, *args and **kwargs have been added to the function signature.

➤ Second, the final line now returns an instance of the class that was created, with the *args and **kwargs passed to the instance.

Now you have an entirely functional class factory, which returns an instance of the form class that it creates. This raises a final point. Now the function is likely indistinguishable from a class to the end developer, unless said end developer inspects the inner workings. Therefore, perhaps it should be presented as one in the naming convention.

```
def CredentialForm(service, *args, **kwargs):
    [...]
```

In Python, functions are normally named with all lowercased letters, and with underscores for word separation. However, this is a function that is being used like a class constructor by developers who actually use it, so by changing the naming convention, you present it as a class name.

Conveniently, the name also matches the name of the class used for the instances, because the first argument to the metaclass' constructor, 'CredentialForm', is the internal name of the class.

And, this is Python. If it looks like a duck and quacks like a duck. . .

SUMMARY

The power of class factories shows itself when it is necessary to have class attributes be determined at runtime, rather than at coding time. The Python language is able to handle this situation precisely because classes are first-class objects, and can be created similarly to how any other object is created.

On the other hand, classes containing unknown attributes add some uncertainty. Their methods must be written to allow for an attribute to be present or absent, where, in other cases, the presence of the attribute may be able to be assumed.

The ability to declare classes at runtime is extremely powerful, but brings with it a tradeoff in simplicity. This is fine. When you encounter a situation where class factories are the right answer, it is often salient, and there is often no other direct way to solve the issue. Put directly, you can be reasonably sure that a class factory is a good approach if it is the *simplest* approach.

That rule holds true for programming generally, but it is a particularly useful one here.

Chapter 7, "Abstract Base Classes," discusses Python strings and bytestrings, and how to manage string data with minimal pain.

Abstract Base Classes

How do you know whether an object you are using conforms to a given specification? The common answer to this in Python is referred to as the "duck typing" model. If it looks like a duck and quacks like a duck, it is probably a duck.

When dealing with programming and objects, this usually translates to verifying that an object implements a given method, or has a given property. If the object has a `quack` method, then you have decent evidence that it is a `Duck`. And, furthermore, if all you need is a `quack` method, it probably does not matter much whether or not it is actually a `Duck`.

This is often a very useful construct, and it flows naturally from Python's loose typing system. It emphasizes questions of composition over questions of identity, `hasattr` over `isinstance`.

Sometimes, however, identity is important. For example, perhaps you are using a library that requires input conforming to a particular identity. Alternatively, sometimes it is too cumbersome to check for a myriad of different properties and methods.

Python 2.6 and Python 3 introduce the concept of *abstract base classes*. Abstract base classes are a mechanism for assigning identity. They are a way of answering, "Is this class fundamentally a `Duck`?" Abstract base classes also provide a mechanism for designating abstract methods, requiring other implementers to provide key functionality that is purposefully not provided in a base implementation.

This chapter explores abstract base classes, why they exist, and how to use them.

USING ABSTRACT BASE CLASSES

The fundamental purpose for abstract base classes is to provide a somewhat formalized way to test whether an object conforms to a given specification.

How do you determine whether you are working with a `list`? That is quite easy—call `isinstance` on the variable against the list class, and it returns either `True` or `False`.

```
>>> isinstance([], list)
True
>>> isinstance(object(), list)
False
```

On the other hand, does the code you are writing really require a `list`? Consider the case where you are simply reading a list-like object, but never modifying it. In such cases, you could accept a `tuple` instead.

The `isinstance` method does provide a mechanism to test against multiple base classes, as shown here:

```
>>> isinstance([], (list, tuple))
True
>>> isinstance((), (list, tuple))
True
>>> isinstance(object(), (list, tuple))
False
```

However, this is not really what you want, either. After all, a custom sequence class would also be entirely acceptable, assuming that it uses a `__getitem__` method that accepts ascending integers and slice objects (such as `QuerySet` methods in Django). So, simply using `isinstance` against the classes that you have explicitly identified may generate false negatives, not allowing objects that should be allowed.

Of course, it is possible to test for the presence of a `__getitem__` method.

```
>>> hasattr([], '__getitem__')
True
>>> hasattr(object(), '__getitem__')
False
```

Again, this is not a sufficient solution. Unlike the `isinstance` checks, it does not generate false negatives. Instead, it generates false positives, because list-like objects are not the only objects that implement `__getitem__`.

```
>>> hasattr({}, '__getitem__')
True
```

Fundamentally, simply testing for the presence of certain attributes or methods is sometimes not a sufficient way to determine that the object conforms to the parameters you seek.

Abstract base classes provide a mechanism to *declare* that one class derives identity from another (whether or not it actually does). This is done without any actual object inheritance or any changes to method resolution order. Its purpose is declarative; it provides a way for an object to *assert* that it conforms to a protocol.

Additionally, abstract base classes provide a way to *require* that a subclass implements a given protocol. If an abstract base class requires a given method to be implemented, and a subclass does not implement that method, then the interpreter will raise an exception when attempting to create the subclass.

DECLARING A VIRTUAL SUBCLASS

Python 2.6, 2.7, and all versions of Python 3 provide a module, `abc` (which stands for "abstract base classes") that provides the tools for using abstract base classes.

The first thing that the `abc` module provides is a metaclass, called `ABCMeta`. Any abstract base classes, regardless of their purpose, must use the `ABCMeta` metaclass.

Any abstract base class can arbitrarily declare that it is an *ancestor* (not a descendent) of any arbitrary concrete class, including concrete classes in the standard library (even those implemented in C). It does this using the `register` method, which `ABCMeta` provides on its instances. (Remember, these are the classes themselves, which use `ABCMeta` as their metaclass.)

Consider an abstract base class that registers itself as an ancestor of `dict`. (Note that the following code uses the Python 3 metaclass syntax.)

```
>>> import abc
>>> class AbstractDict(metaclass=abc.ABCMeta):
...     def foo(self):
...         return None
...
>>> AbstractDict.register(dict)
<class 'dict'>
```

This does not cause any changes to the `dict` class itself. What explicitly does *not* happen here (and this is critical to note) is that `dict`'s method resolution does not change. You do not suddenly find that `dict` got a `foo` method.

```
>>> {}.foo()
Traceback (most recent call last):
  File "<stdin>", line 1, in <module>
AttributeError: 'dict' object has no attribute 'foo'
```

What this *does* do is make `dict` objects also identify as `AbstractDict` instances, and `dict` itself now identifies as an `AbstractDict` subclass.

```
>>> isinstance({}, AbstractDict)
True
>>> issubclass(dict, AbstractDict)
True
```

Note that the converse is not the case. `AbstractDict` is not a subclass of `dict`.

```
>>> issubclass(AbstractDict, dict)
False
```

Why Declare Virtual Subclasses?

To understand why you would want to do this, recall the example at the beginning of the chapter where you wanted to read from a list-like object. It needs to be iterable like `list` or `tuple`, and it needs to have a `__getitem__` method that takes integers. On the other hand, you do not necessarily want to have a restriction of only accepting `list` or `tuple`.

Abstract base classes provide a very good, extensible mechanism for that. A previous example showed that you can use `isinstance` to check against a tuple of classes.

```
>>> isinstance([], (list, tuple))
True
```

This is not really extensible, however. If you are checking against `list` or `tuple` in your implementation, and someone using your library wants to send something else that acts list-like but does not subclass `list` or `tuple`, that person is up a creek.

Abstract base classes provide the solution to this problem. First, define an abstract base class and register `list` and `tuple` to it, as shown here:

```
>>> import abc
>>> class MySequence(metaclass=abc.ABCMeta):
...     pass
...
>>> MySequence.register(list)
<class 'list'>
>>> MySequence.register(tuple)
<class 'tuple'>
```

Now, alter the `isinstance` check to check against `MySequence` instead of against `(list, tuple)`. It will still return `True` when a `list` or `tuple` is checked, and `False` for other objects.

```
>>> isinstance([], MySequence)
True
>>> isinstance((), MySequence)
True
>>> isinstance(object(), MySequence)
False
```

Thus far, you have the same situation as before. But, there is one crucial difference. Consider the case where another developer is using a library that expects a `MySequence` object, and, therefore, expects a `list` or `tuple`.

When `(list, tuple)` is hard-coded in the library, there is nothing that the developer can do. However, `MySequence` is an abstract base class that the library is defining. That means that the developer can import it.

Once the developer is able to import it, the custom class that is sufficiently list-like can simply be registered with `MySequence`:

```
>>> class CustomListLikeClass(object):
...     pass
...
>>> MySequence.register(CustomListLikeClass)
<class '__main__.CustomListLikeClass'>
>>> issubclass(CustomListLikeClass, MySequence)
True
```

The developer is able to pass the `CustomListLikeClass` instance into the library that expects a `MySequence`. Now, when the library does its `isinstance` checks, the check passes, and the object is allowed.

Using *register* as a Decorator

As of Python 3.3, the `register` method provided by classes using the `ABCMeta` metaclass can also be used as a decorator.

If you are creating a new class that should be registered as a subclass of an `ABCMeta`, you normally register it like this (using the `MySequence` abstract base class defined in the previous example):

```
>>> class CustomListLikeClass(object):
...     pass
...
>>> MySequence.register(CustomListLikeClass)
<class '__main__.CustomListLikeClass'>
```

Note, however, that the `register` method returns the class that is passed to it. It works this way so that `register` can also be used as a decorator. It is accepting a callable and returning a callable (in this case, the exact same callable).

The following code will have an identical effect:

```
>>> @MySequence.register
... class CustomListLikeClass(object):
...     pass
...
>>>
```

You can confirm this by doing the same `issubclass` check as you did before.

```
>>> issubclass(CustomListLikeClass, MySequence)
True
```

It is worth noting that this decorator behavior was added in Python 3.3. In Python 2, as well as in Python 3.2 and below, the `register` method on abstract base classes returned `None`, rather than returning the class that was passed to it.

This means that it is unable to be used as a decorator in these versions. If you are writing code that is intended to be cross-compatible with Python 2 and Python 3, or if you are writing code that may run on an older version of Python 3, you should avoid using `register` as a decorator.

__subclasshook__

For most purposes, using a class with the `ABCMeta` metaclass and then using the `register` method that `ABCMeta` provides is an entirely sufficient way to get what you need. However, you may have a case where manual registration of every intended subclass is not tenable.

Classes created with the `ABCMeta` metaclass may optionally define a special magic method called `__subclasshook__`.

The `__subclasshook__` method must be defined as a class method (using the `@classmethod` decorator) and takes a single additional positional argument, which is the class being tested. It can return three values: `True`, `False`, or `NotImplemented`.

The case for `True` and `False` is salient enough. The `__subclasshook__` method returns `True` if the tested class should be considered a subclass, and `False` if it should not be considered a subclass.

Consider the traditional duck typing paradigm. The fundamental concern in the duck-typing paradigm is whether an object has certain methods or attributes (whether it "quacks like a duck"), rather than whether it subclasses this or that class. An abstract base class could implement this concept with __subclasshook__, as shown here:

```
import abc


class AbstractDuck(metaclass=abc.ABCMeta):
    @classmethod
    def __subclasshook__(cls, other):
        quack = getattr(other, 'quack', None)
        return callable(quack)
```

This abstract base class is declaring that any class with a quack method (but not a non-callable quack attribute) should be considered its subclass, and nothing else should be.

```
>>> class Duck(object):
...     def quack(self):
...         pass
...
>>>
>>> class NotDuck(object):
...     quack = 'foo'
...
>>> issubclass(Duck, AbstractDuck)
True
>>> issubclass(NotDuck, AbstractDuck)
False
```

An important thing to note here is that when the __subclasshook__ method is defined, it takes precedence over the register method.

```
>>> AbstractDuck.register(NotDuck)
<class '__main__.NotDuck'>
>>> issubclass(NotDuck, AbstractDuck)
False
```

This is where NotImplemented comes in. If the __subclasshook__ method returns NotImplemented, then (and only then) the traditional route of checking to see if a class has been registered is checked.

Consider the following modified AbstractDuck class:

```
import abc


class AbstractDuck(metaclass=abc.ABCMeta):
    @classmethod
    def __subclasshook__(cls, other):
        quack = getattr(other, 'quack', None)
        if callable(quack):
            return True
        return NotImplemented
```

The only change made here is that if there is not a `quack` method, the `__subclasshook__` method returns `NotImplemented` instead of `False`. Now, the registry is checked, and a class that has been previously registered will come back as a subclass.

```
>>> issubclass(NotDuck, AbstractDuck)
False
>>> AbstractDuck.register(NotDuck)
<class '__main__.NotDuck'>
>>> issubclass(NotDuck, AbstractDuck)
True
```

Essentially, the first example says, "It is an `AbstractDuck` if it quacks like a duck," and the second example says, "It is an `AbstractDuck` if it quacks like a duck … or if it just says flat out that it is an `AbstractDuck`."

Of course, note that if you do this, you must be able to handle anything that you receive. It does you no good to make the `quack` method optional if you rely on being able to call it!

So, what is the value of doing this? It would be easy enough simply to do a `hasattr` or `callable` check on the methods you need.

In a relatively straightforward case, it is probably actually a hindrance to use an abstract base class. For example, it would simply add unnecessary complexity to use one as a stand-in to check for the presence of a single method.

For non-trivial cases, there is some value. First, there is value in compartmentalization. The abstract base class defines a single place for the overall test to live. Any code using a subclass of the abstract base class simply uses the `issubclass` or `isinstance` function. This ensures that as needs evolve, there is a single place for the conformity-checking code to live.

Also, the availability of `NotImplemented` as a return value for `__subclasshook__` adds some power. It provides a mechanism to say that while there are ways to definitively pass or definitively fail to match the given protocol, there is also the way for a custom class author to explicitly opt in.

DECLARING A PROTOCOL

Another major value in abstract base classes is in their capability to declare a protocol. In the previous examples, you learned how an abstract base class can be used to cause a class to be able to *declare* that it should be able to pass a type check test.

However, abstract base classes can also be used to *define* what a subclass must offer. This is similar to the concept of interfaces in some other object-oriented languages, such as Java.

Other Existing Approaches

You can approach this fundamental problem without using abstract base classes. Because abstract base classes are a relatively new language feature, several of these approaches are quite common.

Using *NotImplementedError*

Consider a class that is built with certain functionality, but which intentionally leaves out a critical method so that this method may be implemented by subclasses.

```
from datetime import datetime


class Task(object):
    """An abstract class representing a task that must run, and
    which should track individual runs and results.
    """
    def __init__(self):
        self.runs = []

    def run(self):
        start = datetime.now()
        result = self._run()
        end = datetime.now()
        self.runs.append({
            'start': start,
            'end': end,
            'result': result,
        })
        return result

    def _run(self):
        raise NotImplementedError('Task subclasses must define '
                                  'a _run method.')
```

The purpose of this class would be to run some kind of task and track when those runs happened. It is easy to intuitively understand how it could also provide logging or similar functionality.

What the base `Task` class does *not* provide, however, is a task body. It is up to subclasses to do this. Instead, the `Task` class provides a shell method, _run, which does nothing except raise `NotImplementedError` with a useful error message. Any subclass that fails to override _run will most likely hit this error, which is also what you get if you attempt to call `run` on `Task` itself.

```
>>> t = Task()
>>> t.run()
Traceback (most recent call last):
  File "<stdin>", line 1, in <module>
  File "<stdin>", line 10, in run
  File "<stdin>", line 20, in _run
NotImplementedError: Task subclasses must define a _run method.
```

Using Metaclasses

This is not the only way to declare a protocol. Another common way to do this is by using a metaclass.

```
from datetime import datetime, timezone


class TaskMeta(type):
    """A metaclass that ensures the presence of a _run method
```

```
        on any non-abstract classes it creates.
        """
        def __new__(cls, name, bases, attrs):
            # If this is an abstract class, do not check for a _run method.
            if attrs.pop('abstract', False):
                return super(TaskMeta, cls).__new__(cls, name, bases, attrs)

            # Create the resulting class.
            new_class = super(TaskMeta, cls).__new__(cls, name, bases, attrs)

            # Verify that a _run method is present and raise
            # TypeError otherwise.
            if not hasattr(new_class, '_run') or not callable(new_class._run):
                raise TypeError('Task subclasses must define a _run method.')

            # Return the new class object.
            return new_class


class Task(metaclass=TaskMeta):
    """An abstract class representing a task that must run, and
    which should track individual runs and results.
    """
    abstract = True

    def __init__(self):
        self.runs = []

    def run(self):
        start = datetime.now(tz=timezone.utc)
        result = self._run()
        end = datetime.now(tz=timezone.utc)
        self.runs.append({
            'start': start,
            'end': end,
            'result': result,
        })
        return result
```

This is similar to the previous example, but with a couple of subtle differences. The first difference is that the Task class itself, while it can still be instantiated, no longer declares a _run method at all, so the public-facing run method would raise AttributeError.

```
>>> t = Task()
>>> t.run()
Traceback (most recent call last):
  File "<stdin>", line 1, in <module>
  File "<stdin>", line 12, in run
AttributeError: 'Task' object has no attribute '_run'
```

The more important distinction, however, lies with subclasses. Because the metaclass has a __new__ method that runs when the subclass is created, the interpreter will no longer allow you to create a subclass without a _run method.

```
>>> class TaskSubclass(Task):
...     pass
...
Traceback (most recent call last):
  File "<stdin>", line 1, in <module>
  File "<stdin>", line 16, in __new__
NotImplementedError: Task subclasses must define a _run method.
```

The Value of Abstract Base Classes

Both of these approaches are valuable, but it is also fair to criticize them for being somewhat *ad hoc*.

Abstract base classes provide a more formal way to present the same pattern. They provide a mechanism to declare a protocol using an abstract class, and subclasses must provide an implementation that conforms to that protocol.

The abc module provides a decorator called @abstractmethod, which designates that a given method must be overridden by all subclasses. The method body may be empty (pass), or may contain an implementation that the subclass methods may choose to call using super.

Consider a Task class that uses the @abstractmethod decorator in lieu of a custom metaclass.

```python
import abc
from datetime import datetime, timezone


class Task(metaclass=abc.ABCMeta):
    """An abstract class representing a task that must run, and
    which should track individual runs and results.
    """
    def __init__(self):
        self.runs = []

    def run(self):
        start = datetime.now(tz=timezone.utc)
        result = self._run()
        end = datetime.now(tz=timezone.utc)
        self.runs.append({
            'start': start,
            'end': end,
            'result': result,
        })
        return result

    @abc.abstractmethod
    def _run(self):
        pass
```

Again, this is *mostly* identical to the previous two examples, but ever so slightly different from both. First, note that the Task class itself is unable to be instantiated.

```
>>> t = Task()
Traceback (most recent call last):
  File "<stdin>", line 1, in <module>
TypeError: Can't instantiate abstract class Task with abstract methods _run
```

This is distinct from the `NotImplementedError` approach, which would have allowed the base `Task` class to be instantiated.

Similarly, it is distinct from both of the previous approaches in that the error case for a subclass that does not properly override the `_run` method is slightly different. In the first example, using `NotImplementedError`, you end up having `NotImplementedError` raised at the point where the `_run` method is called. In the second example, using a custom `TaskMeta` metaclass, `TypeError` is raised when the offending subclass is created.

When using an abstract base class, the interpreter is perfectly happy to create a subclass that does not implement all (or even any) of the abstract methods in the base class.

```
>>> class Subtask(Task):
...     pass
...
>>>
```

What the interpreter is *not* willing to do, however, is instantiate it. In fact, it gives the exact same error as the `Task` class gives, which is logically exactly what you expect.

```
>>> st = Subtask()
Traceback (most recent call last):
  File "<stdin>", line 1, in <module>
TypeError: Can't instantiate abstract class Subtask with abstract methods _run
```

However, once you define a subclass that overrides the abstract methods, it works just fine, and you are able to instantiate your subclass.

```
>>> class OtherSubtask(Task):
...     def _run(self):
...         return 2 + 2
...
>>>
>>> ost = OtherSubtask()
>>> ost.run()
4
```

And, if you inspect the `runs` attribute, you will see that information about the run has been saved, as shown here:

```
>>> ost.runs
[{'result': 4, 'end': datetime.datetime(…), 'start': datetime.datetime(…)}]
```

This is actually a very useful approach to this problem, for several reasons. First (and probably most important), this approach is formalized rather than ad hoc. Abstract base classes were specifically proposed as a solution to fill this particular need, pursuant to the notion that, ideally, there should be one and only one "correct" way to do it.

Second, the `@abstractmethod` decorator is very simple, and avoids a lot of potential errors that can crop up if you're attempting to write boilerplate code. As an example, what if, in your `TaskMeta` metaclass, you accidentally only check for the presence of `_run` in the `attrs` dictionary, but do not allow for the presence of `_run` in the superclass? This is an easy mistake to make, and it would result in `Task` subclasses that are not themselves subclassable unless you manually override `_run` every time. With the `@abstractmethod` decorator, you get the right behavior without having to put too much thought into it.

Finally, this approach makes it very easy to have intermediate implementations. Consider an abstract base class that has 10 abstract methods instead of one. It is entirely reasonable to have an entire sub-class tree, where higher subclasses on the chain implement some common methods, but leave other methods in their abstract state for *their* subclasses to implement. In fairness, you can do this with the custom metaclass approach also (by declaring every intermediate class `abstract = True` in the `TaskMeta` example). However, when using `@abstractmethod`, you basically get exactly the behavior you want intuitively.

Of course, there is one big reason *not* to use an abstract base class if you need this type of functionality, which is if you need to support versions of Python that do not yet have `abc`. This is becoming more rare, though, because `abc` was added in Python 2.6, and many Python packages do not support versions of Python older than 2.6.

Abstract Properties

It is also possible for properties (that is, methods that use the `@property` decorator) to be declared as abstract. However, the correct approach to this depends slightly on what versions of Python you are supporting.

In Python 2.6 through 3.2 (including any code that must be cross-compatible with these versions), the correct approach is to use the `@abstractproperty` decorator, which is provided by the `abc` module.

```
import abc


class AbstractClass(metaclass=abc.ABCMeta):
    @abc.abstractproperty
    def foo(self):
        pass
```

In Python 3.3, this approach is deprecated, because `@abstractmethod` has been updated to be able to work alongside `@property`. Therefore, having a special decorator to provide both is now redundant. Thus, the following example is identical to the previous one, but only in Python 3.3 and up:

```
import abc


class AbstractClass(metaclass=abc.ABCMeta):
    @property
    @abc.abstractmethod
    def foo(self):
        pass
```

Attempting to instantiate a subclass of `AbstractClass` that does not override the `foo` method will raise an error.

```
>>> class InvalidChild(AbstractClass):
...     pass
...
>>> ic = InvalidChild()
Traceback (most recent call last):
  File "<stdin>", line 1, in <module>
TypeError: Can't instantiate abstract class InvalidChild with abstract methods foo
```

However, a subclass that overrides the abstract method is able to be instantiated.

```
>>> class ValidChild(AbstractClass):
...     @property
...     def foo(self):
...         return 'bar'
...
>>>
>>> vc = ValidChild()
>>> vc.foo
'bar'
```

Abstract Class or Static Methods

As with properties, you may want to combine the `@abstractmethod` decorator with either a class method or static method (that is, a method decorated with `@classmethod` or `@staticmethod`).

This is a little bit trickier. Python 2.6 through 3.1 simply do not provide a way to do this at all. Python 3.2 does provide a way, using the `@abstractclassmethod` or `@abstractstaticmethod` decorators. These work similarly to the previous abstract properties example.

Python 3.3 then alters this by changing `@abstractmethod` to be compatible with the `@classmethod` and `@staticmethod` decorators, and deprecates the Python 3.2 approach.

In this case, because most code written for Python 3 usually is only written to be compatible with Python 3.3 and up (you learn more about this in Chapter 10, "Python 2 Versus Python 3"), most likely what you want to do is simply use the two decorators separately. However, if you need compatibility with Python 3.2, and *do not* need compatibility with any previous versions of Python (including any versions of Python 2), then those decorators are available to you.

Consider the following abstract class using the Python 3.3 syntax:

```
class AbstractClass(metaclass=abc.ABCMeta):
    @classmethod
    @abc.abstractmethod
    def foo(cls):
        return 42
```

Subclassing this class without overriding the method will work as usual, but the subclass is unable to be instantiated.

```
>>> class InvalidChild(AbstractClass):
...     pass
...
>>> ic = InvalidChild()
Traceback (most recent call last):
  File "<stdin>", line 1, in <module>
TypeError: Can't instantiate abstract class InvalidChild with abstract methods foo
```

The abstract method itself can actually be called directly without error, though.

```
>>> InvalidChild.foo()
42
```

Once the abstract method is overridden in a subclass, that subclass is able to be instantiated.

```
>>> class ValidChild(AbstractClass):
...     @classmethod
...     def foo(cls):
...         return 'bar'
...
>>> ValidChild.foo()
'bar'
>>> vc = ValidChild()
>>> vc.foo()
'bar'
```

BUILT-IN ABSTRACT BASE CLASSES

In addition to providing the `abc` module that enables you to build your own abstract base classes, the Python 3 standard library also provides a small number of abstract base classes built into the language, particularly for opting in a special class to a common pattern (such as a sequence, mutable sequence, iterable, and so on). The most commonly used, which are for collections, live in the `collections.abc` module.

Most of these built-in abstract base classes provide both abstract and non-abstract methods, and are often an alternative to subclassing a built-in Python class. For example, subclassing `MutableSequence` may be a superior alternative to subclassing `list` or `str`.

The provided abstract base classes can be divided into two basic categories: those that require and check for a single method (such as `Iterable` and `Callable`), and those that provide a stand-in to a common built-in Python type.

Single-Method ABCs

Python provides five abstract base classes that contain one abstract method each, and whose `__subclasscheck__` methods simply check for the presence of that method. They are as follows:

➤ Callable (`__call__`)

➤ Container (`__contains__`)

➤ Hashable (`__hash__`)

➤ Iterable (`__iter__`)

➤ Sized (`__len__`)

Any class that contains the appropriate method is automatically considered to be a subclass of the relevant abstract base class.

```
>>> from collections.abc import Sized
>>>
>>> class Foo(object):
```

```
...      def __len__(self):
...          return 42
...
>>> issubclass(Foo, Sized)
True
```

Similarly, classes may subclass the abstract base classes directly, and are expected to override the relevant method.

```
>>> class Bar(Sized):
...     pass
...
>>> b = Bar()
Traceback (most recent call last):
  File "<stdin>", line 1, in <module>
TypeError: Can't instantiate abstract class Bar with abstract methods __len__
```

In addition to these five classes, there is one more. `Iterator` is slightly special. It inherits from `Iterable`, provides an implementation for __iter__ (which just returns itself and can be overridden), and adds an abstract method called __next__.

Alternative-Collection ABCs

Another major type of built-in abstract base classes in Python 3 are those that serve to identify subclasses that serve a similar role as the major Python collection classes: `list`, `dict`, and `set`.

There are six of these classes, divided into three categories with two in each category (one immutable class and one mutable one).

The first category is `Sequence` and `MutableSequence`. These abstract base classes are intended for collections that generally act like Python tuples or lists, respectively. The `Sequence` abstract base class requires __getitem__ and __len__. However, it also provides implementations for a lot of other common methods you use with list and tuples, such as __contains__ and __iter__ (among others). The idea here is that you can subclass `Sequence` and define just the things you need, and Python provides you with the other common functionality of sequences. Of course, `list`, `tuple`, and `set` are considered to be subclasses of `Sequence`.

`MutableSequence` is similar, but adds the notion of modifying the sequence in-place. Therefore, it adds __setitem__, __delitem__, and `insert` as abstract methods, and provides functionality for `append`, `pop`, and the like. The principle is still the same—you must define just the things you fundamentally need to have a mutable sequence, and Python provides list-like methods for the rest. As you probably expect, `list` and `set` are already considered to be subclasses of `MutableSequence` out of the box.

The other two categories are `Mapping` and `Set`, which come with `MutableMapping` and `MutableSet`, as you would expect. `Mapping`s are intended for dictionary-like objects (similar to `dict`, and `dict` is considered a subclass), whereas `Set`s are intended for unordered collections (similar to `set`, and `set` is considered a subclass). In both cases, they specify some key methods (with names corresponding to those of `dict` and `set`) as abstract, and provide implementations for the remainder.

Using Built-In Abstract Base Classes

The key purpose for these abstract base classes is to provide a means to test for common types of collections. Rather than testing to see if you have a `list`, test for a `MutableSequence` (or just a `Sequence` if you do not need to modify it). Rather than testing for `dict`, test for a `MutableMapping`.

This makes your code more flexible. If someone who is using your library *does* have a need to make a list-like object or a dictionary-like object for individual purposes, that person can still pass this to your code, which can use it without any extra work. This allows your code to test to make sure you are getting the kind of object you expect to get, and allows others the flexibility to pass in compatible objects, which may not be the exact ones you anticipated.

Additional ABCs

There are other abstract base classes in the standard library not covered in detail here. In particular, the `numbers` module contains abstract base classes for implementing many different kinds of numbers.

SUMMARY

The primary importance of abstract base classes is that they provide a formal and dynamic way to answer the question, "Are you getting the kind of object you think you are getting?" It addresses some of the shortcomings of both simply testing for the presence of certain attributes and simply testing for particular classes. This is valuable.

It is worth remembering, however, that much like the more ad hoc approaches that preceded them, abstract base classes are still very much a gentlemen's agreement. The Python interpreter will catch some obvious violations (such as failing to implement an abstract method in a subclass). However, it is the responsibility of implementers to ensure that their subclasses do the right thing. There are many things that abstract base classes do not check. For example, they do not check method signatures or return types.

The lesson here is that just because a class implements an abstract base class does not guarantee that it does so correctly, or in the way that you expect. This is nothing new. Just because a class has a particular method does not mean that said method does the right thing. It is easy to inspect whether an object has a `quack` method. It is far more difficult to determine whether the `quack` method actually makes the object quack like a duck.

This is fine, however. Part of writing software in a dynamic language like Python is that you accept that these kinds of gentlemen's agreements exist. There is still tremendous value in having a formalized and streamlined way to declare and to determine whether an object conforms to a type or protocol. Abstract base classes provide this.

Chapter 8, "Strings and Bytestrings," explores the world of Unicode and ASCII strings, and how to handle them effectively in Python programs.

PART III
Data

Strings and Unicode

One of the more common sources of pain when writing Python applications is the handling of string data, specifically when strings contain characters outside of common Latin characters.

One of the first standards developed for representing string data is known as *ASCII*, which stands for *American Standard Code for Information Interchange*. ASCII defines a dictionary for representing common characters such as "A" through "Z" (in both upper- and lowercase), the digits "0" through "9," and a few common symbols (such as period, question mark, and so on).

However, ASCII relies upon an assumption that each character maps to a single byte, and, therefore, runs into trouble because there are far too many characters. As a result, a standard known as *Unicode* is now used to render text.

In Python, there are two different kinds of string data: *text strings* and *byte strings*. It is also possible to convert one type to the other. It is important to understand which kind of data you are dealing with, and to consistently keep the kinds of data straight.

In this chapter, you learn about the difference between text strings and byte strings, and how the types are implemented in both Python 2 and Python 3. You also learn how to deal with common problems that can pop up when you're working with string data within Python programs.

TEXT STRING VERSUS BYTE STRING

Data is consistently stored in *bytes*. Character sets such as ASCII and Unicode are responsible for using byte data to render the appropriate text.

ASCII's approach to this is straightforward. It defines a mapping table, and each character corresponds to 7 bits. A common superset of ASCII, latin-1 (discussed in more detail later), maintains this system, but uses 8 bits. Ordinarily, you represent bytes as either a decimal or hexadecimal number. Therefore, whenever the ASCII codec encounters the byte represented by the decimal number 65 (or hex 0x41), it knows that this corresponds to the character A.

In fact, Python itself defines two functions for converting between a single integer byte and the corresponding character: `ord` and `chr`. The abbreviation "ord" stands for "ordinal." The `ord` function takes a character and returns the integer corresponding to that character in the ASCII table, as shown here:

```
>>> ord('A')
65
```

The `chr` method does the opposite. It accepts an integer and returns the corresponding character on the ASCII table, as shown here:

```
>>> chr(65)
'A'
>>> chr(0x41)
'A'
```

The fundamental problem with ASCII is its assumption of a 1:1 mapping between characters and bytes. This is a serious limitation, because 256 characters is not nearly enough to include the various glyphs in different languages. Unicode solves this problem by using up to 4 bytes to represent each character.

String Data in Python

The Python language actually has two different kinds of strings: one for storing text, and one for storing raw bytes. A *text string* stores data internally as Unicode, whereas a *byte string* stores raw bytes and displays ASCII (for example, when sent to `print`).

Adding to the confusion, Python 2 and Python 3 use different (but overlapping) names for their text strings and byte strings. The Python 3 terminology makes more sense, so you should learn it and then translate to Python 2 when working there.

Python 3 Strings

In Python 3, the text string type (which stores Unicode data) is called `str`, and the byte string type is called `bytes`. Instantiating a string normally gives you a `str` instance, as shown here:

```
>>> text_str = 'The quick brown fox jumped over the lazy dogs.'
>>> type(text_str)
<class 'str'>
```

If you want to get a `bytes` instance, you prefix the literal with the `b` character.

```
>>> byte_str = b'The quick brown fox jumped over the lazy dogs.'
>>> type(byte_str)
<class 'bytes'>
```

It is possible to convert between a `str` and a `bytes`. The `str` class includes an `encode` method, which converts into a `bytes` using the specified codec. In most cases, you want to use UTF-8 as a codec when encoding data. The `encode` method takes a required argument, which is the string representing the appropriate codec.

```
>>> text_str.encode('utf-8')
b'The quick brown fox jumped over the lazy dogs.'
```

Similarly, the `bytes` class includes a `decode` method, which also takes the codec as a single, required argument, and returns a `str`. Decoding is a more interesting issue, though. It is insufficient to dogmatically say that you should always decode data as UTF-8, because data from another source may not have been *encoded* as UTF-8. You must decode data according to how it was encoded. You learn more about this later in this chapter.

Python 3 will never attempt to implicitly convert between a `str` and a `bytes`. Its approach is to require you to explicitly convert between text strings and byte strings with the `str.encode` and `bytes.decode` methods (a practice that requires you to specify a codec). For most applications, this is a preferable behavior, because it helps you avoid getting into situations where programs work when given common English text, but fail when running into unexpected characters.

This also means that text strings containing only ASCII characters are not considered to be equal to byte strings containing only ASCII characters.

```
>>> 'foo' == b'foo'
False
>>>
>>> d = {'foo': 'bar'}
>>> d[b'foo']
Traceback (most recent call last):
  File "<stdin>", line 1, in <module>
KeyError: b'foo'
```

Attempting to do nearly any operation on a text string and byte string together will raise `TypeError`, as shown here:

```
>>> 'foo' + b'bar'
Traceback (most recent call last):
  File "<stdin>", line 1, in <module>
TypeError: Can't convert 'bytes' object to str implicitly
```

One exception to this behavior is the `%` operator, which is used for string formatting in Python. Attempting to interpolate a text string into a byte string will raise `TypeError` as expected.

```
>>> b'foo %s' % 'bar'
Traceback (most recent call last):
  File "<stdin>", line 1, in <module>
TypeError: unsupported operand type(s) for %: 'bytes' and 'str'
```

On the other hand, interpolating a byte string into a text string does work, but does not return the intuitively desired response.

```
>>> 'foo %s' % b'bar'
"foo b'bar'"
```

What is occurring here is that the operator takes the `b'bar'` value, which is a `bytes`. It first looks for a `__str__` method, which the `bytes` object actually does have. It returns the text string `"b'bar'"`, with the `b'` prefix and `'` suffix. This is the same value returned by `__repr__`.

Python 2 Strings

Python 2 strings mostly work similarly, but with some subtle but very important distinctions.

The first distinction is the name of the classes. The Python 3 `str` class is called `unicode` in Python 2. In and of itself, this is fine. However, the Python 3 `bytes` class is called `str` in Python 2. This means that a Python 3 `str` is a text string, whereas a Python 2 `str` is a byte string. If you are using Python 2, it is critically important to understand this distinction.

Instantiating a string with no prefix gives you a `str` (remember, this is a byte string!) instance.

```
>>> byte_str = 'The quick brown fox jumped over the lazy dogs.'
>>> type(byte_str)
<type 'str'>
```

If you want a text string in Python 2, you prefix the string literal with the u character, as shown here:

```
>>> text_str = u'The quick brown fox jumped over the lazy dogs.'
>>> type(text_str)
<type 'unicode'>
```

Unlike Python 3, Python 2 does attempt to implicitly convert between text strings and byte strings. The way that this works is that if the interpreter encounters a mixed operation, it will first convert the byte string to a text string, and then perform the operation against the text strings.

It works this way so that an operation against a byte string and a text string will return a text string:

```
>>> 'foo' + u'bar'
u'foobar'
```

The interpreter performs this implicit decoding using whatever the default encoding is. On Python 2, this is almost always ASCII. Python defines a method, `sys.getdefaultencoding`, which provides the default codec for implicitly converting between text strings and byte strings.

```
>>> import sys
>>> sys.getdefaultencoding()
'ascii'
```

This means that many of the previous Python 3 examples show distinctly different behavior in Python 2.

```
>>> 'foo' == u'foo'
True
>>>
>>> d = {u'foo': u'bar'}
>>> d['foo']
u'bar'
```

str.encode and unicode.decode

One somewhat bizarre aspect of Python 2's string-handling behavior is that text strings actually have a `decode` method, and byte strings actually have an `encode` method.

You never want to use these.

The theoretical purpose of these methods is to ensure that you don't worry too much about what the input variable is. Simply call `encode` to change either kind of string into a byte string, or `decode` to change either kind of string into a text string.

In practice, however, this can be both disastrous and very confusing, because if the method receives the "wrong" kind of input string (that is, a string already of the desired output type), it will attempt two conversions, and attempt the implicit one using ASCII.

Consider this Python 2 example:

```
>>> text_str = u'\u03b1 is for alpha.'
>>>
>>> text_str.encode('utf-8')
'\xce\xb1 is for alpha.'
>>>
>>> text_str.encode('utf-8').encode('utf-8')
Traceback (most recent call last):
  File "<stdin>", line 1, in <module>
UnicodeDecodeError: 'ascii' codec can't decode byte 0xce in position 0:
    ordinal not in range(128)
```

It seems quite bizarre to be asking to encode something as UTF-8 and to get an error back complaining that the text is unable to be *decoded as ASCII*. But this is the implicit conversion that Python 2 is attempting to do in order to run `encode` (a method intended for text strings) on a byte string.

To the interpreter, the final line is equivalent to the following:

```
text_str.encode('utf-8').decode('ascii').encode('utf-8')
```

That is never what you want.

It seems simple enough not to do this, but the way you encounter an error like this is not to bluntly run `encode` twice (as this example does), but rather to run `encode` or `decode` without first checking to see what kind of data you have. In Python 2, text strings and byte strings intermingle frequently, and it is *very* easy to get one when you expected the other.

unicode_literals

If you are using Python 2.6 or greater, you can make part of this behavior track the Python 3 behavior if you choose to do so. Python defines a special module called `__future__`, from which you can preemptively opt-in to future behavior.

In this case, importing `unicode_literals` causes string literals to follow the Python 3 convention, although the Python 2 class names are still used.

```
>>> from __future__ import unicode_literals
>>> text_str = 'The quick brown fox jumped over the lazy dogs.'
>>> type(text_str)
<type 'unicode'>
>>> bytes_str = b'The quick brown fox jumped over the lazy dogs.'
>>> type(bytes_str)
<type 'str'>
```

Once `from __future__ import unicode_literals` is invoked, a string literal with no prefix in Python 2.6 or greater becomes a text string (`unicode`), and a `b` prefix creates a byte string (Python 2 `str`).

Doing this does *not* forward-port other aspects of Python 2's string handling to the Python 3 behavior. The interpreter will still attempt to implicitly convert between text strings and byte strings, and ASCII is still the default encoding.

Nonetheless, most strings specified in code are intended to be text strings rather than byte strings. Therefore, if you are writing code that does not need to support versions of Python below Python 2.6, it is very wise to use this.

six

The fact that Python 2 and Python 3 provide different class names for text strings and byte strings can be a source of confusion, although the transition to the much clearer Python 3 nomenclature is an important one.

To help cope with this, the popular Python library `six`, which is centered around writing modules that run correctly in both Python 2 and Python 3 (and which is covered in much more detail in Chapter 10, "Python 2 Versus Python 3"), provides aliases for these types so that they can be consistently referenced in code that must run on both platforms. The class for text strings (`str` in Python 3 and `unicode` in Python 2) is aliased as `six.text_type`, whereas the class for byte strings (`bytes` in Python 3 and `str` in Python 2) is aliased as `six.binary_type`.

STRINGS WITH NON-ASCII CHARACTERS

Most Python programs, and nearly any program that handles user input (whether it be direct input, from a file, from a database, and so on) must be able to handle arbitrary characters, including those not found on the ASCII table. Converting ASCII characters between text strings and byte strings is trivial (in the `utf-8` codec, it is actually a no-op). The complexity arrives when non-ASCII characters are in play, especially if text strings and byte strings are being used without sufficient regard to which is which.

Observing the Difference

Consider a text string that contains non-ASCII characters, such as the text string in the following code, which says "Hello, world" Google-translated into Greek (note that this is Python 3 code):

```
>>> text_str = 'Γεια σας, τον κόσμο.'
>>> type(text_str)
<class 'str'>
```

The first thing to note about this text string is that it cannot be encoded to a `bytes` instance using the `ascii` codec at all.

```
>>> text_str.encode('ascii')
Traceback (most recent call last):
  File "<stdin>", line 1, in <module>
UnicodeEncodeError: 'ascii' codec can't encode characters in position 0-3:
    ordinal not in range(128)
```

This is because ASCII does not have Greek characters, so the ASCII codec does not have any way to translate them into raw byte data. This is fine, though, because that is what the utf-8 codec is for, as shown here:

```
>>> text_str.encode('utf-8')
b'\xce\x93\xce\xb5\xce\xb9\xce\xb1 \xcf\x83\xce\xb1\xcf\x82,
\xcf\x84\xce\xbf\xce\xbd \xce\xba\xcf\x8c\xcf\x83\xce\xbc\xce\xbf.'
```

Several things are worth noting at this point. First and foremost, this is the first string you have encountered where the text string and the byte string *look* substantially different. The repr of the text string looks like human-readable Greek, whereas the repr of the byte string looks like it is intended to be machine-readable.

Also, notice that the lengths of the strings are actually not the same.

```
>>> byte_str = text_str.encode('utf-8')
>>> len(text_str)
20
>>> len(byte_str)
35
```

Why is this? Remember the problem that Unicode exists to solve: ASCII assumes a 1:1 correlation between bytes and characters, which puts a substantial limitation on the number of characters available.

Unicode allows for many more characters to exist by breaking out of this limitation. UTF-8 characters are variable length. A single Unicode character may be as small as a single byte (for the characters on the ASCII table), or as large as 4 bytes.

In the case of the example Greek text, most characters are 2 bytes, which is why the len of the byte string is almost double the len of the text string. However, the spaces, period, and comma (visible in the byte string as such) are all ASCII characters, and only take 1 byte each.

Unicode Is a Superset of ASCII

Why do the text strings and byte strings that only contain ASCII characters look so similar when printed, but the Unicode strings look so different?

By convention, you print the bytes in the ASCII range as their ASCII characters. Additionally, Unicode is structured in such a way as to make it an exact superset of ASCII. This means that the characters in the Latin alphabet, as well as the common punctuation symbols, are represented the same way in Unicode strings as well as byte strings.

This has another important meaning. Any valid ASCII text is also valid Unicode text.

OTHER ENCODINGS

Unicode is not the only encoding available to convert between raw byte data and a readable textual representation. Many others have been put forward, and some are in common use.

One common encoding is formally known as the ISO-8859 standard, and colloquially called `latin-1`. (For clarity, the remainder of this chapter will use "Latin-1" to refer to this rather than ISO-8859.)

Like Unicode, this encoding is a superset of ASCII, and adds support for glyphs found in many different languages other than English. However, as its name suggests, it is designed only to support languages that rely on Latin glyphs for their letters, and is not suitable for rendering languages that use other alphabets (such as Greek, Chinese, Japanese, Russian, or Korean, among others).

It would not actually be possible to render the previous Greek string using the `latin-1` codec, as the following Python 3 example demonstrates:

```
>>> text_str = 'Γεια σας, τον κόσμο.'
>>> text_str.encode('latin-1')
Traceback (most recent call last):
  File "<stdin>", line 1, in <module>
UnicodeEncodeError: 'latin-1' codec can't encode characters in position 0-
    3: ordinal not in range(256)
```

Encodings Are Not Cross-Compatible

It is important to recognize that while many encodings are structured as supersets of ASCII, they are often not compatible with one another. Outside of ASCII, there is little or no overlap between the `latin-1` and `utf-8` codecs.

Consider the difference in byte strings encoded using each codec.

```
>>> text_str = 'El zorro marrón rápido saltó por encima ' + \
...            'de los perros vagos.'
>>> text_str.encode('utf-8')
b'El zorro marr\xc3\xb3n r\xc3\xa1pido salt\xc3\xb3 por encima de los
    perros vagos.'
>>> text_str.encode('latin-1')
b'El zorro marr\xf3n r\xe1pido salt\xf3 por encima de los perros vagos.'
```

Because of this, a string encoded using one codec is unable to be decoded using the other codec. If you try to take a byte string representing text encoded using `latin-1` and decode it as `utf-8`, the Unicode codec will realize that it is encountering an invalid character sequence and fail.

```
>>> text_str.encode('latin-1').decode('utf-8')
Traceback (most recent call last):
  File "<stdin>", line 1, in <module>
UnicodeDecodeError: 'utf-8' codec can't decode byte 0xf3 in position 13:
    invalid continuation byte
```

Worse, if you try to take a byte string representing text encoded with `utf-8` and decode it as `latin-1`, the (more permissive) codec will successfully return a text string, but with garbled text.

```
>>> text_str.encode('utf-8').decode('latin-1')
'El zorro marrÃ³n rÃ¡pido saltÃ³ por encima de los perros vagos.'
```

It is impossible to infer based on the content of a byte string what encoding is in use. However, many common document formats and data-transfer protocols provide a mechanism to declare what encoding is in use. On the other hand, it is also possible that a document will incorrectly specify its character encoding.

READING FILES

Files always store bytes. Therefore, to use textual data read in from files, you must decode it into a text string.

Python 3

In Python 3, files are ordinarily decoded automatically for you. Consider the following file with Unicode text, encoded using UTF-8:

```
Hello, world.
Γεια σας, τον κόσμο.
```

Opening and reading this file in Python 3 gives you a text string (not a byte string).

```
>>> with open('unicode.txt', 'r') as f:
...     text_str = f.read()
...
>>> type(text_str)
<class 'str'>
```

This code example is making a few critical assumptions that are important to understand.

The biggest assumption being made is how to decode the file. Text files do not declare how they are encoded. There is no way for the interpreter to know whether it is getting UTF-8 text, Latin-1 text, or something else entirely.

Python 3 decides which encoding should be used based on what kind of system it is running on. A function is available to expose this: `locale.getpreferredencoding()`. On Mac OS X and on most Linux systems, the preferred encoding is UTF-8.

```
>>> import locale
>>> locale.getpreferredencoding()
'UTF-8'
```

However, most Windows systems use a different encoding called Windows-1252 or CP-1252 to encode text files, and running the same code in Python 3 on Windows reflects this.

```
>>> import locale
>>> locale.getpreferredencoding()
'cp1252'
```

It is important to note explicitly that the preferred encoding that `locale.getpreferredencoding()` provides is based on how the underlying system operates. It is *reflective*, not *prescriptive*. A text file with special characters saved on almost any system (using that system's default tools) and then opened using `open` in Python 3 will probably be decoded correctly.

However, files are not opened solely on the same type of system on which they are created. This is where the assumption becomes problematic.

Specifying Encoding

Python 3 enables you to explicitly declare the encoding of a file by providing an optional `encoding` keyword argument to `open`. This argument accepts a codec, specified as a string, similar to `encode` and `decode`.

Because the example Unicode file is stipulated as being encoded using UTF-8, you can explicitly tell the interpreter to decode it as such.

```
>>> with open('unicode.txt', 'r', encoding='utf-8') as f:
...     text_str = f.read()
...
>>> type(text_str)
<class 'str'>
```

Because the file was encoded as UTF-8, and the UTF-8 codec was used to decode it, the text string contains the expected data.

```
>>> text_str
'Hello, world.\nΓεια σας, τον κόσμο.\n'
```

Reading Bytes

Another implicit assumption being made (which logically precedes which codec to use to decode the file) is that the file should be decoded at all.

You may want to read in the file as a byte string instead of as a text string. There are two common reasons to do this. The most common reason is if you are accepting non-textual data (for example, if you are reading in an image). However, another potential reason is for reading text files with an uncertain encoding.

To read in a byte string instead of a text string, add the character b to the second string argument sent to open. For example, consider reading in the same file containing Unicode as a byte string, as shown here:

```
>>> with open('unicode.txt', 'rb') as f:
...     byte_str = f.read()
...
>>> type(byte_str)
<class 'bytes'>
```

Examining the byte_str variable shows the raw bytes in the string for the second line of text.

```
>>> byte_str
b'Hello, world.\n\xce\x93\xce\xb5\xce\xb9\xce\xb1 \xcf\x83\xce\xb1\xcf\x82,
    \xcf\x84\xce\xbf\xce\xbd \xce\xba\xcf\x8c\xcf\x83\xce\xbc\xce\xbf.\n'
```

This variable can be decoded just as if it were a byte string provided from any other source.

```
>>> byte_str.decode('utf-8')
'Hello, world.\nΓεια σας, τον κόσμο.\n'
```

This can be a useful strategy for dealing with a file whose encoding is uncertain. The data can be safely read from the file as bytes, and then the program can attempt to determine programmatically how to decode it.

Python 2

In Python 2, the read method will always return a byte string, regardless of how the file was opened.

```
>>> with open('unicode.txt', 'r') as f:
...     byte_str = f.read()
...
>>> type(byte_str)
<type 'str'>
```

Note that the b modifier was not used in the second argument to open, but a str instance (which is a byte string in Python 2) was returned anyway.

You can get a text string by using decode, just like on a byte string that comes from any other source.

```
>>> byte_str
'Hello, world.\n\xce\x93\xce\xb5\xce\xb9\xce\xb1 \xcf\x83\xce\xb1\xcf\x82,
    \xcf\x84\xce\xbf\xce\xbd \xce\xba\xcf\x8c\xcf\x83\xce\xbc\xce\xbf.\n'
>>>
>>> byte_str.decode('utf-8')
u'Hello, world.\n\u0393\u03b5\u03b9\u03b1 \u03c3\u03b1\u03c2,
    \u03c4\u03bf\u03bd \u03ba\u03cc\u03c3\u03bc\u03bf.\n'
```

Because Python 2 always provides byte strings, the open function does not have an encoding keyword argument, and attempting to provide one will raise TypeError.

If you are writing code that is intended to be run on Python 2, the best and safest way to do so is to always open files in binary mode (using b) and, if you are expecting textual data, decode it yourself.

READING OTHER SOURCES

Textual data is read from many different places, not only from files. Modern programs receive direct user input, accept input over protocols (such as HTTP), read out of databases, and transfer data using serialization formats such as Extensible Markup Language (XML) or JavaScript Object Notation (JSON).

Python provides many libraries and tools for reading data of many types, and from many sources. For example, the json module available in Python 2.6 and later is able to serialize and deserialize JSON data. Furthermore, numerous third-party packages are available that read data from other types or sources. For example, the pyyaml library reads YAML files, and the psycopg2 library reads and writes data from PostgreSQL databases.

Most (but not all) of these libraries return text strings. However, it is your responsibility to familiarize yourself with the libraries you use and to know whether you are getting text strings or byte strings. Also, some libraries may behave differently on different versions of Python, returning byte strings on Python 2 and text strings on Python 3. It is very important to make sure you keep them straight!

SPECIFYING PYTHON FILE ENCODINGS

Many document formats do provide a means to declare what codec is being used to encode text. For example, an XML file may begin like this:

```
<?xml version="1.0" encoding="UTF-8"?>
```

This is a common way to begin an XML file. Pay attention to the encoding attribute. This declares that textual data is encoded using UTF-8. Because the XML file declares that this is the encoding it uses, programs that read XML will use UTF-8 to decode any text it finds from bytes to text.

Sometimes it is necessary for Python source files to declare an encoding. For example, suppose a Python source file includes a string literal containing Unicode characters. On Python 2, the interpreter assumes that Python source files are encoded using ASCII, and this will actually fail.

Consider the following Python module saved as `unicode.py`:

```
text_str = u'Γεια σας, τον κόσμο.'
print(text_str)
```

Running this module in Python 3.3 or greater (because Python 3.0-3.2 lack the u prefix) works without any issues.

```
$ python3.4 unicode.py
Γεια σας, τον κόσμο.
```

However, running the same module in Python 2 will fail with a syntax error on the first line, because the Python 2 interpreter wants ASCII.

```
$ python2.7 unicode.py
  File "unicode.py", line 1
SyntaxError: Non-ASCII character '\xce' in file unicode.py on line 1, but
    no encoding declared; see http://www.python.org/peps/pep-0263.html
    for details
```

As the error message suggests, Python modules actually can declare an encoding, similar to how an XML file might do so. By default, Python 2 expects files to be encoded as ASCII, and Python 3 expects files to be encoded as UTF-8.

To override this, Python enables you to include a comment at the top of a module, formatted in a particular way. The interpreter will read this comment and use it as an encoding declaration.

The format for specifying the encoding for a Python file is as follows:

```
# -*- coding: utf-8 -*-
```

You can use any codec that can be passed to `encode` and `decode` here. So, values such as `ascii`, `latin-1`, and `cf-1252` are all acceptable (assuming, of course, that the file is encoded that way).

Consider the same module with a `coding` declaration:

```
# -*- coding: utf-8 -*-
text_str = u'Γεια σας, τον κόσμο.'
print(text_str)
```

If you run this modified file under Python 2, it will now succeed instead of raising a syntax error.

```
$ python2.7 unicode.py
Γεια σας, τον κόσμο.
```

Note that, if you choose to manually specify an encoding for a Python module, it is your responsibility to ensure that the encoding you specify is actually correct. Like any other document format, Python modules are not exempt from the possibility of declaring one encoding while actually using another.

If you accidentally specify the wrong encoding, your strings will come out as garbage. Consider what happens if the same file is declared to be encoded using `latin-1` (when it is actually using `utf-8` characters).

```
# -*- coding: latin-1 -*-
text_str = u'Γεια σας, τον κόσμο.'
print(text_str)
```

Running this in either Python 2 or Python 3.3+ will produce the same result, which is complete garbage.

```
$ python3.4 unicode.py
Î"ÎµÎ¹Î± ÏƒÎ±Ï,, Ï„Î¿Î½ Î°ÏÏƒÎ¼Î¿.
```

Because the `latin-1` codec can accept almost any byte stream, it does not actually recognize that this is not `latin-1` encoded text, and cheerfully returns bad data. Some codecs (such as `utf-8`) are more strict, in which case you would get an exception instead. The latter situation is preferable, but neither is what you want. It is critical to declare encodings correctly.

Note also that this is dependent on your terminal's capability to display these characters. If you have a terminal that does not support Unicode, this will likely raise an exception.

STRICT CODECS

One key advantage of `utf-8` as a codec is that, in addition to supporting the entire range of Unicode characters, it also is a "strict" codec. This means that it does not just take any byte stream and decode it. It can usually detect that non-Unicode byte streams are invalid and fail.

This can lead to helpful patterns when you're dealing with a byte stream where the encoding is not known (because there is no way to infer the encoding with certainty). For example, if you think that a byte stream might be `utf-8` and might be `latin-1`, you can try both, as shown here:

```
try:
    text_str = byte_str.decode('utf-8')
except UnicodeDecodeError:
    text_str = byte_str.decode('latin-1')
```

Of course, this is not a panacea. What happens, for example, if you get a byte string encoded as something entirely different? Because `latin-1` is a permissive codec, it will decode it incorrectly.

Suppressing Errors

Sometimes when you are decoding or encoding text using strict codecs (such as `utf-8` or `ascii`), you do not want a strict exception when the codec encounters text that it does not know how to handle.

The `encode` and `decode` methods provide a mechanism to ask a codec to behave differently when it encounters a set of characters that it cannot handle. Both methods take an optional second argument, `errors`, specified as a string. The default value is `strict`, which is what raises exception classes such as `UnicodeDecodeError`. The two other common error handlers are `ignore` and `replace`.

The `ignore` error handler simply skips over any bytes that the codec does not know how to decode. Consider what happens if you attempt to decode your Greek text as ASCII, as shown here:

```
>>> text_str = 'Γεια σας, τον κόσμο.'
>>> byte_str = text_str.encode('utf-8')
>>> byte_str.decode('ascii', 'ignore')
' , .'
```

The ASCII code does not know how to handle any of the Greek characters, but it does know how to handle the spaces and punctuation. Therefore, it preserves those, but strips all of the foreign characters.

The `replace` error handler is similar, but instead of skipping over unrecognized characters, it replaces them with a placeholder character. The exact placeholder character varies slightly based on the situation (whether encoding or decoding, and what codec is in use), but is usually either a question mark (?) or a special Unicode question mark diamond character (�).

Here is the result if you try to decode your Greek text using the `ascii` codec and the `replace` error handler:

```
>>> text_str = 'Γεια σας, τον κόσμο.'
>>> byte_str = text_str.encode('utf-8')
>>> byte_str.decode('ascii', 'replace')
'������� �����, ����� ����������.'
```

And here is the result if you try to encode your Greek text to a byte string using the `ascii` codec and the `replace` error handler:

```
>>> text_str = 'Γεια σας, τον κόσμο.'
>>> text_str.encode('ascii', 'replace')
b'???? ???, ??? ?????.'
```

You may notice that when using the `replace` error handler, the number of replacement characters may not be 1:1 with the number of characters in the actual text string. When decoding a byte string using the `ascii` codec, the codec has no way of knowing how many bytes correspond to each character, so it ends up showing more question marks than there are actual characters in the text string.

Registering Error Handlers

It is possible to register additional error handlers if the built-in ones are insufficient. The `codecs` module (where the default error handlers are defined) exposes a function for registering additional error handlers, named `register_error`. It takes two arguments: the name for the error handler and the actual function that does the error handling.

That function receives the exception that would otherwise be raised, and is responsible for re-raising it, raising another exception, or returning an appropriate string value to be substituted into the resulting string.

The exception instance contains `start` and `end` attributes that correspond to the substring that the codec is unable to encode or decode. It also has a `reason` attribute with a human-readable explanation of the reason why it is unable to encode or decode the characters in question, and an `object` attribute with the original string.

If returning a replacement value, the error function must return a tuple with two elements. The first element is the replacement character or characters, and the second is the position in the original string where encoding or decoding should continue. Usually, this corresponds to the `end` attribute on the exception instance. If you do this, be careful with the `start` position you return. It is very easy to get into an infinite loop scenario.

The following example simply replaces characters with a different substitution character:

```python
import codecs

def replace_with_underscore(err):
    length = err.end - err.start
    return ('_' * length, err.end)
codecs.register_error('replace_with_underscore', replace_with_underscore)
```

This error handler replaces unknown characters, but using underscores rather than question marks. The following is what happens if you decode a byte string with Unicode Greek text using the `ascii` codec and this error handler:

```python
>>> text_str = 'Γεια σας, τον κόσμο.'
>>> byte_str = text_str.encode('utf-8')
>>> byte_str.decode('ascii', 'replace_with_underscore')
'_____ _____, _____ _____.'
```

SUMMARY

Handling string data can be surprisingly frustrating. It is easier than you might expect to create a program that works right up until it encounters textual data that is dissimilar to what it expected.

When possible, try to have as much of your program as possible handle text strings. It is a good idea to decode byte strings as soon as possible after you receive them. Similarly, when writing data out, endeavor to encode your text strings to byte strings as late as possible.

Sometimes decoding is difficult. You may not know how a byte string is encoded, or you may be told an encoding, but be told wrong. This is challenging, and there is no easy solution.

Remember, the Python interpreter is your friend here. If you are dealing with problematic data, and you do not know the encoding, you may be able to interactively decode a sample of it using different codecs until you find something that looks reasonable. Of course, this manual approach assumes that the data you are coding for will always be similar to the sample data you are using.

The key thing to remember when handling string data is to ensure that you always know what kind of string you are dealing with. The worst and most frustrating problems crop up when you expect a text string and receive a byte string, or vice versa. Be sure to keep them straight.

Chapter 9 explores regular expressions, which are a mechanism for searching strings for data that matches a given pattern.

Regular Expressions

Regular expressions are a tool for matching text by looking for a pattern (rather than looking for a text string) in an easy and straightforward manner. For example, you could check for the presence of an exact text string within another text string simply by using the Python in keyword, as shown here:

```
>>> haystack = 'My phone number is 213-867-5309.'
>>> '213-867-5309' in haystack
True
```

Sometimes, however, you do not have the exact text you want to match. For example, what if you want to know whether *any* valid phone number is present in a string? To take that one step further, what if you want to know whether any valid phone number is present in the string, *and* also want to know what that phone number is?

This is where regular expressions are useful. Their purpose is to specify a pattern of text to identify within a bigger text string. Regular expressions can identify the presence or absence of text matching the pattern, and also split a pattern into one or more subpatterns, delivering the specific text within each.

This chapter explores regular expressions (or *regexes*, for short). First, you learn how to perform regular expression searches in Python using the re module. You then explore various regular expressions, beginning with the simple and working toward the more complex. Finally, you learn about regular expression substitution.

WHY USE REGULAR EXPRESSIONS?

You use regular expressions for two common reasons.

The first reason is data mining—that is, when you want to find a pile of text (matching a given pattern) in a bigger pile of text. It is very common to need to identify text that looks like a given type of information (for example, an e-mail address, a URL, a phone number, or the like).

As humans, we identify the type of information being presented based on patterns all the time. A television commercial that shows alphanumeric characters ending in .com or .org is intuitively understood to be presenting a web address. Add an @ character, and it is intuitively understood to be an e-mail address instead.

The second reason is validation. You can use regular expressions to establish that you got the data that you expected. It is generally wise to consider "outside" data to be untrustworthy, especially data from users. Regular expressions can help determine whether or not untested data is valid.

The corollary to this is that regular expressions are valuable tools for coercing data into a consistent format. For example, a phone number can be written in multiple valid ways, and if you are asking for user input, you likely want to accept all of them. However, you really only want to store the actual digits of the phone number, which can then be consistently formatted on display. In addition to being useful for validation, regular expressions are useful for this kind of data coercion.

REGULAR EXPRESSIONS IN PYTHON

The Python standard library provides the re module for using regular expressions.

The primary function that the re module provides is search. Its purpose is to take a regular expression (the needle) and a string (the haystack), and return the first match found. If no match is found at all, re.search returns None.

Consider re.search in action with the simplest regular expression possible, which is a simple alphanumeric string.

```
>>> import re
>>> re.search(r'fox', 'The quick brown fox jumped...')
<_sre.SRE_Match object; span=(16, 19), match='fox'>
```

The regular expression parser's job here is quite simple. It finds the word fox within the string, and returns a match object.

> **NOTE** *The* re *module also provides a function called* match *that appears to be very similar to* search. *It has one important difference: it only searches for a match that starts at the beginning of the string. It is easy (and common) to use re.match by mistake when you actually want to find something anywhere in a string. You are usually best off always using* re.search *and using the ^ anchor (discussed later in this chapter) if you need it.*

Raw Strings

Observant readers may note that the regular expression was specified slightly differently: r'fox'. The r character that precedes the string stands for "raw" (no, it does not stand for "regex").

The difference between a raw string and a regular string is simply that raw strings do not interpret the \ character as an escape character. This means that, for example, it is not possible to escape a quote character to avoid concluding your string.

However, raw strings are particularly useful for regular expressions because the regular expression engine itself needs the \ character for its own escaping at times. Therefore, using raw strings for regular expressions is very common and very useful. In fact, it is so common that some syntax-highlighting engines will actually provide regular-expression syntax highlighting within raw strings.

Match Objects

Match objects have several methods to tell you things about the match. The group method is arguably the most important. It returns a string with the text of the match, as shown here:

```
>>> match = re.search(r'fox', 'The quick brown fox jumped...')
>>> match.group()
'fox'
```

You may be curious why this method is named group. This is because regular expressions can be split into multiple subgroups that call out just a subsection of the match. You learn more about this shortly.

Match objects have several other methods. The start method provides the index in the original string where the match began, and the end method provides the index in the original string where the match ended.

The groups and groupdict methods are used to call out subsections of the regular expression. You learn more about these methods later, during a discussion about regular expressions with backreferences.

Finally, the re attribute contains the regular expression used in the match, the string attribute contains the string used as the haystack, and the pos attribute is set to the position in the string where the search began.

Finding More Than One Match

A limitation of re.search is that it only returns at most one match, in the form of a match object (discussed in more detail shortly). If multiple matches exist within the string, re.search will only return the first one. Often, this is exactly what you want. However, sometimes you want multiple matches if multiple matches exist.

The re module provides two functions for this purpose: findall and finditer. Both of these methods return all non-overlapping matches, including empty matches. The re.findall method returns a list, and re.finditer returns a generator.

However, there is a key difference here. These methods do not actually return a match object. Instead, they return simply the match itself, either as a string or a tuple, depending on the content of the regular expression.

Consider an example of findall:

```
>>> import re
>>> re.findall(r'o', 'The quick brown fox jumped...')
['o', 'o']
```

In this case, it returns a list with two o characters, because the o character appears twice in the string.

BASIC REGULAR EXPRESSIONS

The simplest regular expression is one that contains plain alphanumeric characters—and nothing else. This is actually easy to overlook. Many regular expressions use direct text matching.

The string `Python` is a valid regular expression. It matches that word, and nothing else. Regular expressions, by default, are also case-sensitive, so it will not match `python` or `PYTHON`.

```
>>> re.search(r'Python', 'python')
>>> re.search(r'Python', 'PYTHON')
```

It will, however, match the word in a larger block of text. It will match the word in `Python 3`, or `This is Python code`, or the like, as shown here:

```
>>> re.search(r'Python', 'Python 3')
<_sre.SRE_Match object; span=(0, 6), match='Python'>
>>> re.search(r'Python', 'This is Python code.')
<_sre.SRE_Match object; span=(8, 14), match='Python'>
```

Of course, there is essentially no value in using regular expressions just to match plaintext regular expressions. After all, it would be trivially easy to use the `in` operator to test for the presence of a string within another string, and `str.index` is more than up to the task of telling you where in a larger string a substring occurs.

The power of regular expressions lies in their capability to specify patterns of text to be matched.

Character Classes

Character classes enable you to specify that a single character should match one of a set of possible characters, rather than just a single character. You can denote a character class by using square brackets and listing the possible characters within the brackets.

For example, consider a regular expression that should match either `Python` or `python`: `[Pp]ython`.

What is happening here? The first token in the regular expression is actually a character class with two options: `P` and `p`. Either character will match, but nothing else. The remaining five characters are just literal characters.

What does the following regular expression match?

```
>>> re.search(r'[Pp]ython', 'Python 3')
<_sre.SRE_Match object; span=(0, 6), match='Python'>
>>> re.search(r'[Pp]ython', 'python 3')
<_sre.SRE_Match object; span=(0, 6), match='python'>
```

This regular expression matches the word `Python` in the string `Python 3` and the word `python` in the string `python 3`. It does not make the entire word case-insensitive, though. It does not match the word in all caps, for example.

```
>>> re.search(r'[Pp]ython', 'PYTHON 3')
>>>
```

Another use for this kind of character class is for words with multiple spellings. The regular expression `gr[ae]y` will match either `gray` or `grey`, allowing you to quickly identify and extract either spelling.

```
>>> re.search(r'gr[ae]y', 'gray')
<_sre.SRE_Match object; span=(0, 4), match='gray'>
```

It is also worth noting that character classes like this match *one and exactly one* character.

```
>>> re.search(r'gr[ae]y', 'graey')
>>>
```

Here, the regular expression engine successfully matches the literal g, then the literal r. Next, the engine is given the character class [ae], and matches it against the a. Now, the character class has been matched, and the engine moves on. The next character in the regular expression is a y, but the next character in the string is an e. This is not a match, so the regular expression parser moves on, starting over and looking for a starting g. When it gets to the end of the string and fails to find one, it returns None.

Ranges

Some quite common character classes are very large. For example, consider trying to match any digit. It would be quite unwieldy to provide [0123456789] each time. It would be even more unwieldy to provide every letter, both capitalized and lowercase, each time.

To accommodate for this, the regular expression engine uses the hyphen character (-) within character classes to denote ranges. A character class to match any digit could be written [0-9] instead. It is also possible to use more than one range within a character class, simply by providing the ranges next to one another. The [a-z] character class matches only lowercase letters, and the [A-Z] character class matches only capital letters. These can be combined—[A-Za-z] would match both lowercase and capital letters.

```
>>> re.search(r'[a-zA-Z]', 'x')
<_sre.SRE_Match object; span=(0, 1), match='x'>
>>> re.search(r'[a-zA-Z]', 'B')
<_sre.SRE_Match object; span=(0, 1), match='B'>
```

Of course, you may also want to match the literal hyphen character. This is surprisingly common. Many reasons exist to match (for example) alphanumeric characters, hyphen, and underscore. What happens when you want to do this?

You can escape the hyphen: [A-Za-z0-9\-_]. This will tell the regular expression engine that you want a literal hyphen. However, escaping generally makes things more difficult to read. You can also provide the hyphen as either the first or last character in the character class, as in [A-Za-z0-9_-]. In this case, the engine will interpret the character as a literal hyphen.

Negation

The character classes shown thus far are all defined by what characters may occur. However, you may want to define a character class by what characters may not occur.

You can invert a character class (meaning that it will match any character other than those specified) by beginning the character class with a ^ character.

```
>>> re.search(r'[^a-z]', '4')
<_sre.SRE_Match object; span=(0, 1), match='4'>
>>> re.search(r'[^a-z]', '#')
```

```
<_sre.SRE_Match object; span=(0, 1), match='#'>
>>> re.search(r'[^a-z]', 'X')
<_sre.SRE_Match object; span=(0, 1), match='X'>
>>> re.search(r'[^a-z]', 'd')
>>>
```

In this scenario, the regular expression parser looks for literally any character other than a through z. Therefore, it matches against numbers, capital letters, and symbols, but not lowercase letters.

It is important to note specifically what the regular expression is looking for here. It is looking for the presence of a character that does not match any of the characters in the character class. It is not looking for (and will not match) the absence of a character.

Consider the regular expression n[^e]. This means the character n followed by any character that is not an e.

```
>>> re.search(r'n[^e]', 'final')
<_sre.SRE_Match object; span=(2, 4), match='na'>
```

In this case, it matches against the word final, and the match is na. The a character is part of the match, because it is a single character that is not an e.

The regular expression will fail to match if it follows an n followed by an e, as you expect.

```
>>> re.search(r'n[^e]', 'jasmine')
>>>
```

Here, the regular expression engine gets to the only n in the string but cannot match the next character, because it is an e, and thus there is no match.

However, the regular expression also will not match against an n at the end of the string.

```
>>> re.search(r'n[^e]', 'Python')
>>>
```

The regular expression finds the n in the word Python. However, that is as far as it gets. There is no character remaining in the string to match against [^e], and, therefore, the match fails.

Shortcuts

Several common character classes also have predefined shortcuts within the regular expression engine. If you want to define "words," your instinct may be to use [A-Za-z]. However, many words use characters that fall outside of this range.

The regular expression engine provides a shortcut, \w, which matches "any word character." How "any word character" is defined varies somewhat based on your environment. In Python 3, it will essentially match nearly any word character in any language. In Python 2, it will only match the English word characters. In both cases, it also matches digits, _, and -.

The \d shortcut matches digit characters. In Python 3, it matches digit characters in other languages. In Python 2, it matches only [0-9].

The \s shortcut matches whitespace characters, such as space, tab, newline, and so on. The exact list of whitespace characters is greater in Python 3 than in Python 2.

Finally, the \b shortcut matches a zero-length substring. However, it only matches it at the beginning or end of a word. This is called the *word boundary* character shortcut.

```
>>> re.search(r'\bcorn\b', 'corn')
<_sre.SRE_Match object; span=(0, 4), match='corn'>
>>> re.search(r'\bcorn\b', 'corner')
>>>
```

The regular expression engine matches the word corn here when it is by itself, but fails to match the word corner, because the trailing \b does not match (because the next character is e, which is a word character).

It is worth noting that these shortcuts work both within character classes and outside of them. For example, the regular expression \w will match any word character.

```
>>> re.search(r'\w', 'Python 3')
<_sre.SRE_Match object; span=(0, 1), match='P'>
```

Because re.search only returns the first match, it matches the P character and then completes. Consider the result of re.findall using the same regular expression and string.

```
>>> re.findall(r'\w', 'Python 3')
['P', 'y', 't', 'h', 'o', 'n', '3']
```

Note that the regular expression matches every character in the string except the space. The \w shortcut does include digits in the Python regular expression engine.

The \w, \d, and \s shortcuts also include *negation shortcuts:* \W, \D, and \S. These shortcuts match any character other than the characters in the shortcut. Note again that these still require a character to be present. They do not match an empty string.

There is also a negation shortcut for \b, but it works slightly differently. Whereas \b matches a zero-length substring at the beginning or end of a word, \B matches a zero-length substring that is not at the beginning or end of a word. This essentially reverses the corn and corner example from earlier.

```
>>> re.search(r'corn\B', 'corner')
<_sre.SRE_Match object; span=(0, 4), match='corn'>
>>> re.search(r'corn\B', 'corn')
>>>
```

Beginning and End of String

Two special characters designate the beginning of a string and end of a string.

The ^ character designates the beginning of a string, as shown here:

```
>>> re.search(r'^Python', 'This code is in Python.')
>>> re.search(r'^Python', 'Python 3')
<_sre.SRE_Match object; span=(0, 6), match='Python'>
```

Notice that the first command fails to produce a match. This is because the string does not start with the word Python, and the ^ character requires that the regular expression match against the beginning of the string.

Similarly, the `$` character designates the end of a string, as shown here:

```
>>> re.search(r'fox$', 'The quick brown fox jumped over the lazy dogs.')
>>> re.search(r'fox$', 'The quick brown fox')
<_sre.SRE_Match object; span=(16, 19), match='fox'>
```

Again, notice that the first command fails to produce a match, because although the word `fox` appears, it is not at the end of the string, which the `$` character requires.

Any Character

The `.` character is the final shortcut character. It stands in for any single character. However, it only serves this role outside a bracketed character class.

Consider the following simple regex using the `.` character:

```
>>> re.search(r'p.th.n', 'python 3')
<_sre.SRE_Match object; span=(0, 6), match='python'>
>>> re.search(r'p..hon', 'python 3')
<_sre.SRE_Match object; span=(0, 6), match='python'>
```

In each of these cases, the period steps in for one single character. In the first example, the regular expression engine finds the character `.` in the regular expression. In the string, it sees a `y`, and matches and continues to the next character (a `t` against a `t`).

In the second case, the same fundamental thing is happening. Each period character matches *one and exactly one* character. It matches the `y` and the `t`, and then this consumes both of the periods, and the regular expression engine continues to the next character (this time, an `h` against an `h`).

Note that there is one character that the `.` does not match, which is newline (`\n`). It is possible to make the `.` character match newline, however, which is discussed later in this chapter.

Optional Characters

Thus far, all of the regular expressions you have seen have involved a 1:1 correlation between characters in the regular expression itself and characters in the string being searched.

Sometimes, however, a character may be optional. Consider again the example of a word with more than one correct spelling, but this time, the inclusion of a letter is what separates the two spellings, such as "color" and "colour," or "honor" and "honour."

You can specify a character, character class, or other atomic unit within a regular expression as optional by using the `?` character, which means that the regular expression engine will expect the token to occur either zero times or once.

For example, you can match the word "honor" with its British spelling "honour" by using the regular expression `honou?r`.

```
>>> import re
>>> re.search(r'honou?r', 'He served with honor and distinction.')
<_sre.SRE_Match object; span=(15, 20), match='honor'>
>>> re.search(r'honou?r', 'He served with honour and distinction.')
<_sre.SRE_Match object; span=(15, 21), match='honour'>
```

In both cases, the regular expression contains four literal characters, hono. These match the hono in both honor and honour. The next thing that the regular expression hits is an optional u. In the first case, the u is absent, but this is okay because the regular expression marks it as optional. In the second case, the u is present, which is also okay. In both cases, the regular expression then seeks a literal r character, which it finds, therefore completing the match.

Repetition

Thus far, you have learned only about characters (or character classes) that occur once and exactly once, or that are entirely optional (occurring zero times or once). However, sometimes you need the same character or character class to repeat.

You may expect a character class to recur a set number of consecutive times, such as in a phone number. American phone numbers comprise the country code 1 (often omitted), an area code, which is three digits, then the seven-digit phone number, with the third and fourth digit of the latter separated by a hyphen, period, or similar.

You can designate that a token must repeat a given number of times with {N}, where the N character corresponds to the number of times the token should repeat.

The following uses a regular expression to identify a seven-digit, local phone number (ignore the country code and area code for the moment): [\d]{3}-[\d]{4}.

```
>>> re.search(r'[\d]{3}-[\d]{4}', '867-5309 / Jenny')
<_sre.SRE_Match object; span=(0, 8), match='867-5309'>
```

In this case, the regular expression engine starts by looking for three consecutive digits. It finds them (867), and then moves on to the literal hyphen character. Because this hyphen character is not within a character class, it carries no special meaning and simply matches the literal hyphen. The regular expression then finds the final four consecutive digits (5309) and returns the match.

Repetition Ranges

Sometimes, you may not know exactly how many times the token ought to repeat. Phone numbers may contain a static number of digits, but lots of numeric data is not standardized this way.

For example, consider credit card security codes. Credit cards issued in the United States contain a special security code on the back, often called a "CVV code." Most credit card brands use three-digit security codes, which you can match with [\d]{3}. However, American Express uses four-digit security codes ([\d]{4}).

What if you want to be able to match both of these cases? Repetition ranges come in handy here. The syntax here is {M,N}, where M is the lower bound and N is the upper bound.

It is worth noting here that the bounds are inclusive. If you want to match three digits or four digits, the correct syntax is [\d]{3,4}. You might be tempted (based on using Python slices) to believe that the upper bound is exclusive (and that you should use {3,5} instead). However, regular expressions do not work this way.

```
>>> re.search(r'[\d]{3,4}', '0421')
<_sre.SRE_Match object; span=(0, 4), match='0421'>
```

```
>>> re.search(r'[\d]{3,4}', '615')
<_sre.SRE_Match object; span=(0, 3), match='615'>
```

In both cases, the regular expression engine finds a series of digits that matches what it expects, and returns a match.

When given the choice to match three characters *or* four characters, where either is a valid match, how does the regular expression engine decide? The answer is that, under most circumstances, the regular expression engine is "greedy," meaning that it will match as many characters as possible for as long as it can. In this simple case, that means that if there are four digits, four digits will be matched.

Occasionally, this behavior is undesirable. By placing a ? character immediately after the repetition operator, it causes that repetition to be considered "lazy," meaning that the engine will match as few characters as possible to return a valid match.

```
>>> re.search(r'[\d]{3,4}?', '0421')
<_sre.SRE_Match object; span=(0, 3), match='042'>
```

The re-use of the ? character for another purpose does not cause any ambiguity for the parser, because the character comes after repetition syntax, rather than a token to be matched against.

Note that the ? in this situation *does not* serve to make the repeated segment optional. It simply means that, given the opportunity to match three or four digits, it will elect only to match three.

> **NOTE** *Note that the* ? *character used to make a token optional is essentially an exact alias for* {0,1}.

Open-Ended Ranges

You also may encounter cases where there is no upper bound for the number of times that a token may repeat. For example, consider a traditional street address. This usually starts with a number (for the moment, hand-wave the exceptions and assert that they always do), but the number could be any arbitrary length. There is nothing technically invalid about an eight-digit street number.

In these cases, you can leave off the upper bound, but retain the , character to designate that the upper bound is ∞. For example, {1,} designates one or more occurrences with no upper bound.

```
>>> re.search(r'[\d]{1,}', '1600 Pennsylvania Ave.')
<_sre.SRE_Match object; span=(0, 4), match='1600'>
```

This syntax also works if you do not want to specify a lower bound, in which case, the lower bound is assumed to be 0.

Shorthand

You can use two shorthand characters in designating common repetition situations. You can use the + character in lieu of specifying {1,} (one or more). Similarly, you can use the * character in lieu of specifying {0,} (zero or more).

Therefore, the previous example could be rewritten using +, as shown here:

```
>>> re.search(r'[\d]+', '1600 Pennsylvania Ave.')
<_sre.SRE_Match object; span=(0, 4), match='1600'>
```

Using + and * generally makes for a regular expression that is easier to read, and is the preferred syntax in cases where they are applicable.

GROUPING

Regular expressions provide a mechanism to split the expression into groups. When using groups, you are able to select each individual group within the match in addition to getting the entire match. You can specify groups within a regular expression by using parentheses.

The following is an example of a simple, local phone number. However, this time, each set of digits is a group.

```
>>> match = re.search(r'([\d]{3})-([\d]{4})', '867-5309 / Jenny')
>>> match
<_sre.SRE_Match object; span=(0, 8), match='867-5309'>
```

As before, you can use the group method on the match object to return the entire match.

```
>>> match.group()
'867-5309'
```

The re module's match objects provide a method, groups, which returns a tuple corresponding to each individual group.

```
>>> match.groups()
('867', '5309')
```

By breaking your regular expression into subgroups like this, you can quickly get not just the entire match, but specific bits of data within the match.

It is also possible to get just a single group, by passing an argument to the group method corresponding to the group you want back (note that group numbers are 1-indexed).

```
>>> match.group(2)
'5309'
```

By using groups, you can take a phone number formatted in a variety of different ways and extract only the data that matters, which is the actual digits of a phone number.

```
>>> re.search(
...     r'(\+?1)?[ .-]?\(?([\d]{3})\)?[ .-]?([\d]{3})[ .-]?([\d]{4})',
...     '(213) 867-5309')
<_sre.SRE_Match object; span=(0, 14), match='(213) 867-5309'>

>>> re.search(
...     r'(\+?1)?[ .-]?\(?([\d]{3})\)?[ .-]?([\d]{3})[ .-]?([\d]{4})',
...     '213-867-5309')
<_sre.SRE_Match object; span=(0, 12), match='213-867-5309'>

>>> re.search(
```

```
...         r'(\+?1)?[ .-]?\(?([\d]{3})\)?[ .-]?([\d]{3})[ .-]?([\d]{4})',
...         '213.867.5309')
<_sre.SRE_Match object; span=(0, 12), match='213.867.5309'>

>>> re.search(
...         r'(\+?1)?[ .-]?\(?([\d]{3})\)?[ .-]?([\d]{3})[ .-]?([\d]{4})',
...         '2138675309')
<_sre.SRE_Match object; span=(0, 10), match='2138675309'>

>>> re.search(
...         r'(\+?1)?[ .-]?\(?([\d]{3})\)?[ .-]?([\d]{3})[ .-]?([\d]{4})', '+1
...         (213) 867-5309')
<_sre.SRE_Match object; span=(0, 17), match='+1 (213) 867-5309'>

>>> re.search(
...         r'(\+?1)?[ .-]?\(?([\d]{3})\)?[ .-]?([\d]{3})[ .-]?([\d]{4})', '1
...         (213) 867-5309')
<_sre.SRE_Match object; span=(0, 16), match='1 (213) 867-5309'>

>>> re.search(
...         r'(\+?1)?[ .-]?\(?([\d]{3})\)?[ .-]?([\d]{3})[ .-]?([\d]{4})',
...         '1-213-867-5309')
<_sre.SRE_Match object; span=(0, 14), match='1-213-867-5309'>
```

This regular expression is a bit more complicated than what you have encountered already. Consider each distinct part by itself, however, and it is easier to parse.

The first segment is `(\+?1)?[ .-]?`. This is first looking for the United States country code in almost any format you may encounter it (+1 or 1, and then possibly a hyphen).

The second segment is `\(?([\d]{3})\)?[ .-]?`, and it grabs the area code, and the optional hyphen or whitespace that may follow it. The area code may optionally be provided in parentheses (as is common with U.S. phone numbers).

The remainder of the regular expression is the final seven digits of the phone number, and is the same as what you have already seen.

Regardless of how the phone number is formatted, the regular expression is capable of matching it. And although the full match is still formatted based on the original data provided, the groups are consistently the same.

```
>>> match = re.search(
...         r'(\+?1)?[ .-]?\(?([\d]{3})\)?[ .-]?([\d]{3})[ .-]?([\d]{4})',
...         '213-867-5309')
>>> match.groups()
(None, '213', '867', '5309')

>>> match = re.search(
...         r'(\+?1)?[ .-]?\(?([\d]{3})\)?[ .-]?([\d]{3})[ .-]?([\d]{4})',
...         '+1 213-867-5309')
>>> match.groups()
('+1', '213', '867', '5309')
```

The only difference between the groups is based on what was provided for the country code. If it is omitted, then it is not captured either, and `None` is provided in its place. The second through fourth groups consistently contain the three (intra-national) segments of the phone number.

The Zero Group

Up until this point, the examples have consistently used the `group` method to return the entire match, rather than just a single group. In fact, it may seem like very odd nomenclature indeed to have to call the `group` method to get back the entire match in the first place.

Why does it work this way? The purpose of the `group` is actually to return a single group from the match. It takes an optional argument, which is the number of the group to return. If the argument is omitted (as the examples had consistently been doing), it defaults to `0`.

In regular expressions, the groups are counted based on their position in the regular expression, starting with `1`.

The `0` group is special, and corresponds to the entire match. This is why groups are 1-indexed. By calling `group` with no argument, you are asking for group `0` and, therefore, getting the entire match back.

Named Groups

In addition to having positionally numbered groups, the Python regular expression engine also provides a mechanism for naming groups. This functionality was actually originally introduced by the Python regular expression implementation, although many other languages have picked it up at this point.

The syntax for a named group is to add `?P<group_name>` immediately after the opening `(` character. You could specify the local phone number regular expression to use named groups by rewriting it as `(?P<first_three>[\d]{3})-(?P<last_four>[\d]{4}`.

```
>>> match = re.search(r'(?P<first_three>[\d]{3})-(?P<last_four>[\d]{4})',
...                    '867-5309')
>>> match
<_sre.SRE_Match object; span=(0, 8), match='867-5309'>
```

First of all, note that named groups are also still positional groups. You can (if you choose) still look up the groups this way:

```
>>> match.groups()
('867', '5309')
>>> match.group(1)
'867'
```

Using named groups opens up two more ways to look up a group. First, the name of the group can be passed as a string to the `group` method.

```
>>> match.group('first_three')
'867'
```

Additionally, match objects provide a `groupdict` method. This method is similar in most ways to the `groups` method, except that it returns a dictionary instead of a tuple, and the dictionary keys correspond to the names of the groups.

```
>>> match.groupdict()
{'first_three': '867', 'last_four': '5309'}
```

It is worth noting that groupdict, like groups, does not return the entire match; it only returns the subgroups. Also, if you have a mix of named groups and unnamed groups, the unnamed groups are not part of the dictionary returned by groupdict.

```
>>> match = re.search(r'(?P<first_three>[\d]{3})-([\d]{4})', '867-5309')
>>> match.groups()
('867', '5309')
>>> match.groupdict()
{'first_three': '867'}
```

In this case, only the first group (named first_three) is a named group, and the second group is a numbered group only. Therefore, when groups is called, both groups are returned in the tuple. However, when groupdict is called, only the first_three group is included in the result.

Named groups are quite valuable for maintenance reasons. You may reference a group in code later. If you use primarily named groups, adding a new group to the regular expression to account for a change does not then require updating group numbers later in code, because the existing names stay the same.

Referencing Existing Groups

The regular expression engine also provides a mechanism to reference a previously matched group. Sometimes, you may be looking for a subsequent occurrence of the same submatch.

For example, if you are trying to parse a block of XML, you may want to very permissively look for any valid opening tag, such as <([\w_-]+)>. However, you want to ensure that the same closing tag exists.

It is insufficient to simply repeat this pattern a second time. On the one hand, it will correctly match patterns that you want.

```
>>> re.search(r'<([\w_-]+)>stuff</([\w_-]+)>', '<foo>stuff</foo>')
<_sre.SRE_Match object; span=(0, 16), match='<foo>stuff</foo>'>
```

On the other hand, it would also match patterns that should not actually match.

```
>>> match = re.search(r'<([\w_-]+)>stuff</([\w_-]+)>', '<foo>stuff</bar>')
>>> match
<_sre.SRE_Match object; span=(0, 16), match='<foo>stuff</bar>'>
>>> match.group(1)
'foo'
>>> match.group(2)
'bar'
```

Here, the regular expression engine correctly sees <foo> as an opening XML tag, matches it, and assigns the text foo to the subgroup. It then matches the literal characters stuff, and then goes to match the closing XML tag.

At this point, what you intuitively want is for the match to fail, because the closing XML tag is </bar>, which is not the same as the opening tag of <foo>.

The regular expression engine does not do that, however. It has simply been told to match the `</` and `>` wrapping characters, and then word characters in between. Because bar fulfills this requirement, the engine matches it, assigns it to the second subgroup, and returns a match.

What you really want at this point is for the regular expression engine to require the same submatch as was used in the first group. This should make a string of `<foo>stuff</foo>` match, but a string of `<foo>stuff</bar>` fail to match.

The regular expression engine provides a way to do this using *backreferences*. Backreferences refer to a previously matched group within a regular expression, and cause the regular expression parser to expect the same match text to occur again.

You backreference numbered groups using `\N`, where N is the group number. Therefore, `\1` will match the first group, `\2` the second group, and so on. This syntax is capable of matching up to the first 99 groups.

Consider the following XML regular expression that uses a backreference:

```
>>> match = re.search(r'<([\w_-]+)>stuff</\1>', '<foo>stuff</foo>')
>>> match
<_sre.SRE_Match object; span=(0, 16), match='<foo>stuff</foo>'>
>>> match.groups()
('foo',)
```

Notice that there is only one subgroup now. In the previous example, there were two, both containing the text foo. In this case, however, a backreference has replaced the second group.

A much more important distinction, however, is what this regular expression does not match.

```
>>> re.search(r'<([\w_-]+)>stuff</\1>', '<foo>stuff</bar>')
>>>
```

In this case, the regular expression engine successfully matches up to the closing XML tag. However, because bar is not the same text as foo, the match fails.

> **WARNING** *You should not actually use custom regular expressions to parse XML. Use* lxml *or a similar tool instead. For parsing HTML, use a package like* BeautifulSoup. *The purpose of this example is solely to explain how this type of backreference works.*

LOOKAHEAD

Earlier, you learned about negated character classes, which enable you to match any character other than those in the class. As mentioned before, this method makes the character or characters matched by the negated character class be part of the match, and it will not match the absence of any character at all.

There is, however, a mechanism to accept or reject a match based on the presence or absence of content after it, without making the subsequent content part of the match. This is called *lookahead*.

The previous example of a negated character class was n[^e]—an n followed by a character that is not an e. This matched na in final, failed to match anything in jasmine, and failed to match anything in Python.

A similar regular expression that instead uses negative lookahead would employ the syntax n(?!e).

```
>>> re.search(r'n(?!e)', 'final')
<_sre.SRE_Match object; span=(2, 3), match='n'>
>>> re.search(r'n(?!e)', 'jasmine')
>>> re.search(r'n(?!e)', 'Python')
<_sre.SRE_Match object; span=(5, 6), match='n'>
```

These results are slightly different than when a negated character class was used. In the first example, using the word final, the regular expression again matches, but the match is different. While the negated character class made the a character part of the match, negative lookahead does not, and the match comes back as just the n character.

The second result is the most similar. The n in jasmine matches the n character in the regular expression. However, because the n is followed by an e, it is disqualified, and the match fails.

The final result is the most different, because this match actually succeeds, where it did not with a negated character class. The regular expression engine matches the n in Python. It then reaches the end of the string. Because that n is not followed by an e, the match succeeds and is returned.

It is worth noting that while this may look like group syntax, in this case, a group is not saved.

```
>>> match = re.search(r'n(?!e)', 'final')
>>> match
<_sre.SRE_Match object; span=(2, 3), match='n'>
>>> match.groups()
()
```

The regular expression engine also supports a different kind of lookahead, called a *positive lookahead*. This requires that the match be followed by the character or characters in question, but nonetheless does not make those characters part of the match.

The syntax for positive lookahead simply replaces the ! character with =. Consider this regular expression:

```
>>> re.search(r'n(?=e)', 'jasmine')
<_sre.SRE_Match object; span=(5, 6), match='n'>
```

In this case, the regular expression engine matches the n in the word jasmine. After doing so, it verifies that the subsequent character is an e, as the regular expression requires. Because it is, the match is complete and returned. As before, no group is created by the lookahead.

Without the e, the match fails, as shown here:

```
>>> re.search(r'n(?=e)', 'jasmin')
>>>
```

In this case, the regular expression engine again matches the n, but disqualifies the match because it is not followed by an e.

FLAGS

Sometimes, you need to slightly tweak the behavior of the regular expression engine. The regular expression engines in most languages, including Python, offer a small number of flags that modify the behavior of the entire expression.

The Python engine offers several flags that can be sent to a regular expression when using `re.search` or similar functions. In the case of `re.search`, it takes a third argument for flags.

Case Insensitivity

The simplest and most straightforward flag is `re.IGNORECASE`, which causes the regular expression to become case-insensitive.

```
>>> re.search(r'python', 'PYTHON IS AWESOME', re.IGNORECASE)
<_sre.SRE_Match object; span=(0, 6), match='PYTHON'>
```

When using `re.IGNORECASE`, the match will still be returned using the case of the string in which it was found, and not the case of the regular expression.

`re.IGNORECASE` is also aliased to `re.I`.

ASCII and Unicode

You may recall that there is a difference between how some character shortcuts work between Python 2 and Python 3. For example, `\w` in Python 3 matches word characters in nearly any language, rather than just the Latin alphabet.

The `re` module provides flags to make Python 2 follow the Python 3 behavior, and also flags to make Python 3 follow the Python 2 behavior.

The `re.UNICODE` (aliased to `re.U`) flag forces the regular expression engine to follow the Python 3 behavior. This flag is defined in both Python 2 and Python 3, so it is safe to use it in code designed to run on either platform. Note that if you try to use a byte string with `re.U` in Python 3, the parser will raise an exception.

The `re.ASCII` (aliased to `re.A`) flag forces the regular expression to follow the Python 2 behavior. Unlike `re.UNICODE`, the `re.ASCII` flag is not available in Python 2. If you need `re.ASCII` in code that runs under both Python 2 and Python 3, use the appropriate character classes instead, or do a version check before applying the flag.

Dot Matching Newline

The `re.DOTALL` flag (aliased to `re.S` to match the terminology used in Perl and elsewhere) causes the `.` character to match newline characters in addition to all other characters.

```
>>> re.search(r'.+', 'foo\nbar')
<_sre.SRE_Match object; span=(0, 3), match='foo'>
>>> re.search(r'.+', 'foo\nbar', re.DOTALL)
<_sre.SRE_Match object; span=(0, 7), match='foo\nbar'>
```

In the first command, the regular expression engine must match one or more of any character. It matches `foo`, and then it reaches a line break and stops, because `.` does not normally match line breaks.

However, in the second command, `re.DOTALL` is passed, and the line break character is included in what `.` matches against. Therefore, the regular expression engine (being greedy) keeps going until it reaches end of string, and the entire string is returned as the match.

Multiline Mode

The `re.MULTILINE` flag (aliased to `re.M`) causes the `^` and `$` characters, which normally would only match against the beginning or end of the string (respectively), to instead match against the beginning or end of any line within the string.

```
>>> re.search(r'^bar', 'foo\nbar')
>>> re.search(r'^bar', 'foo\nbar', re.MULTILINE)
<_sre.SRE_Match object; span=(4, 7), match='bar'>
```

In the first command, the `^` character is only able to match against the beginning of the string. Therefore, the word `bar` does not match, because it is not the first thing in the string.

In the second command, however, the `re.MULTILINE` flag is used. Therefore, the `^` character merely requires the beginning of a line. Because a newline character immediately precedes `bar`, it matches and the match is returned.

Verbose Mode

The `re.VERBOSE` flag (aliased to `re.X`) allows for complicated regular expressions to be expressed in a more readable way.

This flag does two things. First, it causes all whitespace (other than in character classes) to be ignored, including line breaks. Second, it treats the `#` character (again, unless it's inside a character class) as a comment character.

This allows for easy annotation of regular expressions, which can be valuable as they become complicated. The following two commands are equivalent:

```
>>> re.search(r'(?P<first_three>[\d]{3})-(?P<last_four>[\d]{4})', '867-5309')
<_sre.SRE_Match object; span=(0, 8), match='867-5309'>
>>> re.search(r"""(?P<first_three>[\d]{3})    # The first three digits
...                  -                         # A literal hyphen
...                  (?P<last_four>[\d]{4})     # The last four digits
...           """, '867-5309', re.VERBOSE)
<_sre.SRE_Match object; span=(0, 8), match='867-5309'>
```

Debug Mode

The `re.DEBUG` flag (not aliased) dumps some debugging information out to `sys.stderr` while compiling a regular expression.

```
>>> re.search(r'(?P<first_three>[\d]{3})-(?P<last_four>[\d]{4})',
        '867-5309', re.DEBUG)
subpattern 1
  max_repeat 3 3
```

```
        in
           category category_digit
literal 45
subpattern 2
   max_repeat 4 4
      in
         category category_digit
<_sre.SRE_Match object; span=(0, 8), match='867-5309'>
```

Using Multiple Flags

Occasionally, you may need to use more than one of these flags at once. To do this, join them with the | (bitwise OR) operator. For example, if you need both the re.DOTALL and re.MULTILINE flags, the correct syntax is re.DOTALL | re.MULTILINE or re.S | re.M.

Inline Flags

It is also possible to use flags within a regular expression itself by beginning the regular expression with special syntax. This uses the short-form flag, and looks like this:

```
>>> re.search('(?i)FOO', 'foo').group()
'foo'
```

Note the (?i) at the beginning. This is the equivalent of using the re.IGNORECASE flag. However, this syntax is usually less preferable to sending flags explicitly. Also, the long form of the flags will not work. (?ignorecase) is not valid and will raise an exception.

SUBSTITUTION

The regular expression engine is not limited to simply identifying whether a pattern exists within a string. It is also capable of performing string replacement, returning a new string based on the groups in the original one.

The substitution method in Python is re.sub. It takes three arguments: the regular expression, the replacement string, and the source string being searched. Only the actual match is replaced, so if there is no match, re.sub ends up being a no-op.

re.sub enables you to use the same backreferences from regular expression patterns within the replacement string. Consider the task of stripping irrelevant formatting data from a phone number:

```
>>> re.sub(r'(\+?1)?[ .-]?\(?([\d]{3})\)?[ .-]?([\d]{3})[ .-]?([\d]{4})',
...        r'\2\3\4',
...        '213-867-5309')
'2138675309'
```

Because this regular expression matches nearly any phone number and groups only the actual digits of the phone number, you will get back the same data regardless of how the original number was formatted.

```
>>> re.sub(r'(\+?1)?[ .-]?\(?([\d]{3})\)?[ .-]?([\d]{3})[ .-]?([\d]{4})',
...        r'\2\3\4',
...        '213.867.5309')
'2138675309'
```

```
>>> re.sub(r'(\+?1)?[ .-]?\(?([\d]{3})\)?[ .-]?([\d]{3})[ .-]?([\d]{4})',
...         r'\2\3\4',
...         '2138675309')
'2138675309'

>>> re.sub(r'(\+?1)?[ .-]?\(?([\d]{3})\)?[ .-]?([\d]{3})[ .-]?([\d]{4})',
...         r'\2\3\4',
...         '(213) 867-5309')
'2138675309'

>>> re.sub(r'(\+?1)?[ .-]?\(?([\d]{3})\)?[ .-]?([\d]{3})[ .-]?([\d]{4})',
...         r'\2\3\4',
...         '1 (213) 867-5309')
'2138675309'

>>> re.sub(r'(\+?1)?[ .-]?\(?([\d]{3})\)?[ .-]?([\d]{3})[ .-]?([\d]{4})',
...         r'\2\3\4',
...         '+1 213-867-5309')
'2138675309'
```

The replacement string is not limited to just using the backreferences from the string; other characters are interpreted literally. Therefore, re.sub can also be used for formatting. For example, what if you want to display a phone number rather than store it, but you want to display it in a consistent format? re.sub can handle that, as shown here:

```
>>> re.sub(r'(\+?1)?[ .-]?\(?([\d]{3})\)?[ .-]?([\d]{3})[ .-]?([\d]{4})',
...         r'(\2) \3-\4',
...         '+1 213-867-5309')
'(213) 867-5309'
```

Everything here is the same as in the previous examples, except for the replacement string, which has gained the parentheses, space, and hyphen. Therefore, so has the result.

COMPILED REGULAR EXPRESSIONS

One final feature of Python's regular expression implementation is *compiled regular expressions*. The re module contains a function, compile, which returns a compiled regular expression object, which can then be reused.

The re module caches regular expressions that it compiles on the fly, so in most situations, there is no substantial performance advantage to using compile. It can be extremely useful for passing regular expression objects around, however.

The re.compile function returns a regular expression object, with the compiled regular expression as data. These objects have their own search and sub methods, which omit the first argument (the regular expression itself).

```
>>> regex = re.compile(
...     r'(\+?1)?[ .-]?\(?([\d]{3})\)?[ .-]?([\d]{3})[ .-]?([\d]{4})'
... )
>>> regex.search('213-867-5309')
```

```
<_sre.SRE_Match object; span=(0, 12), match='213-867-5309'>
>>> regex.sub(r'(\2) \3-\4', '+1 213.867.5309')
'(213) 867-5309'
```

Also, there is one other advantage to using `re.compile`. The `search` method of regular expression objects actually allows for two additional arguments not available on `re.search`. These are the starting and ending positions of the string to be searched against, enabling you to exempt some of the string from consideration.

```
>>> regex = re.compile('[\d]+')
>>> regex.search('1 mile is equal to 5280 feet.')
<_sre.SRE_Match object; span=(0, 1), match='1'>
>>> regex.search('1 mile is equal to 5280 feet.', pos=2)
<_sre.SRE_Match object; span=(19, 23), match='5280'>
```

The values sent are available as the `pos` and `endpos` attributes on the match objects returned.

SUMMARY

Regular expressions are extremely useful tools for finding, parsing, and validating data. They often look intimidating to those who have not used them before, but they are manageable if taken piece by piece.

In addition, mastering regular expressions will enable you to perform parsing and formatting tasks that are much more difficult without a pattern-matching algorithm.

However, be wary of using regular expressions when they are unnecessary. Sometimes, using a few lines of code with direct string comparison is much more straightforward. Like any tool, regular expressions should be used when they are the appropriate solution, but not when simpler approaches are available to you.

Similarly, bear in mind that regular expressions are often unsuitable for parsing extremely complex structures. If you are parsing a non-trivial document format, you should probably be looking for another library that handles that for you.

Chapter 10 examines testing applications in Python.

PART IV
Everything Else

10

Python 2 Versus Python 3

In several chapters of this book (particularly Chapter 5, "Metaclasses," and Chapter 8, "Strings and Unicode"), you have learned about the differences that exist in the way that Python 2 and Python 3 handle some things.

In fact, Python 3 is a very substantial update to the Python programming language. Throughout its history, Python has stressed strong backward compatibility, eschewing changes that are likely to break large amounts of existing code. That does not mean that the language never deprecates anything, of course, but backward compatibility is a strong focus.

Python 3.0 is an exception to this. Like developers of any complex language or system, the developers of Python made certain decisions that they later viewed as mistakes. Therefore, Python 3.0 can properly be seen as an endeavor to fix mistakes at the expense of backward compatibility.

Because existing Python programs are so pervasive, both Python 2 and Python 3 have been supported for some time—to allow the ecosystem time to migrate from the old to the new. Python 2.6 was released roughly concurrently with Python 3.0, and Python 2.7 roughly a year and a half later (a full year after the release of Python 3.1).

Currently, Python 2.7 and even Python 2.6 are still in common use. Therefore, it is important to understand the differences between Python 2 and Python 3, and how to navigate both.

This chapter explores what distinguishes Python 2 and Python 3, and discusses strategies for navigating the dual ecosystem.

CROSS-COMPATIBILITY STRATEGIES

Python 3 introduces a series of backward-incompatible changes (as well as many backward-compatible ones, but this chapter will not focus much on those). Most of these backward-incompatible changes either focus on removing ambiguity, ensuring that there is a single and coherent approach to solving problems, simply updating the language to address quirks, or making Python's behavior more modern.

Because Python 3 was not intended to be a backward-compatible release, there is no expectation that Python 2 code should be able to run unmodified on Python 3. In fact, many valid Python 2 modules will not run in Python 3, or may produce different results, and some may even contain syntax errors.

That said, you can use several strategies to write code for both ecosystems.

The __*future*__ Module

In some cases, useful Python 3 behavior is able to be "back-ported" into Python 2.6 and Python 2.7. You do this using the __future__ module, which has been in the Python language for some time.

The __future__ module provides a mechanism to introduce a feature into the Python language slowly, allowing the feature to be opted into at first, and then eventually becoming the language's default behavior.

For example, this module was used when yield and later with were being added as keywords to Python. Because adding a new keyword to the language will break existing code that may use either term as a variable name, these keywords were introduced slowly. For one Python release, it was possible to opt-in to the new keyword by using a statement such as the following:

```
from __future__ import with_statement
```

In the case of with, this statement became available in Python 2.5. Using it made both with and as become keywords. If you ran code that used either word as an identifier, you would get a warning. Then, in Python 2.6, with and as were always keywords. However, even then, importing with_statement from __future__ is still valid (it is simply a no-op). This allows code that uses with to run in both Python 2.5 and in later versions.

This same principle applies to many features introduced in Python 3. It is possible to opt-in to some or all of their functionality in Python 2.6 and Python 2.7, which makes writing code for both ecosystems more manageable.

As this chapter iterates over specific behaviors that are distinct in Python 2 and Python 3, you will learn about those that can be opted into in Python 2 using this method.

2to3

When Python 3 was first released, the recommended mechanism to handle sharing source code between Python 2 and Python 3 was by using a tool called 2to3.

2to3 is a command-line application that ships with current versions of Python. Its purpose is to attempt to take a module written for Python 2 and provide a patch to convert it into a Python 3 module, or even convert the module automatically. A similar tool, 3to2, is also available (on PyPI) to do the converse.

Consider the following conversion of foo.py, which is a very simple, one-line Python 2 module:

```
$ cat foo.py
print 'foo'
```

This particular module is valid in Python 2 and breaks in Python 3, because `print` in Python 3 is a function rather than a statement (more on that later). Therefore, what works in Python 2 is a syntax error in Python 3.

```
$ python2.7 foo.py
foo
$ python3.4 foo.py
  File "foo.py", line 1
    print 'foo'
              ^
SyntaxError: invalid syntax
```

This is a very straightforward (albeit backward-incompatible) change, and while it may be arduous to try to change this manually throughout an entire codebase, it is something that 2to3 can handle. By running 2to3 on this file, you get some information about what 2to3 thinks must be done.

```
$ 2to3 foo.py
RefactoringTool: Skipping implicit fixer: buffer
RefactoringTool: Skipping implicit fixer: idioms
RefactoringTool: Skipping implicit fixer: set_literal
RefactoringTool: Skipping implicit fixer: ws_comma
RefactoringTool: Refactored foo.py
--- foo.py      (original)
+++ foo.py      (refactored)
@@ -1 +1 @@
-print 'foo'
+print('foo')
RefactoringTool: Files that need to be modified:
RefactoringTool: foo.py
```

By default, 2to3 does not actually do anything. It just tells you what must be done and offers patches. Here, it has found the `print` statement on line 1 and changed it to a function, told you about it, but it didn't actually modify the file and change code (as discussed in the next section).

```
$ cat foo.py
print 'foo'
```

Writing Changes

However, 2to3 is able to write changes that it is certain of. The simplest way to do this is to add a -w flag, which will overwrite the files in-place. (Note again that it will overwrite the files in-place, so you should understand what you are doing.)

```
$ 2to3 -w foo.py
RefactoringTool: Skipping implicit fixer: buffer
RefactoringTool: Skipping implicit fixer: idioms
RefactoringTool: Skipping implicit fixer: set_literal
RefactoringTool: Skipping implicit fixer: ws_comma
RefactoringTool: Refactored foo.py
--- foo.py      (original)
+++ foo.py      (refactored)
@@ -1 +1 @@
-print 'foo'
+print('foo')
RefactoringTool: Files that were modified:
RefactoringTool: foo.py
```

Sure enough, the actual `foo.py` file has been modified on-disk, and now it runs without error in Python 3.

```
$ cat foo.py
print('foo')
$ python3.4 foo.py
foo
```

Limitations

Unfortunately, the `2to3` tool cannot handle every conceivable situation, so simply running `2to3` on a module is not a guarantee that any valid Python 2 module will magically become a valid Python 3 module.

The way that `2to3` works under the hood is that it contains a number of *fixers*, which is its term for a translation layer between certain Python 2 code and its equivalent Python 3 code. For example, there is a fixer called `print` that handles the conversion from `print` statements to `print` functions. It is even possible to enable or disable specific fixers (with `--fix` and `--nofix`, respectively).

Another more fundamental limitation to `2to3` is that using it fundamentally requires the maintenance of two separate codebases, one for Python 2 and one for Python 3. The official recommendation when using `2to3` is that you simply write Python 2 code and constantly convert it to Python 3 for deployment. In practice though, this gets frustrating and is not really viable for most large projects.

There is a better way.

six

`six` is a Python module written by Benjamin Peterson that is intended to provide single-source compatibility between Python 2 and Python 3. In `2to3`, code is written for Python 2, and then a program runs and generates similar Python 3 code. However, `six` follows a different philosophy. Using `six`, you write a single module in Python 3 syntax that also happens to run correctly on Python 2.6 and Python 2.7.

This approach offers several advantages over `2to3`, but the most important distinction is that only one copy of the code must be maintained. The same code runs in both environments. Additionally, `six` is distributed as a single module, making it very easy to include without relying on a dependency manager if needed.

What `six` fundamentally does is provide a unified interface to elements that have changed between Python 2 and Python 3. For example, you learned in Chapter 8 that Python 2's `unicode` class is the same as Python 3's `str` class. The `six` module provides `six.text_type`, which maps to the correct class in either environment.

For example, the following two lines of code are identical in Python 3:

```
>>> str('foo')
>>> six.text_type('foo')
```

Additionally, the following two lines of code are identical in Python 2:

```
>>> unicode('foo')
>>> six.text_type('foo')
```

They key limitation to `six` is that it is often only a viable approach if you do not have to support any version of Python before Python 2.6. Although `six` itself will run previous versions of Python, the inability to backport some Python 3 features from __future__ in Python 2.5 and older means that it is very difficult to ensure consistency of behavior. That said, if you are certain that the features you are using work on older versions of Python, `six` will usually work also.

The good news is that, if you are reading this, it is fairly unlikely that you really need to support versions of Python before Python 2.6, which was released in 2008 and now has near universal adoption. Every modern Linux distribution is on at least Python 2.6, and has been for many years. If you are on Windows, you are probably installing Python yourself, and are unlikely to have any need to be on an older version.

`six` is now the mechanism that most people recommend to handle writing code designed to operate within a Python 2 or Python 3 environment. As this chapter explores differences between Python 2 and Python 3, you will learn what `six`'s syntax is to get the same approach on both environments with a unified interface. If you are writing code that must run in Python 2 and Python 3, this is probably what you will want to use.

CHANGES IN PYTHON 3

Many changes exist between Python 2 and Python 3. Some of them are extremely substantial, whereas others just involve something as simple as renaming a module.

Strings and Unicode

Possibly the most sweeping change to Python 3 is that string literals are Unicode instead of ASCII, and that most of the strings you will receive throughout your programs are generally Unicode.

This change is such a big deal that this book actually devoted considerable space to this topic in Chapter 8, in which you learned about Python's handling of text data in detail. Here is quick review.

In Python 2, string literals are byte strings by default. They are Unicode strings in Python 3. The Python 3 behavior can be backported to Python 2 with `from __future__ import unicode_literals`, and you absolutely should do this if you are writing single-source code for both environments.

Also, the byte string and text string classes have different names. In Python 2, the `str` class is for byte strings, and the `unicode` class is for text strings. In Python 3, these are `bytes` and `str`. This means that a class named `str` exists in both, but it is not the same thing. The `six` module aliases these as `six.binary_type` and `six.text_type`.

> **NOTE** *For more information, see Chapter 8.*

The *print* Function

As shown in the earlier example, Python 3 alters the way that print works. In Python 2, print is a special statement, as shown here:

```
print 'The quick brown fox jumped over the lazy dogs.'
```

By default, print would write to sys.stdout and append \n to the end of the string. However, print could be used to print elsewhere with a special syntax, >>.

```
import sys
print >> sys.stderr, 'The quick brown fox jumped over the lazy dogs.'
```

In Python 3, print has been made a bit more normal. First and foremost, it is now a function, which means it is called like a function, with parentheses.

```
print('The quick brown fox jumped over the lazy dogs.')
```

It is still possible to print to somewhere that is not sys.stdout. The Python 3 print function takes a keyword argument called file (defaulting to sys.stdout), which handles this case.

```
import sys
print('The quick brown fox jumped over the lazy dogs.', file=sys.stderr)
```

In addition, the new print function is more flexible, because you can change the default behavior of appending \n to the string using the end keyword argument.

```
print('The quick brown fox jumped over the lazy dogs.', end='')
```

This would still print to sys.stdout, but not append \n to the end of the string before doing so.

The Python 3 print function is available in Python 2.6 and Python 2.7 in the __future__ module.

```
from __future__ import print_function
```

> **NOTE** *If you are using an even older version of Python,* six *provides the same functionality as* six.print_. *(Note the trailing underscore so as not to interfere with the Python keyword.) The arguments exactly match the arguments of the* print *function. As a reminder, you generally do not want to attempt to do single-source codebases that support Python 2.5 and below.*

Division

In Python 2, a division (/) operation between two integers will return an int. This is a constant source of confusion in Python 2, where most people intuitively expect division of two integers to return a float if appropriate. Consider the following Python 2 code:

```
>>> 4 / 2
2
>>> 5 / 2
2
```

It is counterintuitive that 5 divided by 2 would return 2. The reason why it does is because it is *integer* division. The interpreter is doing the division, getting the correct result of `2.5`, and then flooring it to get an integer to maintain type consistency. However, that is usually not what you actually want in a dynamic language.

You get around this by ensuring that either the dividend or the divisor is a `float`.

```
>>> 5.0 / 2
2.5
```

Python 3 fixes this behavior by having integer division always return a `float`, which is generally what you want in a dynamic language.

```
>>> 4 / 2
2.0
>>> 5 / 2
2.5
```

If you want to get an integer back from a division operation, use the "floor division" operator, `//`, which always returns an integer regardless of the type of the arguments provided.

```
>>> 4 // 2
2
>>> 5 // 2
2
```

The Python 3 behavior is preferable, but backward incompatible. If you are writing code that must run in both environments, the `__future__` module is once again your friend. You can opt into the Python 3 behavior in Python 2.6 and Python 2.7 by using the following:

```
from __future__ import division
```

This is the recommended mechanism for a single-source approach.

Absolute and Relative Imports

The primary way that packages are referenced for use in your Python modules is through importing. However, what actually happens when you issue `import foo`? It depends.

In Python 2, the first thing that the interpreter will try (after the standard library) is a *relative import*. This means that it will look for a module called `foo.py` (or `foo/__init__.py`) in the same directory as the module that is attempting the import. If it finds one, it is done; it runs this module and makes its attributes available, namespaced under `foo`.

If the interpreter does not find such a file (by far the most common case), then it begins looking in every directory on `sys.path` to find a matching module. Under normal circumstances, this will include any installed Python packages. This kind of import is called an *absolute import*.

This behavior can be problematic. For example, simply adding a duplicatively named module in a directory can cause other modules in that directory to break, because suddenly they are performing relative imports rather than absolute ones.

Python 3 alters this behavior by simply removing relative imports as a possibility. All imports are absolute imports. If you want a relative import (which is occasionally desirable), you must explicitly ask for one using a special syntax, which is a leading period.

```
import .foo
```

This tells the interpreter to import a module named `foo` that is a sibling of the current module. In this case, only a relative import is attempted at all. (An import from the standard library is not, nor is an import from modules on `sys.path`.) The interpreter also provides a `..` syntax for reaching up in the directory tree.

The Python 3 behavior here is a safer and more explicit approach, but breaks backward compatibility. If you are maintaining an application or distribution that runs under either Python 2 or Python 3, you can opt into the Python 3 behavior using the `__future__` module, as shown here:

```
from __future__ import absolute_import
```

This will cause your module to use the Python 3 import behavior. Only the standard library or installed modules are considered as places from which to import a module, unless the explicit relative import syntax is used (in which case, only it is considered).

Removal of "Old-Style" Classes

Python 2.2 introduced what were at the time referred to as *new-style classes*. Essentially, these were an attempt to fix certain issues with class hierarchies in Python (in particular, method-resolution order in multiple inheritance cases was broken), unify the data model, and introduce some new features (such as `super`).

In order to preserve backward compatibility with older versions of Python, the interpreter required opting in. Classes in Python 2 were old-style by default.

```
>>> class Foo:
...     pass
...
>>> type(Foo)
<type 'classobj'>
```

You could create a new-style class by explicitly inheriting a class from any new-style class, most notably `object`, which was the top of the new-style class tree.

```
>>> class Foo(object):
...     pass
...
>>> type(Foo)
<type 'type'>
```

In Python 3, old-style classes have been entirely removed. The few old-style classes that remain in the Python 2 standard library have all been converted to new-style classes. Explicitly inheriting classes from `object` is still allowed, but no longer necessary.

You may notice that the examples in this book (including those that are explicitly Python 3 code) all explicitly inherit from `object`. If you are writing code specifically for Python 3, you do not need to do this. However, if you are writing code that should run in either a Python 2 or Python 3 environment, you should simply continue to explicitly subclass `object` as you did in Python 2 code. This still continues to work in Python 3, and means that these classes are always new-style, regardless of which environment they run under.

If you are performing tests to determine whether a variable is a class, `six` makes available `six.class_types`. On Python 2, `six.class_types` is a tuple with `type` and `classobj`, whereas on Python 3 it is a tuple containing only `type`.

Metaclass Syntax

Python 3 also alters the syntax for assigning a custom metaclass to a class. In Python 2, a custom metaclass was assigned to a class using the `__metaclass__` attribute.

```
class Foo(object):
    __metaclass__ = FooMeta
```

In Python 3, the metaclass has become part of the class declaration itself.

```
class Foo(object, metaclass=FooMeta):
    pass
```

These two syntaxes are incompatible. You are unable to use `metaclass` as a keyword in a class declaration in Python 2, and using a `__metaclass__` attribute will do nothing in Python 3.

The `six` library provides a solution to this problem. It makes available two separate mechanisms (`six.with_metaclass` and `six.add_metaclass`) for assigning a metaclass to a class as you create it.

six.with_metaclass

The `six.with_metaclass` function simply takes the desired metaclass and all of the base classes, and returns a stub class from which the new class inherits. Syntactically, it is used like this:

```
class Foo(six.with_metaclass(FooMeta, object)):
    pass
```

What `six` is doing under the hood here is creating an empty class that subclasses `object` and has the `FooMeta` metaclass. It is returning that class, which is then the sole class from which `Foo` inherits. This causes `Foo` to have the `FooMeta` metaclass (on both Python 2 and Python 3) and the appropriate parent classes, but adds a trivial additional base class (the stub class) under the hood.

You can observe this in action by looking at the method resolution order for the new class.

```
>>> import six
>>>
>>> class FooMeta(type):
...     pass
...
>>> class Foo(six.with_metaclass(FooMeta, object)):
...     pass
...
>>> Foo.__mro__
(<class '__main__.Foo'>, <class 'six.NewBase'>, <type 'object'>)
```

Pay particular attention to that center class in the method resolution order: `six.NewBase`. That is the stub class that `six` created. It subclasses `object` (as you told it to in your call to `six.with_metaclass`). If you inspect it, you will see it is where the `FooMeta` metaclass is being picked up.

```
>>> NewBase = Foo.__mro__[1]
>>> NewBase
<class 'six.NewBase'>
>>> type(NewBase)
<class '__main__.FooMeta'>
```

Indeed, inspecting the `Foo` class reveals that it, too, is a `FooMeta`, because it inherits from `NewBase`, which is also a `FooMeta`.

```
>>> type(Foo)
<class '__main__.FooMeta'>
```

six.add_metaclass

The `six` module also provides `add_metaclass`, which achieves the same goal somewhat differently. The first difference is in the API. `add_metaclass` is used as a class decorator.

```
@six.add_metaclass(FooMeta)
class Foo(object):
    pass
```

The result here is essentially the same. You can observe this by checking the type of `Foo` and see that it is a `FooMeta`.

```
>>> type(Foo)
<class '__main__.FooMeta'>
```

However, the way in which this gets done under the hood is different. While `with_metaclass` performs its magic by creating a stub class and placing it in the class hierarchy, `add_metaclass` avoids this. There is no stub class in the method resolution order when you use this method.

```
>>> Foo.__mro__
(<class '__main__.Foo'>, <type 'object'>)
```

The way that `add_metaclass` works under the hood is that the class is ultimately constructed twice. First, a "normal" class is created, and then the decorator receives that class and replaces it with a class constructed with the appropriate metaclass, which it then returns. This is slightly less efficient, but ends with a slightly cleaner result.

Exception Syntax

Much like it did with `print`, Python 3 changes the syntax for exceptions in order to remove an unusual (and somewhat arbitrary) syntax.

Under Python 2, the syntax to raise an exception originally looked like this:

```
raise ValueError, 'Invalid value.'
```

What happens when you issue this statement in Python 2? The interpreter creates a new `ValueError` object and sends the string as its only argument. Once the object is created, the interpreter raises the exception.

In other words, what is really happening is that it is simply a call to create a new instance of a class (in this case, `ValueError`). Therefore, it should look like the following, and in Python 3, it does. The unusual syntax with the comma has been removed in favor of a direct object instantiation.

```
raise ValueError('Invalid value.')
```

Because exceptions are just objects (that happen to subclass `Exception`), and because it was already valid in Python 2 to raise exception objects, the Python 3 syntax shown here works without any modification in Python 2.

You should simply use this syntax all the time, even for code exclusive to Python 2. This means you no longer need to worry about this distinction.

Handling Exceptions

In addition to changing the syntax for how exceptions are raised, Python 3 also introduces a new syntax for how exceptions are handled. In Python 2, the `except` statement looked something like this (again, note the comma):

```
try:
    raise ValueError('Invalid value.')
except ValueError, ex:
    print('%s' % ex)
```

Python 3 alters this syntax to make it slightly clearer. The comma in Python 2 is replaced with the `as` keyword (which was introduced for other, unrelated purposes in Python 2.5).

```
try:
    raise ValueError('Invalid value.')
except ValueError as ex:
    print('%s' % ex)
```

The Python 3 syntax shown here is also valid in Python 2.6 and Python 2.7. If you are writing code that only needs to run on Python 2.6 or later, you should use the `as` keyword in lieu of the old syntax.

Exception Chaining

Python 3 also adds an important new feature to its exception handling, which is *exception chaining*. Essentially, it is sometimes the case that, while the interpreter is handling one exception (in an `except` clause), another exception is raised. In Python 2, all information about the original exception is lost.

In Python 3, this is no longer the case. When the second exception is raised, it is given a `__context__` attribute with the original exception.

Additionally, Python 3 provides a mechanism to explicitly specify another exception as a "cause" for an exception, using a new syntax: `raise...from`.

```
raise DatabaseError('Could not write') from IOError('Could not open file.')
```

This code would create the `DatabaseError` exception and the `IOError` exception. The latter would be assigned as the cause of the former. How this works is that exceptions in Python 3 now have a `__cause__` attribute, normally set to `None`, and that is set to the appropriate exception when this syntax is invoked. The `__cause__` attribute is considered to take precedence over the `__context__` attribute.

When is an appropriate time to use this? The most common case for a situation like this is in frameworks that implement multiple backends for data storage, task execution, or the like, but want to expose a common error class so that the programmer using the framework only has to deal with one type of exception. In Python 2, such a model required that you simply lose the exception data underneath, but in Python 3, it is retained.

Unfortunately, Python 2 does not support such exception chaining at all, and `raise...from` is not valid syntax in Python 2. The `six` library, however, provides `six.raise_from`. It takes two arguments (the two exceptions), and will attach the exception context in Python 3 while simply ignoring the second argument in Python 2. If you are writing code that should run in both environments and want to take advantage of exception chaining in Python 3, you should use `six.raise_from`.

Dictionary Methods

The `dict` class in Python 2 includes three methods that change in Python 3: `keys`, `values`, and `items`. In Python 2, each of these methods returns a `list` object containing the appropriate contents.

```
>>> d = {'foo': 'bar'}
>>> d.keys()
['foo']
```

This is completely fine on small dictionaries, but can present a problem on larger ones (especially with `values` and `items`), because you are making an in-memory copy of what can potentially be a large amount of data.

In most cases, a copy is not what you need. You simply want to iterate over the requested data. A generator (see Chapter 3, "Generators") is a much better solution for this task. In fact, Python 2 provides such generators, which are called `iterkeys`, `itervalues`, and `iteritems`.

```
>>> d = {'foo': 'bar'}
>>> gen = d.iterkeys()
>>> gen
<dictionary-keyiterator object at 0x10732d7e0>
>>> next(gen)
'foo'
>>> next(gen)
Traceback (most recent call last):
  File "<stdin>", line 1, in <module>
StopIteration
```

Additionally, Python 2 also provides *views* for each of these, called `viewkeys`, `viewvalues`, and `viewitems`. These view objects simply refer to the original dictionary. The result is that if the original dictionary changes, the views also change.

In Python 3, only the views remain, and the methods that return a `list` as well as the methods that return only a generator have been removed (the views serve as generators also). In Python 3, however, the view methods now use the original method names of `keys`, `values`, and `items`.

If you are writing code that is intended to run under both Python 2 and Python 3, the `six` module provides `six.viewkeys`, `six.viewvalues`, and `six.viewitems`, which map to the appropriate methods on both Python 2 and Python 3.

Function Methods

Python 2 and Python 3 both provide ways to inspect the properties of functions, such as their names, the code within them, and the arguments that they take. The recommended way to do this is by using the `inspect` module, but code that interacts with function objects directly is quite common, and, therefore, the `six` module provides an interface to it.

Functions in Python have several attributes that were renamed in Python 2.6 (not Python 3.0). Before this point, these attributes were considered to be a private API, so the Python developers decided that allowing the attributes to be renamed in Python 2.6 was acceptable.

The Python 2.5 attribute names were `func_closure`, `func_code`, `func_defaults`, and `func_globals`. In Python 2.6, these are renamed to remove the `func_` prefix, and instead use double underscores (for example, `__closure__`).

Consider the following `__defaults__` tuple for a simple function:

```
>>> def foo(x=5):
...     return x + 3
...
>>> foo.__defaults__
(5,)
```

This tells you that the first optional argument has a default of 5. Because there is only one optional argument, there is only one element in the tuple.

The `six` module provides aliases that will return the correct attribute regardless of what version of Python you are running. These are `six.get_function_closure`, `six.get_function_code`, `six.get_function_defaults`, and `six.get_function_globals`. Each takes the function as its argument, as shown here:

```
>>> import six
>>> six.get_function_defaults(foo)
(5,)
```

Iterators

Python 3 changes the structure of iterators slightly. Under Python 2, iterators were expected to have a `next` method that takes no arguments. In Python 3, this becomes `__next__`.

If you need an iterator that runs correctly under Python 2 and Python 3, the correct solution is to have a `next` method that does nothing but call `__next__`, such as this one:

```
class CompatibleIterator(object):
    def next(self):
        return self.__next__()
```

Any class that subclasses `CompatibleIterator` will now receive a `next` method that does nothing but call `__next__`, which will work properly in both Python 2 and Python 3.

However, the `six` module actually provides such a class, `six.Iterator`. In fact, it works even better than the previous example by providing this implementation on Python 2, but simply aliasing to object on Python 3.

Therefore, if you are building iterators that must run under both Python 2 and Python 3, have them subclass `six.Iterator`, and simply define a __next__ method and *not* a next method.

STANDARD LIBRARY RELOCATIONS

In addition to providing several new features and changes in syntax, Python 3 also moves several modules around within the standard library.

Generally, `six` provides a unified interface to get at the correct module if you are maintaining code that should run under both Python 2 and Python 3. These live in `six.moves`.

Merging "Fast" Modules

Two modules, `pickle` and `StringIO` in Python 2, have two functionally identical copies within the Python 2 standard library. The first is a Python implementation, and the second is a faster implementation written in C.

Python 3 merges both of these together so that there is only a single module, and so developers do not have to think about whether they are using the C implementation or the Python implementation of a particular library. (Such details usually should not be important when using a library.)

io

The `StringIO` and `cStringIO` modules in Python 2 are merged into a single module, `io`.

To facilitate running a single module in both Python2 and Python 3, `six` provides `six.moves.cStringIO`, which aliases the *class* (not the module). Therefore, `six.moves.cStringIO` is equivalent to `cStringIO.StringIO` on Python 2, and `io.StringIO` on Python 3.

For example, the following two imports are equivalent in Python 3:

```
>>> from io import StringIO
>>> from six.moves.cStringIO import StringIO
```

pickle

The `pickle` module is handled similarly. Python 2 provides both the `pickle` and the `cPickle` modules, with the latter generally being substantially faster. Python 3 merges the two together under the name `pickle`. Importing from `cPickle` is no longer valid.

Again, `six` provides an alias to the correct thing, regardless of which version of Python you are running. However, in this case, `six.moves.cPickle` aliases the module rather than the class. This allows you to import particular methods from the `pickle` module.

The following two lines of code are equivalent in Python 3:

```
>>> import pickle
>>> from six.moves import cPickle as pickle
```

The URL Modules

Python 2 has three modules for working with URLs: `urllib`, `urllib2`, and `urlparse`. What belonged in each is one of the great mysteries of life.

In actual practice, these are commonly needed together, so Python 3 has completely re-organized these modules under a single module: `urllib`. The bulk of the methods from the `urlparse` module (which primarily concerned itself with reading URLs and breaking them up into their individual component pieces) now live in `urllib.parse`.

Additionally, several methods that were really about parsing (such as `quote` and `unquote`) have been moved from `urllib` into `urllib.parse`.

The reorganized `urllib` module in Python 3 contains four submodules: `error`, `parse`, `request`, and `response`. The `six` module provides `six.moves.urllib` with the same four submodules, which collect the appropriate methods as they are organized in Python 3.

If you are writing code that should run under either Python 2 or Python 3, and you are using anything under `urllib` or its Python 2 cousins, you should use `six.moves.urllib`.

Renames

Python 3 also renames certain modules, as well as certain built-in functions. Table 10-1 shows a list of common renamed or moved functions, as well as the `six.moves` function that is an alias to both.

TABLE 10-1 Common Renamed or Moved Functions

PYTHON 3	PYTHON 2	`six.moves`
configparser	ConfigParser	Configparser
filter	itertools.ifilter	filter
input	raw_input	input
map	itertools.imap	map
range	xrange	range
functools.reduce	reduce	reduce
socketserver	SocketServer	socketserver
zip	itertools.izip	zip

Other Package Reorganizations

Additionally, many other packages have been reorganized between Python 2 and Python 3, but the less common ones do not have aliases within `six`. These include packages such as `xml` and `tkinter`.

If you are writing a single-source implementation using these, consult the package documentation for information on what items have been moved around.

If you encounter a module or attribute that has been moved, you can tell `six.moves` about it by using the `six.add_move` function. If a module has been moved, send a `six.MovedModule` object to `add_move`.

The `six.MovedModule` constructor takes three arguments: the name of the move (and how it will be referenced when importing from `six.moves`), and then the old module name and new module name, both as strings.

For example, this will cause `six.moves.ttk` to be an alias of `ttk` in Python 2 and `tkinter.ttk` in Python 3:

```
>>> import six
>>> six.add_move(MovedModule('ttk', 'ttk', 'tkinter.ttk'))
```

If an attribute within a module is moved, send a `six.MovedAttribute` object to `six.add_move` instead. The `MovedAttribute` constructor takes two additional arguments, which are the old and new attribute names, as strings.

VERSION DETECTION

Occasionally, you will end up in situations where you encounter something that works differently on Python 2 and Python 3, and there is no easy interface to make your code be the same on both versions.

In such cases, the `six` module provides two constants, `six.PY2` and `six.PY3`. These are set to `True` or `False`, depending on which version of Python is currently running.

SUMMARY

Python 3 is a substantial step forward over Python 2. It makes the language cleaner and faster. On the other hand, because of the backward-incompatibility issues, the Python community has been slow to adopt Python 3.

If you are writing Python 2 code, consider writing it in such a way that it will run unaltered in both Python 2 and Python 3. This will be of huge benefit to you in the future when, eventually, it comes time to port to Python 3.

Additionally, this is a good place to emphasize the importance of automated testing. You are writing code that runs under very different conditions, and you must be as sure as possible that it works the same way under each environment. The way to do this is by having a robust unit test suite, which can automatically run in all supported environments. A functional test suite is probably a prerequisite for attempting to port from Python 2 to Python 3, and it is also a requirement to have a manageable single-source repository of code that runs in both environments.

Chapter 11 examines testing in more detail, including how to test in multiple environments.

11

Unit Testing

When you think about testing the code that you write, the first thing that probably comes to mind is simply running your program directly. If your program executes, you at least know that you do not have any syntax errors (provided every module was imported).

Similarly, if you provide appropriate inputs, and do not get a traceback, you know that your program completes successfully with those inputs. And, if the result matches the result you expect, that is additional inductive evidence that your program works.

This has a couple of key limitations, though. The first is that for a non-trivial program, it is not possible to test every scenario. It is impossible to avoid this limitation, although it is important to be as complete as possible when thinking through potential scenarios to test.

The second limitation (and the one that the bulk of this chapter covers) is time. For most applications, it is not practical to manually test every scenario you imagine for every change that you ever make to your program, because iterating over these scenarios is time-consuming.

It is possible, however, to ameliorate this limitation somewhat by automating your tests. An automated test suite can run while you are absent or working on something else, providing a significant time savings and making it much easier to test your work early and often.

This chapter explores some of the world of testing. Specifically, it focuses on unit testing using the built-in tools provided by the Python standard library (such as `unittest` and `mock`), and some common packages available for testing.

THE TESTING CONTINUUM

So, what is a unit test exactly? Furthermore, how does it differ between a functional test or an integration test or some other kind of test? To answer this, this chapter discusses two different testing scenarios.

The Copied Ecosystem

First, consider a very complete testing environment. If you are writing an application that primarily runs on servers, this might entail a "staging" server that has a copy of relevant data, and where potentially breaking actions can be performed safely. For a script or desktop application, the principle is the same. It runs in an area with a copy of anything it must touch or alter.

In this scenario, everything your program must do mimics what it does in its actual live environment. If you connect to a particular type of database, that database is still present in your test environment (just at a different location). If you get data from a web service, you still make that same request.

Essentially, in the copied ecosystem, any external dependencies your program relies on must still be present and set up in an identical way.

This type of testing scenario is designed not only to test specific code being worked on, but also to test that the entire ecosystem structure that is put in place is viable. Any data that is passed back and forth between different components of your application is actually passed in exactly the same way.

Automated tests that are run against a copied ecosystem such as this are generally called *system tests*. This term signifies the complete duplicated ecosystem under which these tests run. This kind of test is designed not only to test your specific code, but also to detect breaking changes in the external environment.

The Isolated Environment

Another very distinct type of test is one that is intended to test a very specific block of code, and to do so in an isolated environment.

In a copied ecosystem, any external requirements and dependencies (such as a database, external service, or the like) are all duplicated. On the other hand, tests intended to be run in an isolated environment do so generally by hand-waving the interactions between the tested code and the external dependencies, focusing only on what the actual code does.

This sort of hand wave is done by stipulating that an external service or dependency received a given input and returned a given output. The purpose of this kind of test is explicitly not to test the interaction between your application and the other service. Rather, it is to test what your application does with the data it receives from that service.

For example, consider a function that determines a person's age at the time of his or her wedding. It first gets information about the person (birthday and anniversary) from an external database, and then computes the delta between the two dates to determine the person's age at the time.

Such a function might look like this:

```
def calculate_age_at_wedding(person_id):
    """Calculate the age of a person at his or her wedding, given the
    ID of the person in the database.
    """
    # Get the person from the database, and pull out the birthday
    # and anniversary datetime.date objects.
    person = get_person_from_db(person_id)
```

```
anniversary = person['anniversary']
birthday = person['birthday']

# Calculate the age of the person on his or her wedding day.
age = anniversary.year - birthday.year

# If the birthday occurs later in the year than the anniversary, then
# subtract one from the age.
if birthday.replace(year=anniversary.year) > anniversary:
    age -= 1

# Done; return the age.
return age
```

Of course, if you try to actually run this function, it will fail. This function depends on another function, `get_person_from_db`, which is not defined in this example. You intuitively understand from reading the comments and code around it that it gets a specific type of record from a database and returns a dictionary-like object.

When testing a function like this, a copied ecosystem would simply reproduce the database, pull a person record with a particular ID, and test that the function returns the expected age. In contrast, a test in an isolated environment wants to avoid dealing with the database at all. An isolated environment test would declare that you got a particular record, and test the remainder of the function against that record.

This kind of test, which seeks to isolate the code being tested from the rest of the world (and even sometimes the rest of the application itself) is called a *unit test*.

Advantages and Disadvantages

Both of these fundamental types of tests have advantages and disadvantages, and most applications must have some of both types of tests as part of a robust testing framework.

Speed

One of the most important advantages to unit tests that run in an isolated environment is speed. Tests that run against a copied ecosystem often have long setup and teardown processes. Furthermore, the I/O required to pass data between the various components is often one of the slowest aspects of your application.

By contrast, tests that run in an isolated environment are usually extremely fast. In the previous example, the time it takes to do the arithmetic to determine this person's age is far less (by several orders of magnitude) than the time it takes to ask the database for the row corresponding to the person's ID and to pass the data over the pipe.

Having a set of isolated tests that run very fast is valuable, because you are able to run them extremely often and get feedback from running those tests very quickly.

Interactivity

The primary reason why isolated tests are so fast is precisely because they are isolated. Isolated tests stipulate the interactions between various services involved in powering your application.

However, these interactions require testing, too. This is why you also need tests in a copied ecosystem. This enables you to ensure that these services continue to interact the way that you expect.

TESTING CODE

The focus of this chapter is specifically on unit testing. Therefore, how can you write a test that runs the `calculate_age_at_wedding` function in the previous example ? Your goal is to not actually talk to a database to get a record of a person, so you must test the function and provide that information.

Code Layout

In many cases, the best and by far the most straightforward way to handle testing such a function is simply to organize your code in a way that makes it easily testable.

In the example of the `calculate_age_at_wedding` function, you may not need to retrieve a record from the database at all. Depending on your application, it might be fine (and even preferable) to have the function simply accept the full record, rather than the `person_id` variable. In other words, the baton handoff to this function would not happen until the database call already occurred, and the only thing this function would do would be to perform the arithmetic.

Reorganizing in this way would also make the function less opinionated about what kind of data it gets. Any dictionary-like object with the appropriate keys would do.

The following trimmed-down function only does the calculation of the age, and is expected to receive a full person record (where it gets it from is not relevant).

```
def calculate_age_at_wedding(person):
    """Calculate the age of a person at his or her wedding, given the
    record of the person as a dictionary-like object.
    """
    # Pull out the birthday and anniversary datetime.date objects.
    anniversary = person['anniversary']
    birthday = person['birthday']

    # Calculate the age of the person on his or her wedding day.
    age = anniversary.year - birthday.year

    # If the birthday occurs later in the year than the anniversary, then
    # subtract one from the age.
    if birthday.replace(year=anniversary.year) > anniversary:
        age -= 1

    # Done; return the age.
    return age
```

In most ways, this function is almost exactly the same as the previous version. The only thing that has changed is that the call to `get_person_from_db` has been removed (and the comments and docstring updated to match).

Testing the Function

When it comes to testing this function, the problem is now very simple. Just pass a dictionary and make sure you get the correct result.

```
>>> from datetime import date
>>>
>>> person = {'anniversary': date(2012, 4, 21),
...           'birthday': date(1986, 6, 15)}
>>> age = calculate_age_at_wedding(person)
>>> age
25
```

Of course, a couple limitations exist here. First, this is still something that was run manually in the interactive terminal. The value of a unit testing suite is that you run it in an automated fashion.

A second (and even more important) limitation to recognize is that this tests only one input against only one output. Suppose you gutted the function the next day and replaced it with the following:

```
def calculate_age_at_wedding(*args, **kwargs):
    return 25
```

The test would still pass, even though the function would be extremely broken.

Indeed, the test does not even cover some sections of this function. After all, there is an `if` block in the function based on whether or not the birthday falls before or after the anniversary in a calendar year. At a minimum, you would want to ensure that your test takes both pathways.

The following test function handles this:

```
from datetime import date


def test_calculate_age_at_wedding():
    """Establish that the `calculate_age_at_wedding` function seems to
    calculate a person's age at his wedding correctly, given a
    dictionary-like object representing a person.
    """
    # Assert that if the anniversary falls before the birthday in a
    # calendar year, that the calculation is done properly.
    person = {'anniversary': date(2012, 4, 21),
              'birthday': date(1986, 6, 15)}
    age = calculate_age_at_wedding(person)
    assert age == 25, 'Expected age 25, got %d.' % age

    # Assert that if the anniversary falls after the birthday in a calendar
    # year, that the calculation is done properly.
    person = {'anniversary': date(1969, 8, 11),
              'birthday': date(1945, 2, 15)}
    age = calculate_age_at_wedding(person)
    assert age == 24, 'Expected age 24, got %d.' % age
```

Now you have a function that can be run by an automated process. Python includes a test runner, which is explored shortly. Also, this test covers a couple of different permutations of the function.

It certainly does not cover every possible input (it would be impossible to do that), but it provides a slightly more complete sanity check.

However, always remember that the tests are not an exhaustive check. They only test the inputs and outputs that you provide. For example, this test function says nothing about what would happen if the `calculate_age_at_wedding` function were sent something other than a dictionary, or if it were sent a dictionary with the wrong keys, or if `datetime` objects were used instead of `date` objects, or if you were to send an anniversary date that is earlier than the birth date, or any number of other permutations. This is fine. It is simply important to understand what the limits of your tests are.

The *assert* Statement

What about the `assert` statement that the test function is using? Consider what a unit test fundamentally is. A unit test is an assertion or a set of assertions. In this case, you assert that if you send a properly formatted dictionary with specific dates, you get a specific integer result.

In Python, `assert` is a keyword, and `assert` statements are used almost exclusively for testing (although they need not appear exclusively in test code). The `assert` statement expects the expression sent to it to evaluate to `True`. If it does, the `assert` statement does nothing; if it does not, `AssertionError` is raised. You can optionally provide a custom error message to be raised with the `AssertionError`, as the previous example does.

When writing tests, you want to use `AssertionError` as the exception to be raised when a test fails, either by raising it directly, or (usually) by using the `assert` statement to assert the test's pass conditions, because all of the unit testing frameworks will catch the error and handle it appropriately when compiling test failures.

UNIT TESTING FRAMEWORKS

Now that you have your test as a function, the next step is to set up a process to run that test (as well as any others you may write to test the remainder of the application).

Several unit testing frameworks, such as `py.test` and `nose`, are available as third-party packages. However, the Python standard library also ships with a quite robust unit testing framework, available under the `unittest` module in the standard library.

Consider the testing function from the previous example, but structured to be run by the `unittest` module.

```
import unittest
from datetime import date


class Tests(unittest.TestCase):
    def test_calculate_age_at_wedding(self):
        """Establish that the `calculate_age_at_wedding` function seems
        to calculate a person's age at his wedding correctly, given
        a dictionary-like object representing a person.
```

```
"""
# Assert that if the anniversary falls before the birthday
# in a calendar year, that the calculation is done properly.
person = {'anniversary': date(2012, 4, 21),
          'birthday': date(1986, 6, 15)}
age = calculate_age_at_wedding(person)
self.assertEqual(age, 25)

# Assert that if the anniversary falls after the birthday
# in a calendar year, that the calculation is done properly.
person = {'anniversary': date(1969, 8, 11),
          'birthday': date(1945, 2, 15)}
age = calculate_age_at_wedding(person)
self.assertEqual(age, 24)
```

In most ways, this looks the same as what you saw before. However, it has a couple of key differences. The first difference is that you now have a class, which subclasses `unittest.TestCase`. The `unittest` module expects to find tests grouped using `unittest.TestCase` subclasses. Each test must be a function whose name begins with `test`. As a corollary, because the test itself is now a method of the class rather than an unbound function, it now has `self` as an argument.

The other change is that the raw `assert` statements have been replaced with calls to `self.assertEqual`. The `unittest.TestCase` class provides a number of wrappers around `assert` that standardize error messages and provide some other boilerplate.

Running Unit Tests

Now it is time to actually run this test within the `unittest` framework. To do this, save both the function and the test class in a single module, such as `wedding.py`.

The Python interpreter provides a flag, `-m`, which takes a module in the standard library or on `sys.path`, and runs it as a script. The `unittest` module supports being run in this way, and accepts the Python module to be tested. (If you named your module `wedding.py`, this would be `wedding`.)

```
$ python -m unittest wedding
.
------------------------------------------------------------------
Ran 1 test in 0.000s

OK
```

What is happening here? The `wedding` module was loaded, and the `unittest` module found a `unittest.TestCase` subclass. It instantiated the class and then ran every method beginning with the word `test`, which the `test_calculate_age_at_wedding` method does.

The `unittest` output prints a period character (`.`) for a successful test, or a letter for failures (`F`), errors (`E`), and a few other cases, such as tests that are intentionally skipped (`s`). Because there was only one test, and it was successful, you see a single `.` character followed by the concluding output.

Failures

You can observe what happens when a test fails by simply changing the test's condition so that it will intentionally fail.

To illustrate this, add the following method to your `Tests` class:

```
def test_failure_case(self):
    """Assert a wrong age, and fail."""
    person = {'anniversary': date(2012, 4, 21),
              'birthday': date(1986, 6, 15)}
    age = calculate_age_at_wedding(person)
    self.assertEqual(age, 99)
```

This is a similar test, except that it asserts that the age is 99, which is wrong. Observe what happens if you run tests on the module now:

```
$ python -m unittest wedding
.F
======================================================================
FAIL: test_failure_case (wedding.Tests)
Assert a wrong age, and fail.
----------------------------------------------------------------------
Traceback (most recent call last):
  File "wedding.py", line 50, in test_failure_case
    self.assertEqual(age, 99)
AssertionError: 25 != 99


----------------------------------------------------------------------
Ran 2 tests in 0.000s

FAILED (failures=1)
```

Now you have two tests. You have the main test from before, which still passes, and a second test with a bogus age, which fails.

If you ran the function directly, you would just get a standard traceback when `AssertionError` is raised. However, the `unittest` module actually catches this error and tracks the failure, and prints the output nicely at the end of the test run.

This may seem like an unimportant distinction at this point, but if you have hundreds of tests, this difference matters. A Python module will terminate when it comes across the first uncaught exception, so your test run would stop on the first failure. When you're using `unittest`, the tests continue to run, and you get all the failures at once at the end.

The `unittest` output also includes the test function and the beginning of the docstring, so it is easy to go find the failing test and investigate, as well as the full traceback, so you still have the same insight into the offending code.

Errors

Only a small difference distinguishes an error from a failure. A test that raises `AssertionError` is considered to have failed, whereas a test that raises any exception *other than* `AssertionError` is considered to be in error.

Consider what would happen if the `person` variable being tested is an empty dictionary. Add the following function to your `Tests` class in the `wedding` module:

```
def test_error_case(self):
    """Attempt to send an empty dict to the function."""
    person = {}
```

```
        age = calculate_age_at_wedding(person)
        self.assertEqual(age, 25)
```

Now what happens when you run tests?

```
$ python -m unittest wedding
.EF
======================================================================
ERROR: test_error_case (wedding.Tests)
Attempt to send an empty dict to the function.
----------------------------------------------------------------------
Traceback (most recent call last):
  File "wedding.py", line 55, in test_error_case
    age = calculate_age_at_wedding(person)
  File "wedding.py", line 10, in calculate_age_at_wedding
    anniversary = person['anniversary']
KeyError: 'anniversary'

======================================================================
FAIL: test_failure_case (wedding.Tests)
Assert a wrong age, and fail.
----------------------------------------------------------------------
Traceback (most recent call last):
  File "wedding.py", line 50, in test_failure_case
    self.assertEqual(age, 99)
AssertionError: 25 != 99


----------------------------------------------------------------------
Ran 3 tests in 0.000s

FAILED (failures=1, errors=1)
```

Now you have three tests. You have the passing and failing test from earlier, and a test that is in error. Instead of raising `AssertionError`, the error case raised `KeyError`, because the `calculate_age_at_wedding` function expected an anniversary key in the dictionary (and the key was not there).

For most practical purposes, you probably will not actually put much stock in the difference between a failure and an error. They are simply failing tests that fail in slightly different ways.

Skipped Tests

It is also possible to mark that a test should be skipped under certain situations. For example, say that an application is designed to run under Python 2 or Python 3, but a particular test only makes sense in one of the two environments. Rather than have the test fail when it should not, it is possible to declare that a test should run only under certain conditions.

The `unittest` module provides `skipIf` and `skipUnless` decorators that take an expression. The `skipIf` decorator causes the test to be skipped if the expression it receives evaluates to `True`, and the `skipUnless` decorator causes the test to be skipped if the expression it receives evaluates to `False`. In addition, both decorators take a second, required argument, which is a string that describes *why* the test was skipped.

To see skipped tests in action, add the following function to your `Tests` class. (To keep the output shown here down to a reasonable size, the failure and error tests have been removed.)

```
@unittest.skipIf(True, 'This test was skipped.')
def test_skipped_case(self):
    """Skip this test."""
    pass
```

This function is decorated with `unittest.skipIf`. `True` is a valid expression in Python, and obviously evaluates to `True`. Now see what happens when you run the tests:

```
$ python -m unittest wedding
.s
-----------------------------------------------------------------------
Ran 2 tests in 0.000s

OK (skipped=1)
```

The output for a skipped test is an `s`, rather than the traditional period character that denotes a test that passed. The use of a lowercase letter rather than an uppercase one (as in `F` and `E`) signifies that this is not an error condition, and indeed, the complete test run is considered to be a success.

Loading Tests

So far, you have run tests out of a single module, and the tests have lived in the same module where the code that it is testing also lives. This is fine for a trivial example but entirely unfeasible for a large application.

The `unittest` module understands this, and provides an extensible mechanism for programmatically loading tests from a complete project tree. The default class, which is suitable for most needs, is `unittest.TestLoader`.

If you are just using the default test loading class, which is what you want most of the time, you can trigger it by using the word `discover` instead of the module name to be tested.

```
$ python -m unittest discover

-----------------------------------------------------------------------
Ran 0 tests in 0.000s

OK
```

Where did your tests go? The test discovery follows certain rules for determining where it goes to actually look for tests. By default, it expects all files containing tests to be named according to the pattern `test*.py`.

This is what you really want to do anyway. The value of test discovery is that you can separate your tests from the rest of your code. So, if you move the passing test itself from the `wedding.py` file to a new file matching that pattern (for example, `test_wedding.py`), the test discovery system will find it. (Note that you must import the `calculate_age_at_wedding` function explicitly, because it is not in the same module anymore!)

Sure enough, now the test discovery finds the tests:

```
$ python -m unittest discover
.
-----------------------------------------------------------------------
```

```
Ran 1 test in 0.000s

OK
```

MOCKING

To make the `calculate_age_at_wedding` function something that was capable of being easily unit tested, recall how you had to remove part of the function. The idea was that you organize your code to make that function easily testable by doing a database call elsewhere.

Often, organizing your code in a way that makes it easily testable is the ideal approach to this problem, but sometimes it is not possible or wise. Instead of implicitly hand-waving certain functionality by organizing your code around atomic testing, how do you explicitly hand-wave a segment of tested code?

The answer is mocking. *Mocking* is the process of declaring within a test that a certain function call should be stipulated to give a particular output, and the function call itself should be suppressed. Additionally, you can assert that the mocked call that you expect was made in a particular way.

Beginning in Python 3.3, the `unittest` module ships with `unittest.mock`, which contains tools for mocking. If you are using Python 3.2 or earlier, you can use the `mock` package, which you can download from `www.pypi.python.org`.

The API between these is identical, but how you import it obviously changes. If you are using Python 3.3, you want `from unittest import mock`; if you are using the installed package, you want `import mock`.

Mocking a Function Call

Consider again the original function for `calculate_age_at_wedding`, which included a call to retrieve a record from an unspecified database. (If you are following along, you should create a new file.)

```python
def calculate_age_at_wedding(person_id):
    """Calculate the age of a person at his or her wedding, given the
    ID of the person in the database.
    """
    # Get the person from the database, and pull out the birthday
    # and anniversary datetime.date objects.
    person = get_person_from_db(person_id)
    anniversary = person['anniversary']
    birthday = person['birthday']

    # Calculate the age of the person on his or her wedding day.
    age = anniversary.year - birthday.year

    # If the birthday occurs later in the year than the anniversary, then
    # subtract one from the age.
    if birthday.replace(year=anniversary.year) > anniversary:
        age -= 1

    # Done; return the age.
    return age
```

Before, you tested most of this function by actually changing the function itself. You reorganized the code around ease of testability. However, you also want to be able to test code where this is either impossible or undesirable.

First things first. You still do not actually have a get_person_from_db function, so you want to suppress that function call. Therefore, add a function that raises an exception.

```
def get_person_from_db(person_id):
    raise RuntimeError('The real `get_person_from_db` function '
                       'was called.')
```

At this point, if you actually try to run the calculate_age_at_wedding function, you will get a RuntimeError. This is convenient for this example because it will make it very obvious if your mocking does not work. Your test will loudly fail.

Next comes the test. If you just try to run the same test from before, it will fail (with RuntimeError). You need a way of getting around the get_person_from_db call. This is where mock comes in.

The mock module is essentially a monkey-patching library. It temporarily replaces a variable in a given namespace with a special object called a MagicMock, and then returns the variable to its previous value after the scope of the mock is concluded. The MagicMock object itself is extremely permissive. It accepts (and tracks) basically any call made to it, and returns whatever you tell it.

In this case, you want the get_person_from_db function to be replaced with a MagicMock object for the duration of your test.

```
import unittest
import sys

from datetime import date

# Import mock regardless of whether it is from the standard library
# or from the PyPI package.
try:
    from unittest import mock
except ImportError:
    import mock


class Tests(unittest.TestCase):
    def test_calculate_age_at_wedding(self):
        """Establish that the `calculate_age_at_wedding` function seems
        to calculate a person's age at his wedding correctly, given
        a person ID.
        """
        # Since we are mocking a name in the current module, rather than
        # an imported module (the common case), we need a reference to
        # this module to send to `mock.patch.object`.
        module = sys.modules[__name__]

        with mock.patch.object(module, 'get_person_from_db') as m:
            # Ensure that the get_person_from_db function returns
            # a valid dictionary.
            m.return_value = {'anniversary': date(2012, 4, 21),
                              'birthday': date(1986, 6, 15)}
```

```
# Assert that that the calculation is done properly.
age = calculate_age_at_wedding(person_id=42)
self.assertEqual(age, 25)
```

The big new thing going on here is the call to `mock.patch.object`. This is a function that can be used either as a context manager or a decorator, and it takes two required arguments: a module that contains the callable being mocked, and then the name of the callable as a string. In this case, because the function and the test are all contained in a single file (which is not what you would normally do), you must get a reference to the current module, which is always `sys.modules[__name__]`.

The context manager returns a `MagicMock` object, which is m in the previous example. Before you can call the function being tested, however, you must specify what you expect the `MagicMock` to do. In this case, you want it to return a dictionary that approximates a valid record of a person. The `return_value` property of the `MagicMock` object is what handles this. Setting it means that every time the `MagicMock` is called, it will return that value. If you do not set `return_value`, another `MagicMock` object is returned.

If you run tests on this module, you will see that the test passes. (Here, the new module is named `mock_wedding.py`.)

```
$ python -m unittest mock_wedding
.
----------------------------------------------------------------------
Ran 1 test in 0.000s

OK
```

Asserting Mocked Calls

This test passes, but it is still fundamentally incomplete in one important way. It mocks the function call to `get_person_from_db`, and tests that the function does the right thing with the output.

What the test does *not* do is actually verify that the baton handoff to the `get_person_from_db` function actually occurred. In some ways, this is redundant. You know the call happened, because otherwise you would not have received the return value from the mock object. However, sometimes you will mock function calls that do not have a return value.

Fortunately, `MagicMock` objects track calls made to them. Rather than just spitting out the return value and being done, the object stores information about how many times it was called, and the signature of each call. Finally, `MagicMock` provides methods to assert that calls occurred in a particular fashion.

Probably the most common method you will use for this purpose is `MagicMock.assert_called_once_with`. This asserts two things: that the `MagicMock` was called once and exactly once, and that the specified argument signature was used. Consider an augmented test function that ensures that the `get_person_from_db` method was called with the expected person ID:

```
class Tests(unittest.TestCase):
    def test_calculate_age_at_wedding(self):
        """Establish that the `calculate_age_at_wedding` function seems
        to calculate a person's age at his wedding correctly, given
```

```
           a person ID.
           """
           # Since we are mocking a name in the current module, rather than
           # an imported module (the common case), we need a reference to
           # this module to send to `mock.patch.object`.
           module = sys.modules[__name__]

           with mock.patch.object(module, 'get_person_from_db') as m:
               # Ensure that the get_person_from_db function returns
               # a valid dictionary.
               m.return_value = {'anniversary': date(2012, 4, 21),
                                 'birthday': date(1986, 6, 15)}

               # Assert that that the calculation is done properly.
               age = calculate_age_at_wedding(person_id=42)
               self.assertEqual(age, 25)

               # Assert that the `get_person_from_db` method was called
               # the way we expect.
               m.assert_called_once_with(42)
```

The thing that has changed here is that the `MagicMock` object is now being checked at the end to ensure that you got the call to it that you expected. The call signature is simply a single positional argument: `42`. This is the person ID used in the test (just a few lines earlier). It is sent as a positional argument because that is the way the argument is provided in the original function.

```
       person = get_person_from_db(person_id)
```

Notice that `person_id` is provided as a single positional argument, so that is what the `MagicMock` will record.

If you run the test, you will see that it still passes:

```
   $ python -m unittest mock_wedding
   .
   ----------------------------------------------------------------------
   Ran 1 test in 0.000s

   OK
```

What happens if the `MagicMock`'s assertions are incorrect? The tests fail with a useful failure message, as you can see by changing the `assert_called_once_with` argument signature:

```
   $ python -m unittest mock_wedding
   F
   ======================================================================
   FAIL: test_calculate_age_at_wedding (wedding.Tests)
   Establish that the `calculate_age_at_wedding` function seems
   ----------------------------------------------------------------------
   Traceback (most recent call last):
     File "/Users/luke/Desktop/wiley/wedding.py", line 58, in
         test_calculate_age_at_wedding
       m.assert_called_once_with(84)
     File "/Library/Frameworks/Python.framework/Versions/3.4/lib/python3.4/unittest
         /mock.py", line 771, in assert_called_once_with
```

```
        return self.assert_called_with(*args, **kwargs)
      File "/Library/Frameworks/Python.framework/Versions/3.4/lib/python3.4/unittest
          /mock.py", line 760, in assert_called_with
        raise AssertionError(_error_message()) from cause
AssertionError: Expected call: get_person_from_db(84)
Actual call: get_person_from_db(42)


----------------------------------------------------------------
Ran 1 test in 0.001s
```

Here you are told which call the `MagicMock` expected to get, as well as the call it actually received. You would get similar errors if there were no call, or more than one call.

The `assert_called_once_with` method has a close cousin, which is `assert_called_with`. This is identical except for the fact that it does not fail if the `MagicMock` has been called more than once, and it checks the call signature against only the most recent call.

Inspecting Mocks

You can inspect `MagicMock` objects in several other ways to determine what occurred. You may just want to know that it was called, or how many times it was called. You also may want to assert a sequence of calls, or only look at part of the call's signature.

Call Count and Status

A couple of the easiest and most straightforward questions are whether a `MagicMock` has been called, and how many times it has been called.

If you just want to know whether a `MagicMock` has been called at all, you can check the `called` property, which is set to `True` the first time that the `MagicMock` is called.

```
>>> from unittest import mock
>>> m = mock.MagicMock()
>>> m.called
False
>>> m(foo='bar')
<MagicMock name='mock()' id='4315583152'>
>>> m.called
True
```

On the other hand, you may also want to know exactly how many times the `MagicMock` has been called. This is available, too, as `call_count`.

```
>>> from unittest import mock
>>> m = mock.MagicMock()
>>> m.call_count
0
>>> m(foo='bar')
<MagicMock name='mock()' id='4315615752'>
>>> m.call_count
1
>>> m(spam='eggs')
<MagicMock name='mock()' id='4315615752'>
>>> m.call_count
2
```

The `MagicMock` class does not have built-in methods for asserting the presence of a call or a given call count, but the `assertEqual` and `assertTrue` methods that are part of `unittest.TestCase` are more than sufficient for that task.

Multiple Calls

You may also want to assert the composition of multiple calls to a `MagicMock` in one fell swoop. `MagicMock` objects provide the `assert_has_calls` method for this purpose.

To use `assert_has_calls`, you must understand `call` objects, which are provided as part of the mock library. Whenever you make a call to a `MagicMock` object, it internally creates a `call` object that stores the call signature (and appends it to the `mock_calls` list on the object). These `call` objects are considered to be equivalent if the signatures match.

```
>>> from unittest.mock import call
>>> a = call(42)
>>> b = call(42)
>>> c = call('foo')
>>> a is b
False
>>> a == b
True
>>> a == c
False
```

This is actually how `assert_called_once_with` and similar methods work under the hood. They make a new `call` object, and then ensure that it is equivalent to the one in the `mock_calls` list.

The `assert_has_calls` method takes a list (or other similar object, such as a tuple) of `call` objects. It also accepts an optional keyword argument, `any_order`, which defaults to `False`. If this remains `False`, this means that it expects the calls to have occurred in the same sequence that they do in the list. If it is set to `True`, only the presence of each call to the `MagicMock` is relevant, not the order of the calls.

Here is what `assert_has_calls` looks like in action:

```
>>> from unittest.mock import MagicMock, call
>>>
>>> m = MagicMock()
>>> m.call('a')
<MagicMock name='mock.call()' id='4370551920'>
>>> m.call('b')
<MagicMock name='mock.call()' id='4370551920'>
>>> m.call('c')
<MagicMock name='mock.call()' id='4370551920'>
>>> m.call('d')
<MagicMock name='mock.call()' id='4370551920'>
>>> m.assert_has_calls([call.call('b'), call.call('c')])
```

It is worth noting that although `assert_has_calls` does expect the calls to occur in order, it does not require that you send it the entire list of calls. Having other calls on either end of the list is fine.

Inspecting Calls

Sometimes, you may not want to test the entirety of a call signature. Perhaps it is only important that a certain argument be included. This is a little bit more difficult to do. There is no ready-made method for a `call` to declare that it matches anything other than a complete call signature.

However, it is possible to inspect the `call` object itself and look at the arguments sent to it. The way this works is that the `call` class is actually a subclass of `tuple`, and call objects are tuples with three elements, the second and third of which are the call signature.

```
>>> from unittest.mock import call
>>> c = call('foo', 'bar', spam='eggs')
>>> c[1]
('foo', 'bar')
>>> c[2]
{'spam': 'eggs'}
```

By inspecting the `call` object directly, you can get a tuple of the positional arguments and a dictionary of the keyword arguments.

This gives you the capability to test only part of a call signature. For example, what if you want to ensure that the string `bar` was one of the arguments given to the call, but you do not care about the rest of the arguments?

```
>>> assert 'bar' in c[1]
>>> assert 'baz' in c[1]
Traceback (most recent call last):
  File "<stdin>", line 1, in <module>
AssertionError
>>> assert c[2]['spam'] == 'eggs'
```

Once you have access to the positional arguments as a tuple and the keyword arguments as a dictionary, testing for the presence or absence of a single argument is no different than testing for the presence of an element in a list or dictionary.

OTHER TESTING TOOLS

Several other testing tools are available that you may want to consider using as you build out a unit test suite in your applications.

coverage

How do you actually know what code is being tested? Ideally, you want to test as much of your code as possible in each test run, while still maintaining a test suite that runs quickly.

If you want to know just how much of your code your test suite is exercising, you will want to use the `coverage` application, which is available from www.pypi.python.org. Originally written by Ned Batchelder, `coverage` is a tool that keeps track of all of the lines of code in each module that run as your tests are running, and provides a report detailing what code did not run. Of course, `coverage` runs on both Python 2 and Python 3.

The application works by installing a coverage script, and you use coverage run as a substitute for python when invoking a Python script of any kind, including your unit test script. The output will look fundamentally similar.

```
$ coverage run -m unittest mock_wedding
.
----------------------------------------------------------------------
Ran 1 test in 0.000s

OK
```

However, if you look at the directory, you will see that a .coverage file was created in the process. This file contains information about what code in the file actually ran.

You can view this information with coverage report.

```
$ coverage report
Name            Stmts   Miss  Cover
------------------------------------
mock_wedding       22      1    95%
```

This report shows how many statements ran and how many statements are in the file that did not run. So, you know that one statement was omitted, but not which one. Adding -m to the command adds output showing which lines were skipped:

```
$ coverage report -m
Name            Stmts   Miss  Cover   Missing
---------------------------------------------
mock_wedding       22      1    95%    24
```

Now you know that line 24 was the test that did not run. (In the example mock_wedding.py file, line 24 corresponds to the RuntimeError that is raised if the "real" get_person_from_db function was called.)

The coverage application can also write attractive HTML output using the coverage html command. This highlights in red the lines that did not run. Additionally, if you have a statement with multiple branches (such as an if statement), it highlights those in yellow if only one path was taken.

tox

Many Python applications need to run on multiple versions of Python, including both Python 2 and Python 3. If you are writing an application that runs in multiple environments (even just multiple minor revisions), you want to run your tests against all of those environments.

Attempting to run tests manually across every environment you support is likely to be cumbersome. If you need to do this, consider tox. Written by Holger Krekel, tox is a tool that automatically creates virtual environments (using virtualenv) with the appropriate versions of Python (provided you have them installed) and runs the tests within those environments.

Other Test Runners

This chapter has focused primarily on the test runner provided by Python itself, but other alternatives are available. Some, such as `nose` and `py.test`, are quite popular, and add numerous features and hooks for extensibility.

These libraries are easy to adopt even if you already have a robust unit test suite, because both support using `unittest` tests out of the box. However, both libraries support other ways of adding tests to the pool.

Both of these libraries are available on `www.pypi.python.org`, and run on Python 2.6 and up.

SUMMARY

Unit testing is a powerful way to ensure that your code remains consistent over time. It is a useful way to discover when your code changes, and how to make adjustments accordingly.

This is an important facet of any application. Having a robust testing suite makes it easier to detect some bugs and makes you aware when a function's behavior changes, thus simplifying application maintenance.

Chapter 12 examines the `optparse` and `argparse` tools for using Python on the command-line interface (CLI).

12

CLI Tools

Python applications come in all sorts of flavors, including desktop applications, server-side applications, scripts, scientific computing applications, and much more.

Some Python applications must function with the command-line interface (CLI). They may need to ask for input, and receive arguments that are provided when the script is invoked.

This chapter examines `optparse` and `argparse`, the two tools that the Python standard library provides for writing applications that are run from the CLI.

OPTPARSE

`optparse` is the older of the two modules provided by Python, and is nominally considered to be deprecated as of Python 2.7 (when `argparse` was introduced). However, `optparse` is still very widely used, and is necessary for any code intended to support Python 2.6, which is still quite common in the Python ecosystem.

Essentially, `optparse` exists to provide a clear and consistent way to read arguments off of the command line, including positional arguments, as well as options and switches.

A Simple Argument

`optparse` is actually quite easy to understand once you look at an example. Consider the following simple Python script that takes an option from the CLI:

```python
import optparse


if __name__ == '__main__':
    parser = optparse.OptionParser()
    options, args = parser.parse_args()

    print(' '.join(args).upper())
```

This script takes any number of arguments it receives, converts them to all capital letters, and prints them back out to the CLI.

```
$ python echo_upper.py
```

```
$ python echo_upper.py foo bar baz
FOO BAR BAZ
$ python echo_upper.py spam
SPAM
```

The next two sections break down this example.

__name__ == '__main__'

The line `if __name__ == '__main__'` may be an unfamiliar idiom if you have not done much command-line scripting (or come across it in other use cases). In Python, each module has a `__name__` attribute, which is always automatically set to the name of the module that is currently being executed.

The value `__main__` is special. When a module is invoked directly (such as by running it on the command line), the `__name__` attribute is set to this value.

Why test for this? Nearly every `.py` file in Python is importable as a module, and, therefore, could be imported. In CLI scripts, you probably do not want the code to directly run in this case. CLI scripts sometimes contain code such as calls to `sys.exit()` that would terminate the entire program. This module's option and argument-parsing behavior really only makes sense if it is invoked directly. Therefore, this type of code should be placed beneath the `if __name__ == '__main__'` test.

Note that there is nothing magic about the `if` block; it is simply a top-level `if` statement. Other top-level code will still be executed even if the `if` test fails. Additionally, note that it is traditional that such tests be placed at the bottom of the file.

OptionParser

Next, consider the creation of an `OptionParser` instance, followed by the call to its `parse_args` method. The `OptionParser` class is the primary class in the `optparse` module used for taking the arguments and options sent to a CLI command, and making sense of them.

The fundamental way that this works is that you tell the `OptionParser` instance what options you expect and know how to address. Options are strings that start with - or --, such as -v or --verbose. (You learn more about these shortly.) The call to `parse_args` iterates over all of the options that the parser recognizes, and places them in the first variable that `parse_args` returns (which is named `options` in the previous example). Any arguments left over are considered to be positional arguments, and are placed in the second variable (`args` in the previous example), which is a list.

The previous example uses no options, so everything that the parser receives is considered to be a positional argument. The script then takes that list, joins it into a string, converts it to uppercase, and prints it.

One thing to note is that any argument that begins with hyphens is expected to be an option, and `optparse` raises an exception if you try to send an option that the parser does not recognize. Furthermore, the exception is internally handled within `optparse` and calls `sys.exit`, so there is no real way to catch these errors yourself.

```
$ python echo_upper.py --foo
Usage: echo_upper.py [options]

echo_upper.py: error: no such option: --foo
```

Options

Positional arguments are usually not the most intuitive way to get information to a script. They are reasonable when you have one or two, and the script's purpose is straightforward. However, as your script becomes more customizable, you will generally want to use options.

Options provide the following advantages over positional arguments for many use cases:

➤ They can be made (and usually should be made) to be *optional*. Options can have sensible default values that are used when the option is not provided.

➤ Options that also accept values associate a key (the name of the option) with the option value, which enhances readability.

➤ Multiple options can be provided in any order.

Types of Options

A CLI script can accept two common types of options.

One type is sometimes called a *flag* or a *switch*, and is an option that does not require or accept a value along with the option. Essentially, in these cases, it is the presence or absence of the option that determines the script behavior.

Two common examples of such switches are --verbose and --quiet (often also provided as -v and -q, respectively). The script executes normally if these options are absent, but does something different (provides more or less output) if they are present. Note that you generally specify this as --quiet, as opposed to --quiet=true or something similar. The value is implied by the presence of the switch.

Another type of option is one that does expect a value. Most database clients accept options such as --host, --port, and the like. These do not make sense as switches. You do not simply provide --host and expect the database client to infer what the actual host is. You must provide the host-name or IP address that you are connecting to.

Adding Options to *OptionParser*

Once you have an OptionParser instance, you can add an option to it using the add_option method. This comes after the OptionParser instance is instantiated, but before parse_args, which is the final step in the chain.

Consider first the addition of a simple switch, which does not actually expect an argument.

```python
import optparse


if __name__ == '__main__':
    parser = optparse.OptionParser()
    parser.add_option('-q', '--quiet',
        action='store_true',
        dest='quiet',
        help='Suppress output.',
    )
```

This would add support for a `-q` and `--quiet` switch. Note that, in CLI scripts, it is extremely common to have a long-form and short-form version of options, and so `optparse` supports this easily. By providing two different strings as positional arguments to `add_option`, the `add_option` method understands that they are supposed to be accepted, and that they are aliases of one another.

The `action` keyword argument is what specifies that the `--quiet` flag is a flag, and does not expect a variable. If you leave off the `action` keyword argument, the option is assumed to expect a value (more on that in a moment). Setting `action` to `store_true` or `store_false` means that no value is expected, and, if the flag is provided at all, the value is `True` or `False`, respectively.

The `dest` keyword argument is what decides the name of the option in Python. The name of this particular option within the `options` variable is `quiet`. In many cases, you do not have to set this. `OptionParser` infers an appropriate name based on the name of the option itself. However, it is a good idea to always set it explicitly for readability and maintainability.

Finally, the `help` keyword argument sets the help text for this option. It is what a user will see if he or she invokes your script with `--help`. It is wise to always provide this.

It is worth noting that `optparse` automatically adds a `--help` option, and handles it automatically. If you call a script with only the example option and provide `--help`, you get useful output.

```
$ python cli_script.py --help
Usage: cli_script.py [options]

Options:
  -h, --help   show this help message and exit
  -q, --quiet  Suppress output.
```

Options with Values

In addition to switches, sometimes you need options that actually expect values to be provided along with the option. This does add some complexity. The biggest reason for this is that values have types in Python, and the CLI does not have a robust concept of types. Essentially, everything is a string.

First, consider an option that accepts a string, such as a `--host` flag that might be sent to a database client. This option should probably be optional. The biggest use case for database clients is connecting to databases on the same machine, so `localhost` makes for an entirely sensible default.

Here is a complete script that does nothing but reprint the host to standard out:

```
import optparse


if __name__ == '__main__':
    parser = optparse.OptionParser()
    parser.add_option('-H', '--host',
        default='localhost',
        dest='host',
        help='The host to connect to. Defaults to localhost.',
        type=str,
    )
    options, args = parser.parse_args()
```

If you call this script with no arguments, you will see that the default of `localhost` is applicable.

```
$ python optparse_host.py
The host is localhost.
```

By adding a `--host` option, you override this default.

```
$ python optparse_host.py --host 0.0.0.0
The host is 0.0.0.0.
```

If you fail to provide an option, `optparse` will complain.

```
$ python optparse_host.py --host
Usage: optparse_host.py [options]

optparse_host.py: error: --host option requires an argument
```

Focus on the call to `add_option`. Several things are different from your `--quiet` flag. First, you omitted the `action` keyword argument. The default for this (`store`) simply stores the value provided. You can specify this manually if you choose to do so.

Second, you provided a `type`. The `OptionParser` instance actually infers this from the type of the `default` value in most cases (although this does not work if your default value is `None`), so providing it is often optional. Explicitly providing it often makes the code easier to read later. The default for `type` is also `str`.

Finally, you provided a `default`. Most options should be optional, which means they must have a sensible default. In many cases, this default may be `None`. In the case of the host value, you chose `localhost` as a sensible default because having your client and server on the same machine is a common use case.

One other thing is worth pointing out explicitly. The way you read the value off of the `options` variable is not what you might expect—the host value is read as `options.host`. You may have expected the `options` value to be provided as a dictionary, in which case `options['host']` would have been correct. However, the `options` variable is provided using its own special class (called `Values`), and the individual options exist on this object as attributes. Note that, if you want a dictionary, `options.__dict__` will provide you with the corresponding dictionary.

Non-String Values

What about values that are not strings? For example, continuing the example of a database client of some sort, what if the script should accept a port number? Most databases run on a default port (PostgreSQL uses 5432, MySQL uses 3306, and so on), but sometimes such services run on alternate ports.

An option for a port looks similar to an option for a host.

```
parser.add_option('-p', '--port',
    default=5432,
    dest='port',
    help='The port to connect to. Defaults to 5432.',
    type=int,
)
```

The crucial difference here is that the `type` is now specified as `int`. Again, `OptionParser` would infer this from the fact that the `default` value is the integer `5432`.

In this case, `OptionParser` performs the type conversion for you, and raises an appropriate error if it is not able to. Consider a script that takes a host and port, as shown here:

```
import optparse


if __name__ == '__main__':
    parser = optparse.OptionParser()
    parser.add_option('-H', '--host',
        default='localhost',
        dest='host',
        help='The host to connect to. Defaults to localhost.',
        type=str,
    )
    parser.add_option('-p', '--port',
        default=5432,
        dest='port',
        help='The port to connect to. Defaults to 5432.',
        type=int,
    )
    options, args = parser.parse_args()

    print('The host is %s, and the port is %d.' %
        (options.host, options.port))
```

Again, invoking the script without arguments provides both default values. Because the format string uses `%d` rather than `%s`, you know that `options.port` is an integer under the hood.

```
$ python optparse_host_and_port.py
The host is localhost, and the port is 5432.
```

If you try to specify a port value that is not an integer, you get an error.

```
$ python optparse_host_and_port.py --port=foo
Usage: optparse_host_and_port.py [options]

optparse_host_and_port.py: error: option --port: invalid integer value: 'foo'
$ echo $?
2
```

And, of course, if you specify a valid integer, it overrides the default.

```
$ python3 optparse_host_and_port.py --port=8000
The host is localhost, and the port is 8000.
```

Specifying Option Values

Several different idioms exist for how to specify option values on the command line. The `optparse` module attempts to support all of them.

Short-Form Syntax

Short-form options are options that have one hyphen and a single letter, such as -q, -H, or -p. If the option accepts a value (such as -H and -p in the previous example), it must be written immediately after the option. There can optionally be a space between the option and the value (-Hlocalhost and -H localhost are equivalent), and the value can optionally be enclosed by quotes (-H localhost and -H "localhost" are equivalent). However, you cannot use an equal sign between the short-form option and the value.

Here are four valid ways to specify an option value using the short-form syntax:

```
$ python optparse_host_and_port.py -H localhost
The host is localhost, and the port is 5432.
$ python optparse_host_and_port.py -H "localhost"
The host is localhost, and the port is 5432.
$ python optparse_host_and_port.py -Hlocalhost
The host is localhost, and the port is 5432.
$ python optparse_host_and_port.py -H"localhost"
The host is localhost, and the port is 5432.
```

The use of the equal sign in the short-form syntax causes it to be prepended to the value itself, which is not what you want. (Note the = in the output.) For non-string options, you will usually get an error when the parser tries and fails to convert the string to the desired type.

```
$ python optparse_host_and_port.py -H=localhost
The host is =localhost, and the port is 5432.
```

And, in the world of the flat-out bizarre, you could have the following:

```
$ python optparse_host_and_port.py -H="localhost"
The host is =localhost, and the port is 5432.
```

Long-Form Syntax

For the long-form format (that is, --host instead of -H), the supported permutations are slightly different.

There now must be some separator between the option and the option value (unlike -Hlocalhost). This makes intuitive sense. If you provided --hostlocalhost, the parser would never be able to figure out conclusively where the option ended and the value began. The separator can either be a space or an equal sign (so, --host=localhost and --host localhost are equivalent).

Quotes are allowed, but optional (but you will certainly want to use them if the value has spaces).

Here are four valid ways to specify an option value using the long-form syntax:

```
$ python cli_script.py --host localhost
The host is localhost, and the port is 5432.
$ python cli_script.py --host "localhost"
The host is localhost, and the port is 5432.
$ python cli_script.py --host=localhost
The host is localhost, and the port is 5432.
$ python cli_script.py --host="localhost"
The host is localhost, and the port is 5432.
```

Which Syntax Should You Use?

The basic tradeoff between short-form and long-form syntax is that the former is quicker to type on the CLI, whereas the latter is more explicit.

When you are writing CLI scripts, consider supporting both a short-form and a long-form syntax, especially for options that are going to be used frequently. (For infrequently used options, providing only a long-form alias is probably sufficient.)

When you are invoking CLI scripts, if you are doing so in code that is being committed to version control and must be read and maintained over time, consider using only long-form syntax wherever it is available. This makes the CLI command easier to intuit for the person reading the code later.

On the other hand, for one-time commands that you are typing out on a prompt, it likely does not matter.

Positional Arguments

It is also possible to send positional arguments to `optparse`. Actually, any argument that is *not* attached to an option will be considered by the parser to be a positional argument, and is sent to the args variable that is returned from `parser.parse_args()`.

```python
import optparse


if __name__ == '__main__':
    parser = optparse.OptionParser()
    options, args = parser.parse_args()

    print('The sum of the numbers sent is: %d' %
        sum([int(i) for i in args]))
```

Any arguments sent to this script are part of the `args` variable, and the script tries to convert them to integers and add them together.

```
$ python optparse_sum.py 1 2 5
The sum of the numbers sent is: 8
```

Of course, if you sent an argument that cannot be converted to an integer, you will get an exception.

```
$ python optparse_sum.py 1 2 foo
Traceback (most recent call last):
  File "optparse_sum.py", line 8, in <module>
    print('The sum of the numbers sent is: %d' % sum([int(i) for i in args]))
ValueError: invalid literal for int() with base 10: 'foo'
```

Counters

You can use a small number of other types of options besides simple flags and direct value storage. One type that is infrequently used but is sometimes useful is a *counter flag*.

Most flags simply set a Boolean value to `True` or `False`, based on the presence or absence of the flag. A related idiom, however, is to allow specifying a flag multiple times to intensify the effect.

Consider a -v flag that causes a script to be more verbose. Some programs allow -v to be specified repeatedly in order to make the script become even more verbose. For example, a popular configuration tool called Ansible allows you to specify -v up to four times to provide increasingly verbose output.

You do this through a different `action` value that you can provide to `add_option`. Consider this script:

```python
import optparse


if __name__ == '__main__':
    parser = optparse.OptionParser()
    parser.add_option('-v',
        action='count',
        default=0,
        dest='verbosity',
        help='Be more verbose. This flag may be repeated.',
    )
    options, args = parser.parse_args()

    print('The verbosity level is %d, ah ah ah.' % options.verbosity)
```

Notice that the call to `add_option` now specifies `action='count'`. This means that the value will be incremented by one every time the flag is sent.

You can invoke the script to easily see this in action.

```
$ python count_script.py
The verbosity level is 0, ah ah ah.
$ python count_script.py -v
The verbosity level is 1, ah ah ah.
$ python count_script.py -v -v
The verbosity level is 2, ah ah ah.
$ python count_script.py -vvvvvvvvvvv
The verbosity level is 11, ah ah ah.
```

Notice that you have two valid ways to specify the short-form option in this case: -v -v and -vv are equivalent. This is actually true for distinct short-form options as well, provided they do not expect a value.

It is also worth noting that explicitly specifying the `default` value of 0 is important. If you do not specify it explicitly, `OptionParser` uses a default value of `None`, which is usually not what you want. (In this case, the script would raise `TypeError` when it tries to do the string interpolation on the last line.)

Finally, note that if you choose a default value other than 0, the flag functions as an increment, not a flat count. So, if your default value is 1, and you provide two -v flags, the value would be 3 (not 2).

List Values

Sometimes, you may want to accept multiple values for the same option, and provide them to your script as a list. This is fundamentally similar to a count option, except that it takes a value each time, rather than simply incrementing an integer variable.

The following script prints usernames, one at a time:

```
import optparse


if __name__ == '__main__':
    parser = optparse.OptionParser()
    parser.add_option('-u', '--user',
        action='append',
        default=[],
        dest='users',
        help='The username to be printed. Provide this multiple times to '
            'print the username for multiple users.',
    )
    options, args = parser.parse_args()

    for user in options.users:
        print('Username: %s.' % user)
```

Running this with no -u or --user options provided generates no output.

```
$ python echo_usernames.py
$
```

However, you can provide one or more -u or --user options to the script, and regardless of how many, the OptionParser makes them available as a list:

```
$ python echo_usernames.py -u me
Username: me.
$ python echo_usernames.py -u me -u myself
Username: me.
Username: myself.
```

Why Use *optparse?*

Even though it has been deprecated for years, the optparse module is still the most commonly used module for parsing options. Any code that must run on Python 2.6 or earlier, or Python 3.0 through Python 3.2, must use optparse, because its successor, argparse, is only available in Python 2.7 and Python 3.3.

If you are writing code with CLI tools that must work across multiple versions of Python, most likely optparse is still going to be the module you should use for several years to come. Similarly, because many tools you will be using still rely on optparse, it is important that you be able to read code that was designed using it.

On the other hand, be aware that optparse is not receiving future development work, because it is still deprecated. Over time, as the window of Python versions you want to support moves, you may decide to move work done in optparse over to argparse.

ARGPARSE

The second library that Python provides for parsing CLI arguments and options is called argparse. The argparse module is considered to be the successor to optparse (and optparse is officially deprecated). However, the argparse module is still quite new. It was introduced in Python 3.3 and backported to Python 2.7. Therefore, any code that needs to run on earlier versions still must use optparse.

In many ways, argparse is conceptually similar to optparse. The fundamental principles are the same. You create a parser specify and options you expect along with types and sensible defaults; then a parser parses the things it received from the CLI and groups them accordingly.

The class you instantiate to do parsing in the argparse module is ArgumentParser. Although it uses some different syntax than optparse.OptionParser, the principles are quite similar.

The Bare Bones

A basic CLI script that does not support any actual arguments or options now looks like this:

```
import argparse


if __name__ == '__main__':
    parser = argparse.ArgumentParser()
    args = parser.parse_args()

    print('The script ran successfully and did nothing.')
```

One key difference to note, other than the renamed module and class, is that this parse_args method does not return a two-tuple like the optparse equivalent did. Instead, it returns a single object that contains both the positional arguments and options read by the parser.

Another difference lies in the way positional arguments are handled. In optparse, you did not declare positional arguments. The second variable simply contained whatever was "left over" after optparse had parsed the options you told it about. By contrast, argparse is stricter. It expects to be told about positional arguments individually, which makes for a more useful help screen, and also causes it to raise an error if it receives data it does not expect.

Therefore, unlike the initial optparse example, this code actually raises an error if it receives any arguments, rather than throwing them into the "left over" bucket.

```
$ python argparse_basic.py
The script ran successfully and did nothing.
$ python argparse_basic.py foo
usage: argparse_basic.py [-h]
cli_script.py: error: unrecognized arguments: foo
```

Arguments and Options

In argparse, you add both positional arguments and options through the add_argument method of ArgumentParser objects. The interface for this is now unified, which means that positional arguments in argparse have support for being a type other than str, and for having specified defaults.

Option Flags

The first kind of option is a flag, such as -v or --verbose for a verbose mode, or -q or --quiet for a mode that suppresses most or all output. These options do not expect a value. The presence or absence of the option determines the appropriate Boolean in the parser.

The syntax for specifying a flag looks like this:

```
parser.add_argument('-q', '--quiet',
    action='store_true',
    dest='quiet',
    help='Suppress output.',
)
```

If you are familiar with `optparse` (or read the section on `optparse` earlier in this chapter), this will look very familiar to you. Other than the method name, not much has changed so far.

First, note the `action` variable. This is set to `store_true`, which is the reason why the parser will not expect a value. Most options do not need an `action` to be specified (the default is `store`, which stores the value it receives). The specification of `store_true` or `store_false` is the most common way to indicate that an option is a flag and should not accept a value.

The `dest` keyword argument determines how to look up the parsed value (in this case, `True` or `False`) on the object you get back when you call `parse_args`. The string used here will be the attribute name on the object. (So, you would look up this one using `args.quiet`.) In many cases, the `dest` keyword argument is optional. `ArgumentParser` determines an intuitive name based on the name of the option itself. However, it is useful to explicitly provide this for readability and maintainability.

The `help` keyword argument determines what users get if they call your script with `-h` or `--help`. The `ArgumentParser` implicitly provides a help screen attached to these switches, so you should always specify a `help` on your arguments.

Alternate Prefixes

Most CLI scripts use the hyphen (-) character as the prefix for options, and this is what `ArgumentParser` expects by default. However, some scripts may use different characters. For example, a script that is only intended to be run in Windows environments may prefer to use the / character, which is consistent with many Windows command-line programs.

You can change which characters are used for prefixes by providing the `prefix_chars` keyword argument to the `ArgumentParser` constructor, as shown here:

```
import argparse


if __name__ == '__main__':
    parser = argparse.ArgumentParser(prefix_chars='/')
    parser.add_argument('/q', '//quiet',
        action='store_true',
        dest='quiet',
        help='Suppress output.',
    )
    args = parser.parse_args()

    print('Quiet mode is %r.' % args.quiet)
```

In this example, you changed the prefix character to /. Note that this also means that the argument itself (the one passed to `add_argument`) must change accordingly.

Calling this script is still straightforward. You simply must use /q or //quiet (rather than -q or --quiet).

```
$ python argparse_quiet.py
Quiet mode is False.
$ python argparse_quiet.py /q
Quiet mode is True.
```

Viewing the help reflects this:

```
$ python argparse_quiet.py /h
usage: argparse_quiet.py [/h] [/q]

optional arguments:
  /h, //help  show this help message and exit
  /q          Suppress output.
```

Note that, because you changed the prefix character to /, the automatically registered help command is changed along with it.

Options with Values

Options that accept values are fundamentally similar. Consider the following example of a script that accepts a host value (such as a database client), translated into argparse:

```python
import argparse


if __name__ == '__main__':
    parser = argparse.ArgumentParser()
    parser.add_argument('-H', '--host',
        default='localhost',
        dest='host',
        help='The host to connect to. Defaults to localhost.',
        type=str,
    )
    args = parser.parse_args()

    print('The host is %s.' % args.host)
```

Again, if you are already familiar with optparse, you will likely notice just how similar this is. The keyword arguments are the same, and they do the same thing.

The important argument to focus on here is type, which controls what Python type the value is ultimately expected to be. It is common for this to be int or float, and a small number of other types may also make sense.

Parsing arguments when you use argparse is slightly different from when you use optparse. Regardless of whether you use the short-form or the long-form syntax, you can separate the option from the value using a space or an equal sign. The short-form syntax (and only the short-form syntax) also supports not separating the value from the option at all. Both the short-form and the long-form syntax allow quotes around the value.

Therefore, all of these are equivalent:

```
$ python argparse_args.py -Hlocalhost
The host is localhost.
$ python argparse_args.py -H"localhost"
The host is localhost.
$ python argparse_args.py -H=localhost
The host is localhost.
$ python argparse_args.py -H="localhost"
The host is localhost.
$ python argparse_args.py -H localhost
The host is localhost.
$ python argparse_args.py -H "localhost"
The host is localhost.
$ python argparse_args.py --host=localhost
The host is localhost.
$ python argparse_args.py --host="localhost"
The host is localhost.
$ python argparse_args.py --host localhost
The host is localhost.
$ python argparse_args.py --host "localhost"
The host is localhost.
```

Choices

`ArgumentParser` adds the capability to specify that an option may only be one of an enumerated set of choices.

```python
import argparse


if __name__ == '__main__':
    parser = argparse.ArgumentParser()
    parser.add_argument('--cheese',
        choices=('american', 'cheddar', 'provolone', 'swiss'),
        default='swiss',
        dest='cheese',
        help='The kind of cheese to use',
    )
    args = parser.parse_args()

    print('You have chosen %s cheese.' % args.cheese)
```

If you run this script with no arguments, you get the default value as you expect.

```
$ python argparse_choices.py
You have chosen swiss cheese.
```

You can also override the default to any of the available choices in the `choices` tuple.

```
$ python argparse_choices.py --cheese provolone
You have chosen provolone cheese.
```

However, if you attempt to provide a value that is not in the list of available choices, you get an error.

```
$ python argparse_choices.py --cheese pepperjack
usage: argparse_choices.py [-h] [--cheese {american,cheddar,provolone,swiss}]
argparse_choices.py: error: argument --cheese: invalid choice: 'pepperjack'
    (choose from 'american', 'cheddar', 'provolone', 'swiss')
```

Accepting Multiple Values

One additional feature in argparse is the capability to specify that an option accepts more than one argument. You can set an option to accept an unbound number of arguments, or an exact number. You handle this using the nargs keyword argument to add_argument.

The most straightforward use of nargs is to specify that an option takes an exact number of arguments. Consider the following simple script that takes an option that expects exactly two arguments rather than one:

```
import argparse


if __name__ == '__main__':
    parser = argparse.ArgumentParser()
    parser.add_argument('--madlib',
        default=['fox', 'dogs'],
        dest='madlib',
        help='Two words to place in the madlib.',
        nargs=2,
    )
    args = parser.parse_args()

    print('The quick brown {0} jumped over the '
          'lazy {1}.'.format(*args.madlib))
```

Sending an integer to nargs means that the option expects exactly that number of arguments, and will return them as a list. (Note that if you specify a nargs value of 1, you still get a list.)

If you omit the --madlib argument, you get the default list specified in the add_argument call.

```
$ python argparse_multiargs.py
The quick brown fox jumped over the lazy dogs.
```

Similarly, providing two arguments causes them to be substituted in place of the defaults.

```
$ python argparse_multiargs.py --madlib pirate ninjas
The quick brown pirate jumped over the lazy ninjas.
```

However, if you try to provide any number of arguments other than two, the command fails.

```
$ python argparse_multiargs.py --madlib pirate
usage: argparse_multiargs.py [-h] [--madlib MADLIB MADLIB]
argparse_multiargs.py: error: argument --madlib: expected 2 arguments
$ python argparse_multiargs.py --madlib pirate ninjas cowboy
usage: argparse_multiargs.py [-h] [--madlib MADLIB MADLIB]
argparse_multiargs.py: error: unrecognized arguments: cowboy
```

In the first case, the --madlib option was only able to consume one argument, and because it expected two, it fails. In the second case, the --madlib argument successfully consumes both of the arguments it expects, but there is a positional argument left over. The parser does not know what to do with that, so it fails out instead.

You also may want to allow any number of arguments, which you can indicate by providing + or *
to nargs. The + value indicates that the option expects one or more values to be provided, and
* indicates that the option expects zero or more values to be provided.

Consider the following simple addition script:

```
import argparse


if __name__ == '__main__':
    parser = argparse.ArgumentParser()
    parser.add_argument('--addends',
        dest='addends',
        help='Integers to provide a sum of',
        nargs='+',
        required=True,
        type=int,
    )
    args = parser.parse_args()

    print('%s = %d' % (
        ' + '.join([str(i) for i in args.addends]),
        sum(args.addends),
    ))
```

If you run this, you can see it provides the following equation:

```
$ python argparse_sum.py --addends 1 2 5
1 + 2 + 5 = 8
$ python argparse_sum.py --addends 1 2
1 + 2 = 3
```

Note that the + value provided to nargs actually means one or more values, not two or more.
This script would gladly accept only a single argument.

```
$ python argparse_sum.py --addends 1
1 = 1
```

Positional Arguments

With argparse (unlike with optparse), you must declare your positional arguments explicitly. If
you do not, the parser expects to have no arguments left over after it completes parsing, and it raises
an error if arguments still remain.

The declaration for positional arguments is equivalent to the declaration for options, except that
the leading hyphen is omitted. As an example, it seems bad form for the --addends option in the
previous example to be an option at all. Options should be optional.

It is easy to provide the same thing as a positional argument.

```
import argparse


if __name__ == '__main__':
    parser = argparse.ArgumentParser()
```

```
parser.add_argument('addends',
    help='Integers to provide a sum of',
    nargs='+',
    type=int,
)
args = parser.parse_args()

print('%s = %d' % (
    ' + '.join([str(i) for i in args.addends]),
    sum(args.addends),
))
```

This is mostly the same, except that the `--addends` argument has been replaced with `addends`, without the double-hyphen prefix. This causes the parser to expect a positional argument instead.

Why provide a name for positional arguments? (After all, `optparse` does not need positional argument names,) The answer is that the name you provide is used in the program's `--help` output.

```
$ python cli_script.py --help
usage: cli_script.py [-h] addends [addends ...]

positional arguments:
  addends        Integers to provide a sum of

optional arguments:
  -h, --help  show this help message and exit
```

Notice that the word `addends` is used in the `usage` line near the top of the help. This provides slightly more insight into what is being expected. Additionally, unlike in help provided by `optparse`, the positional arguments are documented as part of the help screen.

You can invoke this script the same way, except without the `--addends` option.

```
$ python cli_script.py 1 2 5
1 + 2 + 5 = 8
```

Reading Files

A common need when writing CLI applications is to read files. The `argparse` module provides a special class that can be sent to the `type` keyword argument of `add_argument`, which is `argparse.FileType`.

The `argparse.FileType` class expects the arguments that would be sent to Python's `open` function, *excluding* the filename (which is what is being provided by the user invoking the program). If you are opening the file for reading, this may be nothing. `open` defaults to opening files only for reading. However, any arguments after the initial positional argument to `open` can be provided to `FileType`, and they will be passed on to `open`.

Consider the following program that may read a configuration file from a non-default location:

```
import argparse


if __name__ == '__main__':
    parser = argparse.ArgumentParser()
```

```
parser.add_argument('-c', '--config-file',
    default='/etc/cli_script',
    dest='config',
    help='The configuration file to use.',
    type=argparse.FileType('r')
)
args = parser.parse_args()

print(args.config.read())
```

This would read from /etc/cli_script by default, but allow you to specify a different file to read from using the -c or --config-file options. Rather than providing these options as text and forcing you to open the file yourself, you will simply be provided with an open file object:

```
$ echo "This is my config file." > foo.txt
$ python cli_script.py --config-file foo.txt
This is my config file.
```

Note that the file is expected to exist. If it does not, you get an error.

```
$ python cli_script.py --config-file bar.txt
usage: cli_script.py [-h] [-c CONFIG]
cli_script.py: error: argument -c/--config-file: can't open 'bar.txt':
    [Errno 2] No such file or directory: 'bar.txt'
```

Why Use *argparse?*

If you are exclusively using Python 2.7 or Python 3.3 and up, several good reasons exist to use argparse rather than optparse. The argparse module supports essentially all of optparse's features, and adds several additional ones, such as multiple arguments, better support for files, and more.

Additionally, argparse's handling of positional arguments is more consistent with its handling of options, and results in more robust handling as well as a more useful help output.

The only major drawback of argparse is its absence from older versions of Python. If you still need to support Python 2.6 or Python 3.2, you need to stick with optparse for now.

SUMMARY

The optparse and argparse modules provide very good support for reading data from the command line for Python programs that need to do this.

The current transition from optparse to argparse poses a challenge because you may find yourself needing to write code around a deprecated module to support versions of Python that are still in wide use today. If you do work in this area, you will probably need to remain familiar with both modules for some time.

In Chapter 13, you learn about asyncio, a new module in Python 3.4 to support asynchronous work.

13

asyncio

In general, most Python applications are sequential applications. That is, they usually run from a defined entry point to a defined exit point, with each execution being a single process from beginning to end.

This stands in contrast to many more asynchronous languages, such as JavaScript and Go. For example, JavaScript relies heavily on asynchronous work, with any web requests happening in the background being called in a separate thread, and relying on callbacks to run correct functions once data has loaded.

There is no right or wrong answer to whether a language should approach most problems sequentially or asynchronously, but cases certainly exist where one model is more useful than the other for particular problems. This is where the asyncio module comes in. It makes it easy to do asynchronous work in Python when the problem warrants it.

Right now, asyncio is a provisional module. While sweeping, backward-incompatible changes are unlikely (because Python shies away from such things once items have been placed in the standard library), it is likely that asyncio may undergo significant revision in the next couple of Python versions.

The asyncio module was introduced in Python 3.4, and is not available in Python 2. If you are on Python 3.3, you can get it from PyPI; it is not yet in the standard library. Therefore, if you want to use the features provided by asyncio, you will be limiting yourself to newer versions of Python. Similarly, the asyncio module has been under active development over the lifetime of Python 3.4, so you will want to be on the newest incremental revision if possible.

Because most Python applications are sequential applications, several concepts may be foreign to you if you have not done a reasonable amount of work outside of sequential languages. This chapter covers these concepts in detail.

THE EVENT LOOP

The fundamental way that most asynchronous applications work is via an *event loop* that runs in the background. When something needs to run, it is registered to the event loop.

Registering a function to an event loop causes it to be made into a *task*. The event loop is then responsible for running the task as soon as it can get to it. Alternatively, sometimes the event loop is told to wait a certain amount of time, and then run the task.

Although you may not be familiar with writing code that uses event loops, you use programs that depend on them frequently. Almost any server is an event loop. A database server, for example, sits around and waits for connections and queries, and then executes queries as fast as possible. If two different connections provide two different queries, it prioritizes and runs both of them. Desktop applications are also event-driven, displaying a screen that allows input in various places and responding to said inputs. Most video games are also event loops. The game waits for control input and takes action based on it.

A Simple Event Loop

In most cases, you do not need to create an event loop object yourself. You can get a `BaseEventLoop` object by using the `asyncio.get_event_loop()` function. What you will actually get will be a subclass; *which* subclass you get is platform-dependent. You do not need to worry about this implementation detail too much. The API between all of them is the same. However, a few platform-dependent limitations exist.

When you first get the loop object, it will not be running.

```
>>> loop = asyncio.get_event_loop()
>>> loop.is_running()
False
```

Running the Loop

The following event loop does not have anything registered to it yet, but you can run it anyway:

```
>>> loop.run_forever()
```

There is one minor hitch, however. If you ran this, you just lost control of your Python interpreter, because the loop is running in it forever. Press Ctrl+C to get your interpreter back. (Of course, this will stop the loop.)

Unfortunately, `asyncio` does not have a "fire and forget" method to run a loop in a separate thread. For most application code, this is actually not a huge hindrance, because you are probably writing a server or daemon where the purpose of the program is to run the loop in the foreground and have other processes issue commands.

For testing or experimenting, however, this presents a serious challenge, because the majority of `asyncio` methods are not actually thread-safe. For most examples in this chapter, you will get around this by simply not running the loop forever.

Registering Tasks and Running the Loop

Tasks are primarily registered to the loop using `call_soon`, which operates as a FIFO ("first in, first out") queue. Therefore, most examples in this chapter will simply include a final task that stops the loop, as shown here:

```
>>> import functools
>>> def hello_world():
...     print('Hello world!')
...
>>> def stop_loop(loop):
...     print('Stopping loop.')
...     loop.stop()
...
>>> loop.call_soon(hello_world)
Handle(<function hello_world at 0x1003c0b70>, ())
>>> loop.call_soon(functools.partial(stop_loop, loop))
Handle(functools.partial(<function stop_loop at 0x101ccf268>,
    <asyncio.unix_events._UnixSelectorEventLoop
    object at 0x1007399e8>), ())
>>> loop.run_forever()
Hello world!
Stopping loop.
>>>
```

In this example, the `hello_world` function was registered to the loop. Then, the `stop_loop` function was also registered. When the loop was started (with `loop.run_forever()`), it ran both tasks, in order. Because the second task stopped the loop, it exited the loop once the task completed.

Delaying Calls

It is also possible to register a task, but indicate that it should not be called until later. You can do this using the `call_later` method, which takes a delay (in number of seconds) as well as the function to be called.

```
>>> loop.call_later(10, hello_world)
TimerHandle(60172.411042585, <function hello_world at 0x1003c0b70>, ())
>>> loop.call_later(20, functools.partial(stop_loop, loop))
TimerHandle(60194.829461844, functools.partial(
    <function stop_loop at 0x101ccf268>,
    <asyncio.unix_events._UnixSelectorEventLoop object at 0x1007399e8>),
    ())
>>> loop.run_forever()
```

Note that it is possible to have two or more delayed calls come up at the same time. If this happens, they may occur in either order.

Partials

You may have also noticed the use of `functools.partial` in the previous example. Most `asyncio` methods that take functions only take function objects (or other callables), but not arguments to be sent to those functions once they are called. The `functools.partial` method is a solution to that problem. The `partial` method itself takes the arguments and keyword arguments that must be passed to the underlying function when it is called.

For instance, the `hello_world` function in the previous example is actually entirely unnecessary. It is an analogue to `functools.partial(print, 'Hello world!')`. Therefore, the previous example could be written as follows:

```
>>> import functools
>>> def stop_loop(loop):
...     print('Stopping loop.')
...     loop.stop()
...
>>> loop.call_soon(functools.partial(print, 'Hello world! ')
Handle(functools.partial(<built-in function print>, 'Hello world'), ())
>>> loop.call_soon(functools.partial(stop_loop, loop))
Handle(functools.partial(<function stop_loop at 0x101ccf268>,
    <asyncio.unix_events._UnixSelectorEventLoop object
    at 0x1007399e8>), ())
>>> loop.run_forever()
Hello world!
Stopping loop.
>>>
```

Why have partials at all? After all, it is usually easy enough to wrap such calls in functions that do not require arguments. The answer is in debugging. The `partial` object knows what it is calling and with what arguments. This is represented as *data* to the `partial`, and the `partial` uses that data when called to perform the proper function call. By contrast, the `hello_world` function is just that: a function. The function call within it is *code*. There is no way to easily inspect the `hello_world` function and pull out the underlying call.

You can see this difference by creating a partial and then inspecting its underlying function and arguments.

```
>>> partial = functools.partial(stop_loop, loop)
>>> partial.func
<function stop_loop at 0x10223e488>
>>> partial.args
(<asyncio.unix_events._UnixSelectorEventLoop object at 0x102238b70>,)
```

Running the Loop until a Task Completes

It is also possible to run the loop until a task completes, as shown here:

```
>>> @asyncio.coroutine
... def trivial():
...     return 'Hello world!'
```

```
...
>>> loop.run_until_complete(trivial())
'Hello world!'
```

In this example, the `@asyncio.coroutine` decorator transforms this normal Python function into a coroutine, which is covered in more detail later. When you call `run_until_complete`, it registers the task and then runs the loop only until the task completes. Because it is the only task in the queue, it completes and exits the loop, returning the result of that task.

Running a Background Loop

It is possible to run an event loop in the background, using the `threading` module that is available in the Python standard library.

```
>>> import asyncio
>>> import threading
>>>
>>> def run_loop_forever_in_background(loop):
...     def thread_func(l):
...         asyncio.set_event_loop(l)
...         l.run_forever()
...     thread = threading.Thread(target=thread_func, args=(loop,))
...     thread.start()
...     return thread
...
>>>
>>> loop = asyncio.get_event_loop()
>>> run_loop_forever_in_background(loop)
<Thread(Thread-1, started 4344254464)>
>>>
>>> loop.is_running()
True
```

Note that this is a useful idiom for getting started, but is almost certainly not what you will want in your final application. (For example, you will have a hard time *stopping* the loop; `loop.stop` does not work anymore.) It is fine for learning, though.

This loop is still relatively uninteresting. After all, while it is running, it has nothing to do. You have not registered any tasks to it yet. Consider what happens when you register a trivial task to run as soon as possible.

```
>>> loop.call_soon_threadsafe(functools.partial(print, 'Hello world'))
Handle(functools.partial(<built-in function print>, 'Hello world'), ())
>>> Hello world
```

This output might be a bit confusing. First, you called `call_soon_threadsafe`. This tells the loop to run the given function asynchronously as soon as possible. Note that, in most cases, you will simply use the `call_soon` function, because you will not be running the event loop in a thread.

The `call_soon_threadsafe` function returns a `Handle` object. This is an object with one method: `cancel`. It is able to cancel the task entirely if appropriate.

Next, you have the >>> prompt (suggesting that the interpreter expects input), followed by `Hello world`. That was printed from the previous function call, *after* the prompt was written to the screen.

Because event loops are not thread safe, the remainder of the examples in this chapter use other models to explain the concepts.

COROUTINES

Most functions that are used within `asyncio` should be coroutines. A *coroutine* is a special kind of function designed to run within an event loop. Additionally, if a coroutine is created but is never run, an error will be issued to the logs.

> **NOTE** *This discussion documents Python 3.4 specifically. Changes are possible in Python 3.5.*

You can make a function into a coroutine by decorating it with `@asyncio.coroutine`. Consider this example of running a simple coroutine with the event handler's `run_until_complete`:

```
>>> import asyncio
>>> @asyncio.coroutine
... def coro_sum(*args):
...     answer = 0
...     for i in args:
...         answer += i
...     return answer
...
>>> loop = asyncio.get_event_loop()
>>> loop.run_until_complete(coro_sum(1, 2, 3, 4, 5))
15
```

The `coro_sum` function created here is no longer a regular function; it is a coroutine, and it is called by the event loop. It is worth noting that you can no longer call it the regular way and get what you may expect.

```
>>> coro_sum(1, 2, 3, 4, 5)
<generator object coro at 0x104056e10>
```

Coroutines are, in fact, special generators that are consumed by the event loop. That is why the `run_until_complete` method is able to take what appears to be a standard function call. The function is not actually run at that point. The event loop is what consumes the generator and ultimately extracts the result.

What actually happens under the hood essentially looks like this:

```
>>> try:
...     next(coro_sum(1, 2, 3, 4, 5))
... except StopIteration as ex:
```

```
...      ex.value
...
15
```

The generator does not yield any values. It immediately raises `StopIteration`. The `StopIteration` exception is given a value, which is the return value of the function. The event loop is then able to extract this and handle it appropriately.

Nested Coroutines

Coroutines provide a special mechanism to call other coroutines (or `Future` instances, as discussed shortly) in a fashion that mimics that of sequential programming. By using the `yield from` statement, a coroutine can run another coroutine, and the statement returns the result. This is one mechanism available to write asynchronous code in a sequential manner.

The following simple coroutine calls another coroutine using `yield from`:

```
>>> import asyncio
>>> @asyncio.coroutine
... def nested(*args):
...     print('The `nested` function ran with args: %r' % (args,))
...     return [i + 1 for i in args]
...
>>> @asyncio.coroutine
... def outer(*args):
...     print('The `outer` function ran with args: %r' % (args,))
...     answer = yield from nested(*[i * 2 for i in args])
...     return answer
...
>>> loop = asyncio.get_event_loop()
>>> loop.run_until_complete(outer(2, 3, 5, 8))
The `outer` function ran with args: (2, 3, 5, 8)
The `nested` function ran with args: (4, 6, 10, 16)
[5, 7, 11, 17]
```

Here you have two coroutines, with the outer coroutine calling the nested coroutine using the `yield from` syntax. You can see from the output to standard out that both coroutines run, and the final result is returned at the end of `outer`.

Incidentally, what is happening here under the hood is that the `outer` coroutine is actually suspended when it encounters the `yield from` statement. The `nested` coroutine is then placed on the event loop and the event loop runs it. The `outer` coroutine does not continue until `nested` completes and a result is available.

A couple things are worth noting. First, the `yield from` statement returns the result of the coroutine it runs. That is why you see an assignment to a variable in the example.

Second, why would you not simply call the function directly? This would be fine if it were a procedural function, but this is a coroutine. Calling it directly would return a generator rather than the value. You could write `nested` as a standard function, but consider the following situation where you would also want to be able to assign it to the event loop directly.

```
>>> loop.run_until_complete(nested(5, 10, 15))
The `nested` function ran with args: (5, 10, 15)
[6, 11, 16]
```

The capability to have a coroutine call another coroutine using `yield from` addresses this. It increases the capability to reuse coroutines.

FUTURES AND TASKS

Because most work using `asyncio` is done asynchronously, you must contend with how to deal with the results of functions that are run in this manner. The `yield from` statement provides one way to do this, but sometimes, for example, you want to run asynchronous functions in parallel.

In sequential programming, return values are straightforward. You run a function, and it returns its result. However, in asynchronous programming, while the function returns its result as before, what happens to the result then? There is no clear caller to return the result *to*.

Futures

A mechanism for dealing with this particular challenge is the `Future` object. Essentially, a `Future` is an object that is told about the status of an asynchronous function. This includes the status of the function—whether that function is running, has completed, or was canceled. This also includes the result of the function, or, if the function ended by raising an exception, the exception and traceback.

The `Future` is a standalone object. It is independent of the actual function that is running. It does nothing but store the state and result information.

Tasks

A `Task` is a subclass of `Future`, as well as what you will generally be using when programming with `asyncio`. Whenever a coroutine is scheduled on the event loop, that coroutine is wrapped in a `Task`. So, in the previous example, when you called `run_until_complete` and passed a coroutine, that coroutine was wrapped in a `Task` class and then executed. It was the `Task` that stored the result and handled providing it in the `yield from` statement.

The `run_until_complete` method is not the only way (or even the primary way) for a coroutine to be wrapped in a class, however. After all, in many applications, your event loop runs forever. How do tasks get placed on the event loop in such a system?

The primary way you do this is by using the `asyncio.async` method. This method will place a coroutine on the event loop, and return the associated `Task`.

> **NOTE** *If you are running Python 3.4.4+, use* `ensure_future` *rather than* `asyncio.async`. *However, if you are running Python 3.4.3, continue to use* `asyncio`.

To demonstrate this, first get the event loop and write a garden-variety coroutine, as shown here:

```
>>> import asyncio
>>>
>>> @asyncio.coroutine
... def make_tea(variety):
...     print('Now making %s tea.' % variety)
...     asyncio.get_event_loop().stop()
...     return '%s tea' % variety
...
>>>
```

This is still a trivial task, but one new thing here that you have not seen yet is that the task actually stops the event loop. This is simply a nice workaround to dodge the fact that when you *start* the loop (with run_forever), it will run forever.

Next, register the task with the event loop.

```
>>> task = asyncio.async(make_tea('chamomile'))
```

This is all you actually need to do to register the task with the loop, but because the loop is not running, the task is not going to execute for now. Indeed, you can inspect the task object using the done and result methods and see this.

```
>>> task.done()
False
>>> task.result()
Traceback (most recent call last):
  File "<stdin>", line 1, in <module>
  File "/Library/Frameworks/Python.framework/Versions/3.4/lib/python3.4/asyncio/
      futures.py", line 237, in result
    raise InvalidStateError('Result is not ready.')
asyncio.futures.InvalidStateError: Result is not ready.
```

Next, you must start the loop. It is okay to start the loop with run_forever now; the actual task will stop it as soon as the task completes because of the call to loop.stop().

```
>>> loop = asyncio.get_event_loop()
>>> loop.run_forever()
Now making chamomile tea.
>>>
```

Sure enough, the loop starts, runs the task, and then immediately stops. Now if you inspect the task variable, you will get different results.

```
>>> task.done()
True
>>> task.result()
'chamomile tea'
```

Whenever you create a Task object with asyncio.async, you will get a Task object back. You can inspect that object at any time to get the status or result of the task.

CALLBACKS

Another feature of `Future` objects (and therefore `Task` objects, because `Task` subclasses `Future`) is the capability to register callbacks to the `Future`. A *callback* is simply a function (or coroutine) that should execute once the `Future` is done, and which receives the `Future` as an argument.

In some ways, callbacks represent a reversal of the `yield from` model. When a coroutine uses `yield from`, *that coroutine* ensures that the nested coroutine runs before or during its execution. When you register a callback, you are working in the opposite direction. The callback is being attached to the original task, to run *after* the execution of the task.

You can add a callback to any `Future` object by using that object's `add_done_callback` method. Callbacks are expected to take a single argument, which is the `Future` object itself (which will contain the status and result, if applicable, of the underlying task).

Consider the following example of a callback in action:

```
>>> import asyncio
>>> loop = asyncio.get_event_loop()
>>>
>>> @asyncio.coroutine
... def make_tea(variety):
...     print('Now making %s tea.' % variety)
...     return '%s tea' % variety
...
>>> def confirm_tea(future):
...     print('The %s is made.' % future.result())
...
>>> task = asyncio.async(make_tea('green'))
>>> task.add_done_callback(confirm_tea)
>>>
>>> loop.run_until_complete(task)
Now making green tea.
The green tea is made.
'green tea'
```

The first thing that is happening is that you again made a `make_tea` coroutine, identical to the one in the previous example, except that this one does not stop the loop.

Next, notice the `confirm_tea` function. This is a plain function; it is *not* a coroutine. In fact, you cannot send a coroutine as a callback here. It will raise an exception when you run the loop if you try. This function receives the `Future` object (which is the `task` variable in this case) that it is registered to once the callback runs. The `Future` object contains the result of the coroutine—which is that is the `'green tea'` string in this case.

Finally, notice the call to `add_done_callback`. This is where the `confirm_tea` method is assigned as a callback to the task. Also, notice that it is assigned to the *task* (a particular invocation of a coroutine), not the coroutine itself. If another task was registered to the loop with `asyncio.async` that called the same coroutine, it would *not* have this callback.

The output shows that both functions ran, in the order you expected. The return value is the return value from `make_tea`, provided to you because that is how `run_until_complete` works.

No Guarantee of Success

There is one important thing to note. Simply because a `Future` is done does *not* guarantee that it ran successfully. This example simply assumes that `future.result()` will be populated, but that may not be the case. The `Task` could have ended in an exception, in which case, attempting to access `future.result()` will raise that exception.

Similarly, it is possible to cancel a task (using the `Future.cancel()` method or by other means). If this occurs, the task will be marked `Cancelled`, and the callbacks will be scheduled. In this case, attempting to access `future.result()` will raise `CancelledError`.

Under the Hood

Internally, `asyncio` informs the `Future` object that it is done. The `Future` object then takes each of the callbacks registered against it and calls `call_soon_threadsafe` on each of them.

Be aware that there is no guarantee of order when it comes to callbacks. It is entirely possible (and fine) to register multiple callbacks to the same task. However, you do not have any way of controlling which callbacks will be run in which order.

Callbacks with Arguments

One limitation of the callback system is that, as noted, the callback receives the `Future` as a positional argument, and accepts no other arguments.

It is possible to send other arguments to a callback through the use of `functools.partial`. If you do this, however, the callback *must still* accept the `Future` as a positional argument. In practice, the `Future` is appended to the end of the positional arguments list before the callback is called.

Consider the following case of a callback that expects another argument:

```
>>> import asyncio
>>> import functools
>>>
>>> loop = asyncio.get_event_loop()
>>>
>>> @asyncio.coroutine
... def make_tea(variety):
...     print('Now making %s tea.' % variety)
...     return '%s tea' % variety
...
>>> def add_ingredient(ingredient, future):
...     print('Now adding %s to the %s.' % (ingredient, future.result()))
...
>>>
>>> task = asyncio.async(make_tea('herbal'))
>>> task.add_done_callback(functools.partial(add_ingredient, 'honey'))
>>>
>>> loop.run_until_complete(task)
Now making herbal tea.
Now adding honey to the herbal tea.
'herbal tea'
```

This is mostly similar to the previous example. The only significant difference is in how the callback is registered. Instead of passing the function object directly (as you did in the previous example), you instantiate a `functools.partial` object with the positional argument you are sending (`'honey'`).

Again, notice that the `add_ingredient` function is written to accept *two* positional arguments, but the `partial` only specifies one argument. The `Future` object is sent as the *last* positional argument in cases where a `partial` is used. The function signature for `add_ingredient` reflects this.

TASK AGGREGATION

The `asyncio` module provides a convenient way to aggregate tasks. You have two major reasons to do something like this. The first reason is to take some sort of action once *any* task in a set of tasks has completed. The second reason is to take some sort of action once all tasks in the set have completed.

Gathering Tasks

The first mechanism that `asyncio` provides for this purpose is the `gather` function. The `gather` function takes a sequence of coroutines or tasks and returns a single task that aggregates all of them (wrapping any coroutines it receives in tasks as appropriate).

```
>>> import asyncio
>>> loop = asyncio.get_event_loop()
>>>
>>> @asyncio.coroutine
... def make_tea(variety):
...     print('Now making %s tea.' % variety)
...     return '%s tea' % variety
...
>>> meta_task = asyncio.gather(
...     make_tea('chamomile'),
...     make_tea('green'),
...     make_tea('herbal')
... )
...
>>> meta_task.done()
False
>>>
>>> loop.run_until_complete(meta_task)
Now making chamomile tea.
Now making herbal tea.
Now making green tea.
['chamomile tea', 'green tea', 'herbal tea']
>>> meta_task.done()
True
```

In this case, the `asyncio.gather` function received three coroutine objects. It wrapped them all in tasks under the hood, and returned a single task that serves as an aggregation of all three.

Notice that scheduling the `meta_task` object effectively schedules the three tasks gathered underneath it. Once you run the loop, the three subtasks all run.

In the case of a task created with `asyncio.gather`, the result is always a list, and that list contains the results of the individual tasks that were gathered. The order of the list of results is guaranteed to be the same order in which the tasks were gathered (but the tasks are not guaranteed to be run in that order). Therefore, the list of strings you got back are in the same order as the registered coroutines in the `asyncio.gather` call.

The `asyncio.gather` paradigm also provides the opportunity to add a callback to the *set* of tasks as a whole, rather than the individual tasks. What if you only want a callback to run once *all* of the tasks are completed, but it does not matter to you in which order they complete?

```
>>> import asyncio
>>> loop = asyncio.get_event_loop()
>>>
>>> @asyncio.coroutine
... def make_tea(variety):
...     print('Now making %s tea.' % variety)
...     return '%s tea' % variety
...
>>> def mix(future):
...     print('Mixing the %s together.' % ' and '.join(future.result()))
...
>>> meta_task = asyncio.gather(make_tea('herbal'), make_tea('green'))
>>> meta_task.add_done_callback(mix)
>>>
>>> loop.run_until_complete(meta_task)
Now making green tea.
Now making herbal tea.
Mixing the green tea and herbal tea together.
['green tea', 'herbal tea']
```

The first thing that happened when you called `run_until_complete` was that both of the individual tasks gathered into `meta_task` ran, individually. Finally, the `mix` function ran, only after both of the individual tasks had run. This is because the `meta_task` is not considered to be done until after all of its individual tasks are done, so only once both individual tasks complete does it trigger the callback.

You can also see that the `Future` object that the `mix` function received was `meta_task`, not the individual tasks, and, therefore, its `result` method returned a list of both of the individual results.

Waiting on Tasks

Another tool that the `asyncio` module provides is the built-in `wait` coroutine. The `asyncio.wait` coroutine takes a sequence of coroutines or tasks (wrapping any coroutines in tasks) and returns once they are done. Note that the signature here is distinct from `asyncio.gather`. `gather` takes each coroutine or task as a single positional argument, whereas `wait` expects a list.

Additionally, `wait` accepts a parameter to return when *any* of its tasks complete, rather than only returning when all of them do. Regardless of whether this flag is set, the `wait` method always returns a two-tuple, with the first element being the `Future` objects that have completed, and the second element being those that are still pending.

Consider the following example that is similar to how you previously used `asyncio.gather`:

```
>>> import asyncio
>>> loop = asyncio.get_event_loop()
>>>
>>> @asyncio.coroutine
... def make_tea(variety):
...     print('Now making %s tea.' % variety)
...     return '%s tea' % variety
...
>>> coro = asyncio.wait([make_tea('chamomile'), make_tea('herbal')])
>>>
>>> loop.run_until_complete(coro)
Now making chamomile tea.
Now making herbal tea.
({Task(<coro>)<result='herbal tea'>, Task(<coro>)<result='chamomile tea'>}, set())
```

Note a couple of subtle differences here. First, unlike the `gather` method, the `wait` method returns a coroutine. This has its value; you can use it in a `yield from` statement, for example.

On the other hand, you are unable to attach callbacks directly to a coroutine returned from `wait`. If you want to do this, you must wrap it in a task using `asyncio.async`.

Also, the result is different. The `asyncio.gather` function aggregated the results in a list, and returned that. The result for `asyncio.wait` is a two-tuple containing the actual `Future` objects (which themselves contain their results). Additionally, the `Future` objects are reorganized. The `asyncio.wait` routine places them into two sets—one set for those that are done, and another set for those that are not. Because sets are themselves an unordered structure, that means you must rely on the `Future` objects to piece together which result corresponds to which task.

Timeouts

It is possible to have the `asyncio.wait` coroutine return when a specific amount of time has passed, regardless of whether all of the tasks have completed. To do this, you pass the `timeout` keyword argument to `asyncio.wait`.

```
>>> import asyncio
>>> loop = asyncio.get_event_loop()
>>>
>>> coro = asyncio.wait([asyncio.sleep(5), asyncio.sleep(1)], timeout=3)
>>> loop.run_until_complete(coro)
({Task(<sleep>)<result=None>}, {Task(<sleep>)<PENDING>})
```

In this case, you are just using a coroutine provided by the `asyncio` module: `asyncio.sleep`. This simply waits for a given number of seconds, and then returns `None`. The timing in this example is set up so that one of the tasks (the second one) will complete before the `wait` function times out, but the other will not.

The first difference to note is that the second element of the two-tuple now has a task in it; the sleep coroutine that failed to complete in time is still pending. The other, however, did complete, and has a result (None).

The use of timeout does not necessitate that the entire time period designated by timeout must elapse. If all of the tasks complete before time expires, the coroutine will complete immediately.

Waiting on Any Task

One of the biggest features of asyncio.wait is the capability to have the coroutine return when *any* of the Future objects under its care completes. The asyncio.wait function also accepts a return_when keyword argument. By sending it a special constant (asyncio.FIRST_COMPLETED), the coroutine will complete once any task has finished, rather than waiting for every task.

```
>>> import asyncio
>>> loop = asyncio.get_event_loop()
>>>
>>> coro = asyncio.wait([
...     asyncio.sleep(3),
...     asyncio.sleep(2),
...     asyncio.sleep(1),
... ], return_when=asyncio.FIRST_COMPLETED)
>>>
>>> loop.run_until_complete(coro)
({Task(<sleep>)<result=None>},
 {Task(<sleep>)<PENDING>, Task(<sleep>)<PENDING>})
```

In this case, the asyncio.wait call is given a list of three asyncio.sleep coroutines, which will sleep for 3, 2, and 1 seconds. Once the coroutine is called, it runs all the tasks underneath it. The asyncio.sleep coroutine that is only asked to wait for 1 second completes first, which completes the wait. Therefore, you get a two-tuple back with one item in the first set (tasks that are complete), and two items in the second set (tasks that are still pending).

Waiting on an Exception

It is also possible to have a call to asyncio.wait complete whenever it encounters a task that completed with an exception, rather than exiting normally. This is a valuable tool in situations where you want to trap the exceptional cases as early as possible and deal with them.

You can trigger this behavior using the return_from keyword argument as before, but by sending the asyncio.FIRST_EXCEPTION constant instead.

```
>>> import asyncio
>>> loop = asyncio.get_event_loop()
>>>
>>> @asyncio.coroutine
... def raise_ex_after(seconds):
...     yield from asyncio.sleep(seconds)
...     raise RuntimeError('Raising an exception.')
...
>>> coro = asyncio.wait([
...     asyncio.sleep(1),
```

```
...        raise_ex_after(2),
...        asyncio.sleep(3),
... ], return_when=asyncio.FIRST_EXCEPTION)
>>>
>>> loop.run_until_complete(coro)
({Task(<raise_ex_after>)<exception=RuntimeError('Raising an exception.',)>,
  Task(<sleep>)<result=None>},
 {Task(<sleep>)<PENDING>})
```

In this case, the `asyncio.wait` coroutine stopped as soon as a task completed with an exception. This means that the 1-second `asyncio.sleep` completed successfully, and it is in the first set in the return value. The `raise_ex_after` coroutine also completed, so it is in the first set also. However, the fact that it raised an exception caused `wait` to trigger its completion before the 3-second sleep could complete, so it is returned in the second (pending) set.

Sometimes, there may not be any task that actually raises an exception (which is usually a convenient case). In this case, the wait completes once all of the tasks have completed as normal.

```
>>> import asyncio
>>> loop = asyncio.get_event_loop()
>>>
>>> coro = asyncio.wait([
...        asyncio.sleep(1),
...        asyncio.sleep(2),
... ], return_when=asyncio.FIRST_EXCEPTION)
>>>
>>> loop.run_until_complete(coro)
({Task(<sleep>)<result=None>, Task(<sleep>)<result=None>}, set())
```

QUEUES

The `asyncio` module provides several common patterns that are built upon the fundamental building blocks of the event loop and `Future` objects. One of these is a basic queuing system.

A *queue* is a collection of tasks to be processed by a task runner. The Python ecosystem includes several third-party task queue utilities, with the most popular of these probably being `celery`. This is not a fully featured queuing application. Rather, the `asyncio` module provides simply the fundamental queue itself, which application developers can build on top of.

Why is `Queue` part of `asyncio`? This `Queue` class provides methods to be used in a sequential or an asynchronous context.

Consider first a very simple example of a `Queue` in action:

```
>>> import asyncio
>>> queue = asyncio.Queue()
>>> queue.put_nowait('foo')
>>> queue.qsize()
1
>>> queue.get_nowait()
```

```
'foo'
>>> queue.qsize()
0
```

In addition to being trivially simple, there is nothing particularly asynchronous going on here. You did not even bother to get or run the event loop. This is a very direct FIFO queue.

Note the use of the put_nowait and get_nowait methods. These methods are designed to perform the addition or removal of the item to or from the queue immediately. If, for example, you try to call get_nowait on an empty queue, you get a QueueEmpty exception.

```
>>> queue.get_nowait()
Traceback (most recent call last):
  File "<stdin>", line 1, in <module>
  File "/Library/Frameworks/Python.framework/Versions/3.4/lib/python3.4/asyncio/
      queues.py", line 206, in get_nowait
    raise QueueEmpty
asyncio.queues.QueueEmpty
```

The Queue class also provides a method called get. Instead of returning an exception on an empty queue, the get method will patiently wait for an item to be added to the queue, and then retrieve it from the queue and return it immediately. Unlike get_nowait, this method is a coroutine, and runs in an asynchronous context.

```
>>> import asyncio
>>> loop = asyncio.get_event_loop()
>>> queue = asyncio.Queue()
>>>
>>> queue.put_nowait('foo')
>>> loop.run_until_complete(queue.get())
'foo'
```

In this case, an item was already on the queue, so the get method still returns immediately. If there was not an item on the queue yet, a simple call to loop.run_until_complete would never complete, and block your interpreter.

You can use the timeout parameter in asyncio.wait to see this concept in action, though.

```
>>> import asyncio
>>> loop = asyncio.get_event_loop()
>>> queue = asyncio.Queue()
>>>
>>> task = asyncio.async(queue.get())
>>> coro = asyncio.wait([task], timeout=1)
>>>
>>> loop.run_until_complete(coro)
(set(), {Task(<get>)<PENDING>})
```

At this point, there is still nothing on the queue, so the task to get the item off the queue is just continuing indefinitely. You also have the task variable, and can inspect its status.

```
>>> task.done()
False
```

Next, place an item on the queue, as shown here:

```
>>> queue.put_nowait('bar')
```

You will notice that the task still is not done yet, because the event loop is no longer running. The `task` is still registered, though, so register a callback to stop the loop once it completes, and it is possible to start it again.

```
>>> import functools
>>> def stop(l, future):
...     l.stop()
...
>>> task.add_done_callback(functools.partial(stop, loop))
>>>
>>> loop.run_forever()
```

Now, because there was an item on the queue, the task is done, and the task's result is the item on the queue (`'bar'`).

```
>>> task.done()
True
>>> task.result()
'bar'
```

Maximum Size

It is also possible to give a `Queue` object a maximum size, by setting the `maxsize` keyword argument when creating the queue.

```
>>> import asyncio
>>> queue = asyncio.Queue(maxsize=5)
```

If you do this, the `Queue` will not allow any more than the maximum number of items onto the queue. A call to the `put` method will simply wait until a previous item is removed, and then (and only then) will it place the item on the queue. If you call `put_nowait` and the queue is full, it will raise `QueueFull`.

SERVERS

One of the most common uses of the `asyncio` module is to create services that can run as a daemon and accept commands. The `asyncio` module defines a `Protocol` class that is able to fire appropriate events on receiving or losing a connection, and when it receives data.

Additionally, the event loop defines a `create_server` method that opens a socket, allowing data to be sent to the event loop and on to the protocol.

Consider a simple server that can do nothing but add numbers and shut itself down.

```
import asyncio


class Shutdown(Exception):
    pass
```

```python
class ServerProtocol(asyncio.Protocol):
    def connection_made(self, transport):
        self.transport = transport
        self.write('Welcome.')

    def data_received(self, data):
        # Sanity check: Do nothing on empty commands.
        if not data:
            return

        # Commands to this server shall be a single word, with
        # space separated arguments.
        message = data.decode('ascii')
        command = message.strip().split(' ')[0].lower()
        args = message.strip().split(' ')[1:]

        # Sanity check: Verify the presence of the appropriate command.
        if not hasattr(self, 'command_%s' % command):
            self.write('Invalid command: %s' % command)
            return

        # Run the appropriate command.
        try:
            return getattr(self, 'command_%s' % command)(*args)
        except Exception as ex:
            self.write('Error: %s\n' % str(ex))

    def write(self, msg_string):
        string += '\n'
        self.transport.write(msg_string.encode('ascii', 'ignore'))

    def command_add(self, *args):
        args = [int(i) for i in args]
        self.write('%d' % sum(args))

    def command_shutdown(self):
        self.write('Okay. Shutting down.')
        raise KeyboardInterrupt


if __name__ == '__main__':
    loop = asyncio.get_event_loop()
    coro = loop.create_server(ServerProtocol, '127.0.0.1', 8000)
    asyncio.async(coro)
    try:
        loop.run_forever()
    except KeyboardInterrupt:
        pass
```

This is a somewhat long module, but a few details are worth noting. First, the ServerProtocol class subclasses asyncio.Protocol. The connection_made and data_received methods are defined in the superclass, but do nothing. The other three methods are custom.

Remember that when you make a socket connection between machines, you are essentially always sending bytes, not text strings. The `write` method here does that conversion in one place, rather than forcing you to convert to a byte string every time you want to write to the transport.

The guts of this are in the `data_received` method. It takes a line of data and tries to figure out what to do with it. It only understands two basic commands, and anything else is an error.

Finally, the block at the end of the file actually starts up the server, and runs it against the local machine on a particular port. This is all the code you need to start up a server and have it listen for commands.

You can verify that the server receives commands by starting it up and then, in another shell window, using `telnet` to connect to it.

```
$ telnet 127.0.0.1 8000
Trying 127.0.0.1...
Connected to localhost.
Escape character is '^]'.
Welcome.
add 3 5
8
make_tea
Invalid command: make_tea
shutdown
Okay. Shutting down.
Connection closed by foreign host.
```

You have a very simple server. It can accept two commands: `add` and `shutdown`. It can provide errors if you try to issue a command it does not understand. And, the server is, in fact, able to shut itself down.

SUMMARY

Python is, at its core, a sequential language. It is a sequential language that, with `asyncio`, is getting budding asynchronous features built in to the standard library.

One thing that makes `asyncio` valuable is that it enables you to write code that follows sequential patterns, but is actually asynchronous under the hood, by using the `yield from` statement. However, if you intend to write an asynchronous application, you still must understand the advantages and disadvantages of this paradigm.

As you have seen, many things are different. You may not always know in what order tasks will run. It is possible for tasks to be intentionally canceled. Finally, code may be registered to run using a callback system, rather than through direct sequential function calls. All of these things represent a break from "normal" Python programming.

Still, if you have a robust Python 3 application and need certain asynchronous elements, `asyncio` may be the right tool for you.

In Chapter 14, you learn about style norms and recommendations in Python.

Style

Code is read more often than it is written.

Despite this fact, programmers often write code as if they do not expect to have to maintain it or even read it in the future. This leads to code that is incomprehensible when it is read months or years later.

Therefore, one of the most important things you can do as a programmer (in *any* language) is to write readable code.

This chapter explores principles for writing readable code, as well as some of the standards adopted by the Python community at large for writing code in a consistent manner.

PRINCIPLES

Before discussing specific standards that the Python community has adopted, or additional recommendations that have been proposed by others, it is important to consider a few over-arching principles.

Remember that the purpose of readability standards is to improve readability. The rules exist to serve the people reading and writing code, not the other way around.

This section discusses a few principles to keep in mind.

Assume Your Code Will Require Maintenance

It is very easy to believe that the work you are doing at the moment will not require additions or maintenance in the future. This is because it is difficult to anticipate future needs, and it is easy to underestimate your own propensity to introduce bugs. However, very little of the code that you write will simply exist untouched into perpetuity.

If you assume that code that you are writing is going to be "a one-off" and something that you will not have to read, debug, or amend later, it is frighteningly easy to ignore other principles of readable code simply because you believe that "it does not matter this time."

Therefore, preserve a healthy distrust of any instinct you may have that code you write will not need to be maintained. The safe bet is always that you will see that code again. Furthermore, if you do not, someone else will.

Be Consistent

The two aspects of consistency are *internal consistency* and *external consistency*.

Your code should be as internally consistent as possible. This is true both of style and structure. The *style* should be consistent in that any formatting rules should be followed throughout the project. The *structure* should be consistent in that the same types of code should be organized into the same places, so that projects are navigable.

You code should also be externally consistent. Structure your projects and your code similarly to how other people do. If a new developer opens up your project, he or she should not react by saying, "I have never seen anything like this before." Community guidelines matter, because they are what developers will expect to see when they come to your project. Similarly, and for the same reasons, take seriously the standards surrounding how to accomplish common tasks and how to organize code when using certain frameworks.

Think About Ontology, Especially with Data

Ontology basically means "the study of being." In philosophy (where the word is most commonly used), ontology is the study of the nature of reality and existence, and is a subset of metaphysics.

When it comes to writing software applications, ontology refers to a focus on what the various "things" in your application *are*. How do you represent your concepts in your database? What about your class structure?

What this sort of question ultimately affects is the way you write and structure your code. Do you use inheritance or composition to structure the relationship between two classes? In what database table does this or that column belong?

This advice effectively boils down to, "Think before you write." Specifically, think about what the objects in your application are, and how they interact with one another. Your application is a world where objects and data interact. So, what are the rules by which they work together?

Do Not Repeat Yourself

When writing code, consider situations in which you are reusing a value that could change over time. Is that value being used in multiple modules and functions? How much work would it be to change it if it became necessary to do so?

The same principle applies to functions. Do you have a common boilerplate that you find yourself constantly repeating throughout your application? If the boilerplate is longer than a couple of lines, you may want to consider abstracting it out into a function, so that if the need to change it arises, it is manageable to do so.

On the other hand, it is possible to take this principle too far. Not *every* value needs to be defined as a constant in a module (and doing so can impair readability and maintainability). Use wise judgment. Consistently be asking the question, "If this changes, how much work would it be to update it everywhere?"

Have Your Comments Explain the Story

Your code is a story. It is an explanation of what occurs, from beginning to end, as users interact with your program. The program starts in one location (potentially with some input), moves through a series of "choose your own adventure" steps to reach an end point, and then concludes (probably with some output).

Consider adopting a commenting style where every few lines of code is preceded by a comment block explaining what that code is doing. If your code is a story, your comments are an illumination and explanation of that story.

When *narrative commenting* is done well, a reader can parse the code (for example, when trying to troubleshoot a problem or maintain the code) by reading the comments to get the story, then quickly zero in on the code that requires maintenance, and only then focus on the vocabulary of the code itself.

Narrative commenting also helps explain intent. It helps answer the question, "What did the person who wrote this code aim to accomplish?" Occasionally, it will help answer the question, "Why was this done this way?" These are questions you naturally ask when you read code, and providing the answers to those questions aids in understanding.

Therefore, comments should explain the rationale for anything in the code that is not simple and salient. If a somewhat complex algorithm is being used, consider including a link to an article explaining the pattern and providing other examples of its use.

Occam's Razor

The most important principle for writing maintainable code is colloquially known as *Occam's Razor*: the simplest solution is usually the best one. In his "The Zen of Python" web posting (https://www.python.org/dev/peps/pep-0020/), which is a collection of proverbs for programming (for example, type `import this` in a Python console to read it), Tim Peters includes a similar line: "If the implementation is hard to explain, it's a bad idea."

This principle is true in both how your code *works* and how it *looks*. When it comes to how your code works, simple systems are more maintainable. *Simplicity of implementation* means that you are less likely to write esoteric bugs, and that those who come after you to maintain your work (including yourself) are more likely to intuitively understand what is happening and be able to add to the application without hitting unexpected snags.

As far as how your code looks, remember that, as much as is possible, reading code should be about learning the *story* of what the code is doing, not about parsing the vocabulary. The vocabulary is the means, while the story is the end. It is easy to write rules such as, "Do not use ternary operators." However, following rules you can run through a linter (while valuable) is not a sufficient condition for clarity. Focus on writing and organizing code so that it is as simple as possible.

STANDARDS

The Python community largely follows a style guide known as PEP 8 (`https://www.python.org/ dev/peps/pep-0008/`), which is written by Guido van Rossum (the creator of Python) and is adopted by most major Python projects, including the Python standard library.

The universality of the PEP 8 standard is one of its greatest strengths. It has been adopted by so much of the community that you can reasonably expect that most Python code you encounter will conform to it. As you write code this way, it will become easier to read code written similarly.

Trivial Rules

Many of the guidelines in PEP 8 are quite straightforward. Highlights include the following:

➤ Use four spaces for indentation. Do not use literal tabs (`\t`).

➤ Variables should be spelled with underscores, not camel case (`my_var`, not `myVar`). Class names start with a capital letter and are in camel case (for example, `MyClass`).

➤ If a variable is intended to be "internal use only," prefix it with an underscore.

➤ Use a single space around operators (for example, `x + y`, not `x+y`), including assignment (`z = 3`, not `z=3`), except in keyword arguments, in which case, the spaces are omitted.

➤ Omit unnecessary whitespace in lists and dictionaries (`for example, [1, 1, 2, 3, 5]`, not `[ 1, 1, 2, 3, 5 ]`).

Read the Python style guide for additional examples and further discussion on these rules.

Documentation Strings

Remember that, in Python, if the first statement in a function or class is a string, that string is automatically assigned to the special __doc__ variable, and is then used if you call `help` (and in a few other cases).

PEP 8 designates that *docstrings* (as they are colloquially called) should be written as an imperative sentence.

```
"""Do X, Y, and Z, then return the result."""
```

This is contrasted with writing the docstring as a description, which is frowned upon.

```
"""Does X, Y, and Z, then returns the result."""
```

If the docstring is a single line, follow it with an empty line before the body of the class or function begins. If the docstring spans multiple lines, place the closing quotes on their own line in lieu of the empty line.

```
"""Do X, Y, and Z, then call the a() method to transform all the things,
then return the result.
"""
```

Blank Lines

Blank lines are used for logical segmentation.

PEP 8 designates that two blank lines should separate "top level" classes and function definitions in a module.

```
class A(object):
    pass


class B(object):
    pass
```

PEP 8 also designates that after the top level, class and function definitions should be separated by one blank line each.

```
class C(object):
    def foo(self):
        pass

    def bar(self):
        pass
```

It is acceptable to use single blank lines within functions or other blocks of code to delineate logical segments. Consider preceding all such segments with comments explaining the block.

Imports

Python allows both absolute and relative imports. In Python 2, the interpreter will attempt a relative import, and then attempt an absolute import if no relative import matches.

In Python 3, relative imports are given a special syntax—a leading period (.) character—and "normal" imports only attempt absolute imports. The Python 3 syntax is available starting in Python 2.6. Additionally, you can turn off implicit relative imports using `from __future__ import absolute_import`.

You should always stick to absolute imports whenever possible. If you must use a relative import, you should use the explicit style. If you are writing code for Python 2.6 and 2.7, consider explicitly opting in to the Python 3 behavior.

When you are importing modules, each module should be given its own line.

```
import os
import sys
```

However, if you are importing multiple names from the same module, it is perfectly acceptable to group them on the same line.

```
from datetime import date, datetime, timedelta
```

Additionally, although PEP 8 does not mandate this, consider keeping imports grouped by the packages that they come from. Within each group, sort imports by alphabetical order.

Also, when doing imports, do not forget about the ability to alias names that are imported using the as keyword.

```
from foo.bar import really_long_name as name
```

This often allows you to shorten long or unwieldy names that are going to be repeated often. Aliasing is a valuable tool when an import is used frequently, and when the original name is difficult for whatever reason.

On the other hand, remember that when you do this, you are effectively masking the original name within your module, which can reduce clarity if you do it when it is not really necessary. Like any tool, use this with discretion.

Variables

As mentioned earlier, variable names are spelled with underscores, not camel case (for example, my_var, not myVar). Additionally, it is important that variable names be descriptive.

It is generally not appropriate to use extremely short variable names, although there are situations where this is acceptable, such as the iterator variables in loops (for example, for k, v in mydict.items()).

Avoid naming variables after common names already in the Python language, even when the interpreter would allow it. You should never name a variable or a function something like sum or print. Similarly, avoid type names such as list or dict.

If you must name a variable after a Python type or keyword, the convention is to include a trailing underscore; this is explicitly preferable over altering the spelling. For example, if you are passing a class to a function, the function argument should be named class_, not klass. (The exception to this is class methods, which by convention take cls as their initial argument.)

Comments

Comments should be written in English, using complete sentences, and written in a block above the relevant code. You should use correct capitalization, spelling, and grammar.

Also, ensure that comments are kept up to date. If the code changes, the comments may need to change along with it. You do not want to end up with a series of comments that actually contradict the code, which can easily cause confusion.

Modules may include a comment header, usually generated by your version-control system, detailing the version of that file. This can make it easier to see if the file has been changed, and is particularly useful if you are distributing a module for use by others.

Line Length

The single most controversial (and most often rejected) aspect of the Python style guide is its limitations on line length. PEP 8 requires that lines be no longer than 79 characters, and that docstring lines be no longer than 72 characters.

This rule frustrates many developers, who point out that we live in an age of 27-inch monitors and widescreen displays. GitHub, a popular website for sharing code, uses a window with a width of 120 characters.

Proponents point out that many people still use narrower displays or 80-character terminals, or simply do not set their code window up to maximize the screen.

There will likely never be harmony on this issue. You should code to the standards of the projects you are working on. Regardless of whether you conform to a 79-character standard or some greater width, you should know how to wrap code when the situation arises.

The best way to wrap a long single line is by using parentheses, as shown here:

```
if (really_long_identifier_that_maybe_should_be_shorter and
            other_really_long_identifier_that_maybe_should_be_shorter):
    do_something()
```

Whenever it is feasible, use this method instead of using a \ character before the line break. Note that in cases where an operator such as and is being used, it should appear before the line break if possible.

It is also possible to wrap function calls. PEP 8 lists many acceptable ways to do this. The general rule to follow is that indentation of the trailing lines should be consistent.

```
really_long_function_name(
    categories=[
        x.y.COMMON_PHRASES,
        x.y.FONT_PREVIEW_PHRASES,
    ],
    phrase='The quick brown fox jumped over the lazy dogs.',
)
```

When using line continuation within a function call, list, or dictionary, include a trailing comma on the final line.

SUMMARY

Many times, the person coming along a year later and reading your code *will be you*. Memories are never as good as they intuitively seem to be, and code written without a constant eye to readability and maintainability will be naturally difficult to read and maintain.

Throughout this book, you have learned how to use various modules, classes, and structures in the Python language. When deciding how to solve a problem, remember that it often takes more skill to debug code than it does to write it.

Therefore, aim to have your code be as simple as possible, and as readable as possible. You will thank yourself a year from now. Your coworkers and fellow contributors will, too.

INDEX